BLACK AMERICANA
POSTCARD PRICE GUIDE

"COMRADES".

**A Century of History
Preserved on Postcards**

J. L. MASHBURN

COLONIAL HOUSE
ENKA, NORTH CAROLINA USA

Publisher: J. L. Mashburn
Editor: Emma Mashburn

Cover Design: Picture Perfect Publishing, Inc.
Interior Design: Emma Mashburn
Electronic Page Assembly: Picture Perfect Publishing, Inc.

A Colonial House Production

Printed in the United States of America

First Edition

10 9 8 7 6 5 4 3 2 1

Library of Congress Cataloging-in-Publication

Mashburn, J. L. (Joseph Lee)
      Black Americana postcard price guide / J.L. Mashburn
              p. cm.
      Includes bibliographical references and index.
      ISBN 1-885940-01-7
      1. Afro-Americans in art--Catalogs.   2. Postcards--Catalogs
I. Title
NC1878.A37M37   1995   95-38149
741.6'83'075--DC20   CIP

AN IMPORTANT NOTICE TO
THE READERS OF THIS PRICE GUIDE:

The comprehensive nature of compiling data and prices on the thousands of cards, sets and series in this publication gives many probabilities for error. Although all information has been compiled from reliable sources, experienced collectors and dealers, some data may still be questionable.

The author and publisher will not be held responsible for any losses that might occur in the purchase or sale of cards because of the information contained herein.

The author will be most pleased to receive notice of errors so that they may be corrected in future editions.

Contact: J. L. Mashburn, Colonial House, Box 609, Enka NC 28728

CONTENTS

DEDICATION

TO THE MEMORY OF MY WONDERFUL MOTHER

Ella Roberts Mashburn, 1913-1994

ACKNOWLEDGMENTS

Many individuals have made valuable contributions to this publication. Although it is impossible to list everyone, the following have given unselfishly of their time, their expertise, and their concerted effort to make this book as complete and interesting as possible.

Special thanks to **Andreas Brown** for his great support, helpful suggestions, and vital information relating to the rarer cards, as well as the social and historic subject matter concerning them. Also for the use of cards from the Gotham Book Mart collection.

Special thanks also to **Pete Brown** who helped from the very beginning by allowing us to use his great checklists and many cards from his personal collection. He was also very helpful in pricing and editing.

Our sincere thanks to **Russell Hughes** for his unselfish support, and for allowing us to select and use cards from his superb collection.

Special thanks also to **Jim Dismuke**, **Lonny Bauer**, **Carla Zimke**, and **Shirley** and **Dale Hendricks**, who so generously allowed us to scan cards from their personal collections.

Thanks also to all the dealers who allowed Emma and me to gain a lot of information by spending some extra time searching through all their stocks of African American cards.

Most of all I wish to thank my wife **Emma** for the hundreds of hours she has spent putting this book together on the computer. Her work in scanning almost 1000 cards, and painstakingly placing those we selected in their proper location in the book was a major accomplishment. She also did all the typesetting, helped with the design, and edited it. In so many ways I owe this book to her.

A Word About the Reproduction of Postcards in this Book

All images in this edition are the final results of using various computer programs where each card is scanned, photostyled to the best grayscale clarity, and later placed in position in the text. Real photo and black and white cards are best for this process, and images reproduce very well. However, the majority of original postcards were printed in many colors and shades that are sometimes difficult to reproduce in black and white. Because of their historical content, their rarity, or great collector interest, we have intentionally used many cards even though they did not reproduce well.

The card shown above, an unsigned image by Agnes Richardson, has outstanding, vivid colors. A good part of the joy and magic in collecting postcards is to observe the radiant colors produced by the publishers during postcards' Golden Years.

Private Mailing Card
AUTHORIZED BY ACT OF CONGRESS MAY 19, 1898
IL CARD — CARTE POSTALE.

1

INTRODUCTION

BRIEF HISTORY OF THE U.S. POSTCARD

On May 1, 1893, the first American picture postcards were sold or distributed at the World's Colombian Exposition in Chicago. They became extremely popular and widely acclaimed as hundreds of thousands were sold to visitors at the gala event. From this fantastic beginning the future of the picture postcard was assured and it was soon to become one of the country's leading industries.

These postcards, now over 100 years old, pictured beautiful and colorful views of the Exposition buildings and displays and products of countries and manufacturers throughout the world. Other cards were also issued to advertise the Exposition itself and were used by visitors to mail or take back home as proof of their attendance at the event. The beauty of the cards, their small size and low cost, made them a great delight for collectors and gift givers.

Fuelled by the great results of this triumphant beginning for the postcard, manufacturers and merchants started using it to advertise their products and services. The cards were either distributed by salesmen or sent by mail to other manufacturers or merchants. Officials of large cities and tourist resorts, believing in the adage that "a picture is worth a thousand words," commissioned publishers to print multi-view cards of interesting sites in their cities. These soon became single views of all the important buildings and street scenes and points of interest. Big publishers, taking advantage of the new craze, dispatched hordes of photographers to all the big cities and resort areas to take pictures of everything of interest.

The artist and magazine illustrator, heretofore limited to sales of portraits, prints, magazine articles and covers, welcomed the new medium and soon became major contributors. Glamour artists Harrison Fisher, Philip Boileau, the Christys, Charles Dana Gibson, Clarence Underwood and others became household names, and the postcard helped them gain worldwide acclaim.

The collecting of postcards became one of the leading hobbies, not only in the U.S. but throughout the world. Large albums served as a convenient means of displaying and protecting the cards, and almost everyone had one or more in which to store their treasured mementos. This collecting craze era, known as "Postcard's Golden Years," waned and virtually terminated in the 1914-1918 era of World War I. A postcard tariff, imposed by the United States, and intervention of Germany (where almost all were printed for the U.S. Trade) into the war brought an end to the fabulous era.

Many new firms in the U.S. began publishing cards in 1915 but their printing technology was very poor when compared to that produced in Germany. Reproduction of old views and images, and the resulting poor quality, finally sealed the doom for the postcard publisher and collector. With no new treasures to add to collections, the big albums were removed from their familiar station in the living or viewing rooms and placed in the attic or basement trunks. Later generations, with little interest in the hobbies of their ancestors, disposed of many of these beautiful works of art. However, many millions were saved and remain today for the enjoyment of the collector. They also provide excellent material for historians.

HISTORY RECORDED ON POSTCARDS

The events of history, beginning in the early 1890's, are recorded on postcards. The era of the event can be dated in several different ways. The first, and most factual is the postmark date providing that the cards were postally used. The second is the knowledge of knowing when a particular type card was published ... whether it was a (1) Pioneer issue, (2) Private Mailing Card, (3) Undivided Back, (4) Divided Back, (5) White Border, (5) Linen, or (6) Chrome.

Knowing the name of the publisher and when he was in business, as well as his numbering system, can also be a tremendous help in dating a card. For Real Photo cards the process used is normally shown on the back. The means to identify the age and Postcard Eras can be found later in this chapter.

AFRICAN AMERICANS ON POSTCARDS

One of the first postcards portraying African Americans was released at the 1895 Cotton States and International Exposition which was held in Atlanta. The card pictured the Expo's "Negro Building." It was dedicated by Booker T. Washington who had helped persuade Congress to provide funds to build it. It was said to have been built "to show the harmony between blacks and whites living together ... to show the progress being made by the Negro in the south ... and to show the availability of cheap labor to encourage industry to move to the south." All of the cards of this exposition are extremely rare and belong to the "Pioneer Era." The Negro Building card is now valued between $350 and $400, and is among the most prized in the group.

The greater majority of postcards portraying African Americans were published from 1908 through 1914, which were the most prominent of the postcard's "Golden Years." Well known publishers such as Raphael Tuck, Detroit Publishing Co., and Curt Teich, sent their photographers throughout the southeastern cities and countrysides to take pictures of the prominent buildings, important sights, and interesting local inhabitants. The pictures taken of blacks during these expeditions played a prominent role in recording their social history and their life-styles during these early times.

Black history was also recorded on postcards for the U.S. market by hundreds of artists and illustrators, both here and abroad. Many of the better artists pictured them as beautiful, playful children and well-dressed and fun-loving adults, both at work and at play. However, some produced cards that stereotyped them in insensitive ways. These vulgarities continued well into the 1960's before merchants took them off their shelves and refused to sell them.

Many Real Photo postcards which have survived tell a great part of the true story of blacks in the years between 1900-1940. These were normally taken by blacks and were of family members and black events or happenings. They reveal them as particularly proud, well dressed working people in various jobs and positions; of actors, dancers, singers; of babies and children; of the black soldier serving his country; and families attending church and religious functions. They show the minstrels, bands, athletes, and the students in school and college. These photos seem to illustrate the lighter side of their struggles for equality.

HOW TO USE THIS PRICE GUIDE

This price guide has been uniquely designed to serve the needs of both the beginning and advanced collector, as well as the established postcard dealer. Our attempt to provide a comprehensive guide to postcards dating from the 1890's through the 1960's makes it possible for even the novice collector to consult it with confidence and ease in finding each particular listing. The following important explanations summarize the general practices that will help in getting the most benefits from its use.

CATEGORICAL ARRANGEMENT

Cards are arranged by category, and each category is listed in the Table of Contents. In the Artist-Signed category, cards that were drawn or painted are listed in two different sections -- either signed or unsigned. Artists are always listed alphabetically, with the name of their publisher, series number if applicable, and the caption from each card, if any.

The Real Life section includes all cards that were taken with a camera, with the end result being either a color or black and white image. Included in this section are Real Photo images, both personal and commercial. The publisher, if known, is always listed alphabetically; this is followed by the era, series number, and caption from each individual card. This is further explained in "Listings" below.

Topical cards such as advertising, sports, entertainment, and others, are listed separately and are designated whether they are Real Life or Artist-Signed. These are also shown alphabetically with individual listings of some of the most prominent cards and their values. Otherwise, the values listed are for generalized cards in the particular topic or theme.

LISTINGS

Listings may be identified as follows:

1. **SECTION** (Artist-Signed, Real Life, Real Photo, etc.).
2. **ARTIST** (Listed in Bold Capital Letters) when available.
3. **PUBLISHER** (Listed in Bold, either all caps or lower case).
4. **ERA** (Pioneer, PMC, Undivided Back, Divided Back, etc.)

5. **NAME OF SERIES; OR SERIES NUMBER.**
6. **NUMBER OF CARDS IN SET OR SERIES** (Enclosed in Parentheses) when available.
7. **CARD NUMBER**, if any.
8. **CAPTION OR TITLE OF CARD** (Enclosed in Quotation Marks).
9. **PRICE OF 1 CARD IN VERY GOOD CONDITION AND PRICE OF 1 CARD IN EXCELLENT CONDITION.**

Example of above for Artist-Signed Section:

1. **ARTIST-SIGNED**
2. **FRANCES BRUNDAGE**
3. **Raphael Tuck & Sons**
4. Divided Back
5. **2723** "Colored Folks"
6. (6)
7. None
8. "The Church Parade"
9. $40 - 45 and $45 - 50

Example of above for Real Life Section:

1. **REAL LIFE**
2. (Not Applicable)
3. **ALBERTYPE CO.**
4. PMC
5. "Greetings from the Sunny South"
6. (12)
7. None
8. No Caption (e.g., Boy in Straw Hat)
9. $25 - 30 and $30 - 35

ABBREVIATIONS USED IN THIS BOOK

(B&W)	Black and White
(C)	Chromes
(Emb.)	Embossed or Raised Printing
(L)	Linen Finish
(L.L.)	Large Letter Cards, Usually States
(PMC)	Private Mailing Cards
(R.P.)	Real Photo Type
(UndB)	Undivided Backs
(Uns.)	Unsigned

CONDITION AND GRADING OF POSTCARDS

The condition of a postcard, as with old coins, stamps, books, etc., is an extremely important factor in pricing it for the collector, the dealer, and for those having found cards to sell. Damaged, worn, creased, or dirty cards — cards in less than Very Good condition— are almost uncollectible unless they are to be used as a space filler until a better one is found. Collectors should never buy a damaged card if they expect to sell it later on; however, rarity of a card may make any condition acceptable.

It is necessary that some sort of card grading standard be used so that buyer and seller may come to an informed agreement on the value of a card. Two different collectible conditions, **Very Good** and **Excellent,** are used in the **BLACK AMERICANA POSTCARD PRICE GUIDE**. There are, of course, higher and lower grades, but these two will be most normally seen and most normally quoted for postcards sold throughout the hobby.

The standard grading system adapted by most dealers and by the leading postcard hobby publications in the field, *Barr's Post Card News* and *Post Card Collector*, is listed below with their permission:

M—MINT. A perfect card just as it comes from the printing press. No marks, bends, or creases. No writing or postmarks. A clean and fresh card. Seldom seen.

NM—NEAR MINT. Like Mint but very light aging or very slight discoloration from being in an album for many years. Not as sharp or crisp.

EX—EXCELLENT. Like mint in appearance with no bends or creases, or rounded or blunt corners. May be postally used or unused and with writing and postmark only on the address side. A clean, fresh card on the picture side.

VG—VERY GOOD. Corners may be just a bit blunt or rounded. Almost undetectable crease or bend that does not detract from overall appearance of the picture side. May have writing or postal cancellation on address side. A very collectible card.

G—GOOD. Corners may be noticeably blunt or rounded with noticeably slight bends or creases. May be postally used or have writing on address side. Less than VG.

FR—FAIR. Card is intact. Excess soil, stains, creases, writing, or cancellation may affect picture. Could be a scarce card that is difficult to find in any condition.

Postcard dealers always want better condition cards that have no defects. Collectors should keep this in mind if they have cards to sell. Therefore, anyone building a collection should maintain a standard for condition and stick to it. Even if the asking price is a little higher when a card is purchased, it will be worth the cost when it is resold.

VALUATIONS

The postcard values quoted in this publication represent the current retail market. They were compiled with the assistance of some of the leading dealers and collectors in the U.S., dealer pricing at shows, personal dealer communications, from the author's personal purchasing worldwide, from his approval sales, and from his active day-to-day involvement in the postcard field.

Some values were also compiled from observations of listings in auctions, auction catalogs (U.S., Europe, and Great Britain), prices realized and fixed price sales in the fine hobby publications, *Barr's Post Card News* and *Postcard Collector*, and other related publications.

It must be stressed that this price guide and reference work is intended to serve only as an aid in evaluating postcards. It should not be used otherwise. As we all know, actual market conditions change constantly, and prices may fluctuate. The trend for postcards, however, seems to always be to the upside.

Publication of this price guide is not intended to be a solicitation to buy or sell any of the cards listed.

Price ranges for cards in both **Very Good** and **Excellent** conditions are found at the end of each listing. Prices for cards in less than Very Good condition would be much lower, while those grading above Excellent might command relatively higher prices.

Without exception, prices quoted are for **one** card, whether it be a single entity or one card in a complete set or series. Note that after many entries a number is enclosed in parentheses; e.g., (6). This number indicates the total number of cards in a set or in a series. The price listed is for one card in the set and must be multiplied by this number to determine the value of a complete set.

WHY PRICE RANGES ARE QUOTED

For cards graded both **Very Good** and **Excellent**, price ranges are quoted for four major reasons. Any one, or more, of the following can determine the difference in the high or low prices in each of the listing ranges.

1.   Prices vary in different geographical areas across the United States. At this time, they are somewhat higher on the Pacific coast and other western states. They tend to be a little lower in the East and somewhere in-between in the central and midwestern states. For instance, a card with a price range of $6.00-8.00 might sell for $6.00 in the East, $7.00 in the Mid-West and $8.00 in the Far West.

2.   Dealer price valuations also vary. Those who continually set up at postcard shows seem to have a better feel for prices and know which cards are selling well and, therefore, can adjust their prices accordingly. Dealers who sell only by mail, or by mail auction, tend to price their cards (or list estimated values in their auctions) just a bit higher. They usually are able to get these prices because of a wider collector market base obtained by the large number of subscribers served by the nationally distributed postcard auction publications. The publications also reach collectors who are unable to attend shows.

3.   Cards that have been sent on approvals quite often are priced higher than at postcard shows, etc., because the dealer has spent more time in selecting and handling. He is usually working from a customer "want list."

4.   Cards that are in great demand, or "hot" topics, also have wider price ranges; as collector interests rise there is a greater disparity in values because of supply and demand.

5.   Card appearance and the subject in a set or series can also cause a variance in the price range. Printing quality, more beautiful and varied colors, and sharpness of the image may make a particular card much more desirable and, therefore, it will command a higher price.

Cards that have a wide price range usually are those that are presently the "most wanted" and best sellers. Dealers, most often, will only offer a small discount when selling these because they know there is a good market for them. Cards listed with a narrow price range are usually those that have been "hot" but have settled down and established a more competitive trading range. Dealer discounting on these slow-movers tends to be much more prevalent than those in the wide price ranges.

GUIDELINES FOR BUYING AND SELLING CARDS

As noted above, the prices listed in this price guide are retail prices—prices that a collector can expect to pay when buying a card from a dealer. It is up to the collectors to bargain for any available discount from the dealer.

The wholesale price is the price which a collector can expect from a dealer when selling cards. This price will be significantly lower than the retail price. Most dealers try to operate on a 100% markup and will normally pay around 50% of a card's low retail value. On some high-demand cards, he might pay up to 60% or 75% if he wants them badly enough.

Dealers are always interested in purchasing collections and accumulations of cards. They are primarily interested in those that were issued before 1915, but may be induced to take those issued afterwards if they are clean and in good condition.

Collections: Normally, collections are a specialized group or groups of cards that a person has built over the years. They will be in nice condition, without any damage, and may contain some rarities or high-demand cards.

Collectors wanting to sell their cards may need to contact a dealer in order to dispose of them. As noted above, be prepared to sell at approximately 50% of the value of the collection. If you do not know of any dealers, write the **International Federation of Postcard Dealers,** to the attention of Mildred Knoll, Secretary, P. O. Box 3587, Baltimore, Maryland 21214, and enclose a double-stamped, self-addressed #10 envelope for a list of members.

Another source for disposing of your collection would be dealers who advertise in *Barr's Post Card News,* 70 South 6th St., Lansing, IA 52151 or *Postcard Collector,* P.O. Box 1050, Dubuque, IA 52004. Other publications that have postcard sections are *Collectors News*, P. O. Box 156, Grundy Center, IA 50638-0156, *Paper Collectors' Market Place*, P. O. Box 128, Scandinavia, WI 54977, and *The Antique Trader*, P. O. Box 1050, Dubuque, IA 52004. Write to any of these publications and ask for information on subscriptions or sample copies.

Accumulations: Accumulations are usually groups of many different kinds, many different eras, and many different topics ... with the good usually mixed in with the bad. If you have a large accumulation that you wish to sell, your best bet is to contact a dealer as noted above. You may expect only 20% to 30% of value on a group such as this. Many low demand cards are non-sellers and are worthless to a dealer, but he may take them if there are some good cards in the accumulation.

Buying: Without doubt, the best way to buy postcards is to attend a show where there is a large group of dealers. Compare prices among dealers on cards that are of interest to you, and return to those who have the best cards at the lowest price for your purchases. Buy from a dealer in your area if there is one. A good dealer will help you with your collection by searching for cards you need or want. If none are available, many dealers listed in *Barr's Post Card News* and *Postcard Collector* run auctions or will send cards on approval. Also, you might try joining a postcard club. It is possible to find an excellent choice of cards at these meetings because attendees bring material that is of interest to their fellow members.

It is also possible to find cards at Antique Shows, Flea Markets and Antique Shops. You can, however, waste a lot of time and never find suitable cards. It is best to go direct to the source and that would be a postcard dealer or auctioneer. Here you can find a great variety and almost always cards of interest to you.

IDENTIFYING THE AGE OF POSTCARDS

The dating of postcards for years or eras of issue can be accurately determined if the card is studied for identity points. Research has already been done by earlier historians and guidelines have been put into place.

There were seven eras for the postcard industry and each one has distinguishing points to help establish its respective identity. The following helps determine the era of the card in question.

PIONEER ERA (1893-1898)

The Pioneer Era began when picture postcards were placed on sale by vendors and exhibitors at the Colombian Exposition in Chicago, May, 1893. These were very popular and proved to be a great success. The profitable and lasting future of the postcard was greatly

enhanced. The cards from this era are relatively scarce. They can be identified by combinations of the following:
* All have undivided backs.
* None show the "Authorized by Act of Congress" byline.
* Postal cards will have the Grant or Jefferson head stamp.
* Most, but not all, will be multiple view cards.
* The words "Souvenir of ..." or "Greetings from..." appear on many.
* Postage rate, if listed, is usually 2 cents.
* The most common titles will be "Souvenir Card" or "Mail Card."
* Appeared mostly in the big Eastern cities.

PRIVATE MAILING CARD ERA (1898-1901)

The government, on May 19, 1898, gave private printers permission to print and sell postcards. The cards were all issued with the inscription "Private Mailing Card," and today they are referred to as PMC's. It is very easy to identify these because of the inscription. It may be noted that many of the early Pioneer views were reprinted as Private Mailing Cards.

UNDIVIDED BACK ERA (1901-1907)

On December 24, 1901, permission was given for use of the wording "Post Card" to be imprinted on the backs of privately printed cards. All cards during this era had undivided backs and only the address was to appear on the back. The message, therefore, had to be written on the front (picture side) of the card. For this reason, there is writing on the face of many cards; this is becoming more acceptable on cards of this era.

DIVIDED BACK ERA (1907-1915)

This era came into being on March 1, 1907. The divided back made it possible for both the address and the message to be on the back of the card. This prevented the face of the card from being written on and proved to be a great boon for collectors. Normally the view colors or images filled the entire card with no white border.

WHITE BORDER ERA (1915-1930)

The White Border Era brought an end to the postcard craze era. The golden age ended as imports from Germany ceased and publishers in the U.S. began printing postcards to try to fill the void. The cards were very poor quality and many were reprints of earlier Divided Back Era cards. These are easily distinguished by the white border around the pictured area.

LINEN ERA (1930-1945)

Improvements in American printing technology brought improved card quality. Publishers began using a linen-like paper containing a high rag content but used very cheap inks in most instances. Until recently, these cards were considered very cheap by collectors. Now they are very popular with collectors of Roadside America, Blacks, Comics, and Advertising. Views are also becoming more popular as collectors realize that this era too is a part of our history, and these cards help to illustrate the changes in the geographic structure of America.

PHOTOCHROME ERA (1939 to present day)

"Modern Chromes," as they are now called by the postcard fraternity, were first introduced in 1939. Publishers, such as **Mike Roberts**, **Dexter Press, Curt Teich,** and **Plastichrome**, began producing cards that had very beautiful chrome colors and were very appealing to collectors. The growth of this group has been spectacular in recent years, so much so that there are now many postcard dealers who specialize only in chromes.

REAL PHOTO POSTCARDS (1900 to present day)

Real Photo postcards were in use as early as 1900. It is sometimes very hard to date a card unless it has been postally used or dated by the photographer. The stamp box will usually show the process by which it was printed—AZO, EKC, KODAK, VELOX, and KRUXO are some of the principal ones. Careful study of photo cards is essential to make sure they have not been reproduced.

HOW TO DETERMINE CARD VALUES

Values of each card are listed under the headings "VG" (Very Good) and "EX" (Excellent). If there is no value listed for a card, just refer to the one listed immediately above it.

Example: A-3146   10 - 15   15 - 18
             A-3147

The value of A-3147 would be $10 - 15 and $15 - 18.

What is an artist-signed postcard?   It is simply a postcard, reproduced from a painting or sketch by the artist who signed his or her name to the original work. The original work, which included the signature, was first photographed and recolored and then printed as a postcard by various printing methods. If the original was unavailable, they were reproduced from earlier posters, prints, calendars, magazines and books, or from other postcards.

The artist's signature serves as the most important factor in the identification of all artist type postcards. It is also very important for evaluation and, in most instances, makes a card more valuable than an unsigned one.

BLACK STEREOTYPES

The American press and literary magazines of the 1890 to 1920 era basically gave a predominantly vulgar image of African Americans. Whether appearing in news articles, cartoons, fictional works or editorials, they were normally stereotyped as happy-go-lucky, lazy, stupid, superstitious, a thief, a liar, or a drunk. They supposedly loved fun and frolic, dancing, and music. They liked to wear gallant clothes and trinkets. They were also depicted as loving to eat fried chicken, watermelons, yams, and possum.

Artist-drawn comic postcards, probably as much as any other medium, stereotyped them as above, and illustrated them as having heavy thick lips with flat noses, big ears, kinky hair and big feet. Among the artists whose works most accurately depicted these typical features were those painted by H. Horina, Donadini, Jr., and Arthur Thiele. Horina's renditions of the Ullman Series 109, "The National Game," of baseball players in game situations, and Series 106, "In the Colored Swim," which shows a man and woman's escapades while boating, are generally considered the classical stereotypes. The same goes for Thiele's Series 386 Head Studies by FED and Sports Series 871 by Theo Stroefer. However, the anonymously published Series 454 by Donadini, Jr., of fashionably dressed and peculiar acting blacks, are much more so. In addition, Donadini, Jr. probably is also the artist of the unsigned S&M, Germany, Series 1415, which was also produced in the same vulgar vein.

This stereotyping on postcards (and by magazines and press) continued and remained the norm even after the end of the 1900-1915 "Golden Era of the Postcard" to well into the 1950's when, from the urging of the NAACP, the major 5 and 10 cent stores refused to sell them and took them off their card racks. Drug stores and other sales outlets soon followed suit, and black real-life and stereotype comical cards practically disappeared from the scene. This left only those in postcard collections and the remains of old dusty stocks in warehouses as memories of the crude and uncomplimentary phrases of hundreds of captions such as "Coon," "Nigger," "Darkie," "Chocolate Drop," "Pickaninnies," "African Annie," "Colored Cannibal," "Negro Ruffian," and others.

Many publishers were not so blatant as they published black cards picturing happy, playful, and extremely beautiful children, classical ladies, and well-dressed men. They intermingled them with whites, especially with children, and made no note of differing colors or race. Some of the classical works of Frances Brundage, Mabel Lucie Attwell, Ellen Clapsaddle, Ethel Parkinson, Agnes Richardson, and Grace O'Neill, the most revered of the painters and illustrators of beautiful children of the time, depicted them as they were... beautiful, happy and fun-loving children...with no stereotyping, demeaning racial slurs or vulgar captions used by many other artists.

H. D. Sandford did over 25 series, usually in sets of six cards, for Raphael Tuck alone. Although the titles of the series, such as "Happy Little Coons," "Curley Coons," "Seaside Coons," and "Dark Girls and Black Boys," emitted racial overtones, his cards and their captions did otherwise. His children are painted as happy, fun-loving and carefree. The same was true for F.G. Lewin, who did work for many publishers. His children are probably the most loved because they usually portray the little boy-little girl courting relationship in a comical way. It is good that these many postcards were left as historical proof to show that there were also good feelings, pleasant thoughts, and very little bad racial bias among many of the early artists. Postcard historians, with their knowledge of the various postcard eras and the times they represent, are able to trace the history and progress of African Americans throughout this century.

Certainly, much of the history is there--where and how they lived, how they worked, how they strived for equal rights, and their desire to better themselves. Postcards, through all these years, illustrate both the good times and the bad, the segregational and racist attitudes and behavior of some of the whites, the comical satire, the great entertainers and sports heroes...it's all there for the collector of postcards.

	VG	EX
A		
PCK		
"Dinner in Sight"	12 - 15	15 - 18
ALYS		
2946 "Opposites drawn together" (B&W)	8 - 10	10 - 12
ATTWELL, MABEL LUCIE		
Valentine & Sons		
No No. "Mixed Bathing-Ready?"	22 - 25	25 - 28
No No. Mixed Bathing "He Won't come...!"		
614 "O' Help"		
615 "You should have heard him..."		
745 "I Loves Being Alive, I Does"		
883 "A Laugh A Day Keeps..."		
951 "Everybody's Loved by Someone"	30 - 35	35 - 40
A331 "You Do Make I Larf..."	15 - 18	18 - 22
A550 "Strike me, Me's your match..."		
A615 "You should have heard Him..."		
2916 "Stay as Sweet as You Are"		
4417 "We's Not Afraid of the Dark"		
5498 "Meet Kinkie..."		
74418 "If I were the only..."		
"Shall us - Lets."		
"The End of a Perfect Day"		
"There's Lots of Boys About"		

Anonymous Spanish Publisher
   "The Bride"   22 - 25   25 - 28
   Others
      Early Period, Pre-1915   22 - 25   25 - 28
      Middle Period, 1915-30   16 - 18   18 - 22
      Late Period, 1930-50   10 - 12   12 - 15
      Reprints, 60's-70's   2 - 3   3 - 4

B See (Bonte)

T.S.N.
   Series 440   25 - 30   30 - 35
      9 Old Man Sits on Box
      24 Black with Mop

B. F.

Norwood Souvenir Co.
   "Who's a Democrat?"   25 - 30   30 - 35

BACUADA, FRED
   Raphael Tuck   15 - 18   18 - 22

BENSON, HENRY
   Ullman Mfg. Co.

Mabel Lucie Attwell
Valentine's #4417, "We's Not
Afraid of the Dark."

Mabel Lucie Attwell
Anonymous Spanish Publisher

Mabel Lucie Attwell
Valentine's No No., "Mixed Bathing -- He won't come clean!"

514 "No Race Suicide"   6 - 8   8 - 10
527 "Comparing Notes"
BERTIGLIA, A.
Series 518 Blacks-Whites   15 - 18   18 - 22
BISHOP
"What do you know about that?"   8 - 10   10 - 12
BOIRAU (Ca 1934)
"The Blessings of Civilization"   8 - 10   10 - 12
BONTE or B
  E. Nister (UndB)
    Series 71 Signed "B"
      "A Mos' Bligin' Genelman is Massa Nick..." 25 - 30   30 - 35
      "Ida's de Laundress who hangs out clothes..."
      "Moses de' Passon, who Preeches..."
      "Quentin's a spark who allus wuz free..."
    Series 72 Signed "B"
      "Here's Felix a Restin he won' do no work..."
      "Ole Nigger Sam is as black as can be..."
    Series 73 Signed "B"
      "Remus 'de Gentleman Tell a good yarn..."
      "Smilin Miss Utah named after a state..."
    Series 74 Signed "B"
      "Chawlie, de Butler him waits on de table..."
      "Old Uncle Dan'l, who..."
      389 The Cook, with Bowl and Spoon
      404 Mammy

B (Bonte), E. Nister Series 71
"Quentin's a Spark..."

B (Bonte), E. Nister Series 74
"Ole Uncle Dan'l who..."

B (Bonte), E. Nister Series 71
"A Mos' 'bligin' Genelman..."

B (Bonte), E. Nister Series 71
"Moses de Passon who preeches..."

B (Bonte), Theo Stroefer
Series 440, N-16

B (Bonte), Theo Stroefer
Series 440, N-20

Bonte, Theo Stroefer
Series 404, N-4

Bonte, Theo Stroefer
Series 404, N-2

F. Brundage (Uns.), TSN 664
"Du Kennst mein noch lange ..."

F. Buchanan, R. Tuck 9309
"You can see we are here"

Theo Stroefer (T.S.N.)

389 "Cook" Caricature (Same as Nister)	25 - 30	30 - 35
Series 404 Signed "Bonte"		
N-2 Mammy, with Pan of Biscuits	25 - 30	30 - 35
N-4 Mammy, with Pressing Iron		
Others		
Series 440 Signed "B"		
N-2 The Farmer, with Wooden Bucket		
N-16 Man with Chicken Under Coat		
N-20 Man Carries in Fire Wood		

BOOTH, A.

"Mr. Brown with Smith's Wife" (White)	15 - 18	18 - 22

BORISS, MARGRET

AMAG

Series 0322		
Kids Chase Hat	12 - 15	15 - 18
"Powder Me White"		

BROWNE, TOM

Davidson Bros.

Black Man Courts White Lady	12 - 15	15 - 20
"Mrs. Jackson is gone on the corner man..."		

BRUCKMAN, HARRY

Heads of Children	12 - 15	15 - 18

"The Christening"

"Don't Took de Las' Piece."

"Church Parade"

"The Village Choir"

"You is a Chicken" (on slates)

Shown here are five of the six cards in Raphael Tuck Series 2723, "Colored Folks," by Frances Brundage. This is one of her most popular works, and is one of the most desired of all sets of postcards in the entire hobby. The sixth card is entitled "De Proof of de Puddin."

FRANCES BRUNDAGE

Some of the most beautiful black-related cards of the early era were those painted by one of the most famous artists of adorable children, Frances Brundage. Her renditions illustrate beautiful and happy children that were void of racial overtones or demeaning slurs in the titles or captions. Her works published by Raphael Tuck are among the true works of art. "Colored Folks" Series 2723 and "Connoisseur" Series 2816 are duplicate 6-card series and are said to be, along with the 4-card "Funny Folk" Series 4096, among her very best works. They are a prime target of collectors of beautiful children throughout the world.

BRUNDAGE, FRANCES
Raphael Tuck

Oilette Series "Christmas Greetings"		
"The Night Before Christmas" (Uns.)	25 - 28	28 - 32
Series 100 "Valentine" (Uns.)		
"Loving Thoughts"		
Series 101 "Valentine" (Uns.)	22 - 25	25 - 28
"Be My Sweetheart"		
"Who Says I Is?"		
"My Valentine"		
This Series is the same as Series 106 and		
French Series 941 with French captions.		
All three series are unsigned.		
Series 102 "Valentine" (1)	22 - 25	25 - 28
"To Ma Honey"		
Series 103 "Valentine" (1) (Uns.)		
"Git a Move On..."		
Series 107 "Valentine" (2) (Uns.)		
"To My Heart's Beloved"		
"To My Loved One"		
Series 108 Valentines (4) (Uns.)		
Girl - "Does yo' reckon I would do..."		
Boy - "I'm cuttin up now..."		
Boy - "I lubs yo' deah, and dats why..."		
Girl - "I lubs yo' deah, wid my hearts..."		
Series 115 "Valentine" (2) (Uns.)		
Boy Angel - "To My Valentine"	22 - 25	25 - 28
Lovers - "My little love..."		
Series 118 "Little Loves & Lovers" (2) (Uns.)	25 - 28	28 - 32
Girl - "Waitin Fo' Mah Sweetheart"		
Boy - "To Greet Mah Valentine"		
Series 2723 "Colored Folks" (6)	50 - 60	60 - 70
"The Christening"		
"Church Parade"		
"De Proof of de Puddin"		
"Don'! Took de las' piece"		
"The Village Choir"		
Chalk Boards - "You is a Chicken"		
Series 2816; The "Connoisseur" Series		
Duplicates Series 2723.	50 - 60	60 - 70
Series 4096 "Funny Folk" (4)	40 - 50	50 - 60
"I'se Just Been Married"		
"The Pickaninnies Bedtime"		
"Preparing for the Party"		

F. Brundage (Uns.), R. Tuck 118
"To Greet Mah Valentine"

F. Brundage (Uns.), R. Tuck 118
"Waitin' fo' Mah Sweetheart"

F. Brundage (Uns.), R. Tuck 115
"My little love, my little love ..."

F. Brundage (Uns.), R. Tuck 108
"I'm 'cuttin' up now, for it's ..."

"Tubbing Time in Darkie Land"
Series 6616 "Humorous" (Uns.)   20 - 25   25 - 28
"Git a move on..."
Series 8201
     Black Angels   20 - 25   25 - 30
T.S.N. (Theo Stroefer, Nuremburg)
Series 664, "Du Kennst mein noch lange ..."
     Little Girl Looks Though Picket Fence   18 - 22   22 - 26
Others, Signed Brundage   18 - 22   22 - 25
Others, Unsigned   18 - 20   20 - 22
BUCHANAN, FRED
   Raphael Tuck
     "Write Away" Series 9309 (6)   20 - 25   25 - 30
      "Ah haint got nothin much to say"
      "We are having a good time"
      "We are going to have a dance"
      "We have just arrived"
      "We shall not wait"
      Others
BUNNY
     Foxy Grandpa Series   12 - 15   15 - 18
     Blacks Dancing, with Watermelons
BURBROOK
     Big Eyed Boy, "Coon"   15 - 20   20 - 25
BURGER
   Rotograph Co.
     FL 431 "I's only chopping..."   12 - 15   15 - 18
BUXTON, DUDLEY (G.B.)   10 - 12   12 - 15
CADY, HARRISON (PMC)
     "Under the Southern Palm"   12 - 15   15 - 18
CARMICHAEL
   T.P. & Co.
     Series 668 "Anybody Here Seen Kelly?"   12 - 15   15 - 18
CARR, GENE
   Rotograph Co.
     Series 242
      3 "Follow-Master"   12 - 15   15 - 18
CARTER, REG.
   E. Mack (B&W)
     "I'se So Lonely"   8 - 10   10 - 12
CARTER, SYDNEY
   Hildesheimer & Co.
     5192 "How Men Propose"   12 - 15   15 - 18
     5239 "The Dance" Series   12 - 15   15 - 18

"We are going to have a dance"

"We are having a good time"

"We shall not wait"

"We have just arrived"

Fred Buchanan, R. Tuck, "Write Away" Series 9309

CAVALLEY

6539	6 - 8	8 - 10

CHIOSTRI

Ballerini & Fratini

Series 242	40 - 50	50 - 60

CHIVOT

Comical Black/White Boxers	8 - 10	10 - 12

CHRISTIE, G. F.

"Some 'Color' Sergeant"	10 - 12	12 - 15

Int. Art Pub. Co.

"Will Gentleman in Black..."	12 - 15	15 - 18

CHRISTY, F. EARL

Bergman Co. (Sepia)

Man and Woman Golfers with Black Caddie	18 - 22	22 - 25

ELLEN CLAPSADDLE

Ellen H. Clapsaddle was, without doubt, the most prolific of all artists of children during the golden era. She designed hundreds of sets and series of all Holiday Greetings which mainly illustrated lovable and beautiful children. All have the "Clapsaddle" look and can be easily identified whether signed or unsigned.

Most of her children were published by the International Art Publishing Co. and later by Wolf & Co. Also to be found are some foreign issues by Kopal and several issues by unknown German publishers. Her most famous black-related card is from International Art's Halloween Mechanical Series 1236 of a smiling black boy, draped in a white sheet costume and holding a large Jack O' Lantern in his right hand. His arm moves and the Jack O' Lantern rotates for the mechanical effect. "A Jolly Halloween" is the caption. The card is now valued up to $450.00. The remaining three cards in the series are of white children.

Ellen also designed Series 780, a 6-card set of blacks on Valentine's Day Greetings featuring beautiful children and published by International Art. This set was reproduced by an anonymous German publisher, the differences being that the cards were unsigned; each had a cotton background, and some of the captions were changed.

CLAPSADDLE, ELLEN H.

International Art Pub. Co.

Mechanical Series 1236

"A Jolly Halloween"	350 - 400	400 - 450

THE "Agony Column".

MAINLY PERSONAL

WILL Gentleman in black KINDLY make
another appointment with Dark LADY.

G. F. Christie, Int. Art Pub. Co.
"Will Gentleman in Black ..."

HOW MEN PROPOSE.

IN THE "OLE PLANTATION"

Sydney Carter, Hildesheimer 5192
"How Men Propose ..."

Best
Wishes
for a happy
New Year

Ellen Clapsaddle, Int. Art, No No.
"Best Wishes for a happy New ..."

Ah'll twang de banjo, an sing a refrain
Erbout a maiden so fine;
She's jest as sweet as de sugar-cane,
Ma lubly Valentine.

TO MY
VALENTINE

Ellen Clapsaddle, Int. Art
Series 780, "To My Valentine"

No No. 4 of Same Girl Sitting on Bench		
New Year, Valentine, Christmas	16 - 18	18 - 22
Series 780 (6)	22 - 25	25 - 30
"Love's Fair Exchange"		
1 - Boy Offers Ice Cream to Girl		
"To My Valentine" (2)		
1 - Boy with Banjo		
2 - Boy with Top Hat and Cane		
"With Love's Greeting" (3)		
1 - Boy with Straw Hat Walking Left		
2 - Boy Offers Watermelon to Girl		
3 - Girl in Blue Dress Sits on Wooden Box		
Series 781 (4)		
"Affectionate Greetings"		
"My Love to You"		
"True Love"		
"With Fondest Love"		
Unsigned; Elegant Boy/Girl Do Cake Walk	18 - 22	22 - 25
Kopal		
New Year Series (4)	30 - 35	35 - 40
No Captions (2)		
Stewart & Woolf, London		
Series 696		
"A Happy Christmas" (2)	22 - 25	25 - 30
"A Joyful Christmas"		
"With Best Christmas Wishes"		
Boy and Girl W/Slice of Watermelon		
Anonymous, Germany		
Cotton Background, Embossed, Unsigned		
Same Images as Series 780 Above	25 - 30	30 - 35
Boy with Top Hat and Cane		
"With Fondest Love"		
Girl in Blue Dress Sits on Wooden Box		
"My Love to You"		
Boy with Straw Hat Walking Left		
"To the One I Love"		
Boy Playing Banjo		
"To My Valentine"		
Boy Offers Ice Cream to Girl		
"My Valentine Think of Me"		
Boy Offers Watermelon to Girl		
CLARK, A.		
Ullman Mfg. Co.		

E. Clapsaddle, Int. Art Series 780
"With Love's Greeting."

E. Clapsaddle, Anon. German
"To the One I Love."

E. Clapsaddle, Int. Art, Series 1236
"A Jolly Halloween" (Mechanical)

E. Clapsaddle, Anon. German
"My Valentine think of Me"

"Kute Koon Kids" Series 165
    2917 "A Case of Suspended Animation"   15 - 18   18 - 22
    2919 "Jest wait til we grow up"
    2667 "He lubs me - He lubs me not"
    2668 "A Hard Blow"
CLEN DENNING, WILL
  Valentine & Sons
    "The change has benefited..."   8 - 10   10 - 12
COCKRELL
  L. M. Johnson, 1905
    Girl in Sunbonnet   10 - 12   12 - 15
COLOMBO
  GPM
    Series 2048   15 - 18   18 - 22
  Ultra
    Series 2219
      Children, Snails, Spiders
      Boy and Girl with Duck   12 - 14   14 - 16
    Series 2224
    Series 2245
CONNELL
  White City Art Co.
    238 Boy with Rabbit   8 - 10   10 - 12
COOGLER, MARY   (L)
  Asheville Post Card Co.
    E-9639 "Never Min' Me Mr. Gator..."   5 - 6   6 - 8
COOK, A. M.
  DAGB
    Series 636   15 - 18   18 - 22
  C. W. Faulkner
    Series 1413 (6) Children   18 - 22   22 - 25
      "Gee Up"
      "I Lub a Lubly Gal I Do"
      "Oh, Honey"
      "Please I've Come"
      "Shy"
      "You Made Me Lub You"
    Series 1594
      "Pack Up Your Troubles and Smile"   12 - 15   15 - 18
      Others
  ZAHC
    "In Erwartung"   12 - 15   15 - 18
  L. M. Johnson Co.,
    Boy Eating Watermelon   10 - 12   12 - 14

Rose Clark
Ullman Series 165, No. 2917
"A Case of Suspended Animation"

Will ClenDenning
Valentine & Sons
"The change has benefited ..."

COOPER, PHYLLIS
  Raphael Tuck
    Golliwogs "Happy Land" Series 3463
      "I'm very sure you never saw..."   22 - 25   25 - 28
    Series 3464
      "Now what's our game?"
      "Baby, Baby, up so high..."
COWHAM, HILDA (G.B.)
  Raphael Tuck
    Series 1322 "Seaside"
      "The Beach Concert"   15 - 18   18 - 22
CRAMER, RIE
  Roukens & Erhert   15 - 18   18 - 22
CRANE
    Chicken Thief in Bear Trap   8 - 10   10 - 12
CUNNINGHAM
  Central News Co.
    "September Evening"   6 - 8   8 - 10
CURTIS, E.
  Raphael Tuck
    Valentine Series 3, "From Many Lands"   8 - 10   10 - 12

Chiostri (Unsigned)
Ballerini & Fratini No. 242
No Caption

Colombo, GPM Series 2048
Boy with Black Doll

Phyllis Cooper, R. Tuck 3463
"I'm very sure you never saw ..."

"De Trouble of True Lub"
"I Lubs Yo' Ma Honey"
DOMERGE, GABRIEL
    Real Photo-types of Josephine Baker   100 - 120   120 - 140
    (See **Entertainers** Section)
DONADINI, JR., Dresden
    Series 454 (6)   25 - 28   28 - 32
        "The Voice that Breathed O'er Eden"
        Tall Lady with Hurt Child Walking Behind
        Surprised Man Washes Foot
        Well Dressed Dude with Suitcase
        Man Singing from "Sleep, Darling Sleep"
DWIG
    Raphael Tuck
        Series 180 "Never"
        "Never insult a mule behind his back..."   18 - 22   22 - 25
E.O.
    B & R   15 - 18   18 - 22
E.O.B.
    B.K.W.I., Vienna
        Series 466
            Quarreling   15 - 18   18 - 22
            Harmonica Playing
            Others
ELLAM
    Hold-to-Light Transparency
        Minstrel Man with Tambourine   40 - 50   50 - 60
    Raphael Tuck   12 - 15   15 - 18
ELLIOTT, H.
    Blacks Go Hunting   12 - 15   15 - 18
ERICKSON
    "That Dear Little Fellow"   6 - 8   8 - 10
    "And this he calls Love"
FAL
    Girl Rides Red Wooden Horse   18 - 22   22 - 25
F.E.M.
    Guildhall
        Series 519
        "Rear in Arrears"   6 - 8   8 - 10
    Raphael Tuck
        Series 8497   12 - 15   15 - 18
        Series 10002
        Series 10062 "The Dawn of Love"
        "There's nothing half so sweet..."

Donadini, Jr., Anon. Publisher
Series 454, No Caption

Donadini, Jr., Anon. Publisher
Series 454, No Caption

Donadini, Jr., Anon. Publisher
Series 454, No Caption

Donadini, Jr., Anon. Publisher
Series 454, No Caption

DWIG, R. Tuck Series 180
"Never insult a mule behind ..."

WF (Wally Fialkowski)
AMV 1913, "Liebe macht blind"

FIALKOWSKI, WALLY (Austria)
   AMV   12 - 15   15 - 18
FLC
   F.A. Moss
      "Say, Honey, Hain't yo never..."   6 - 8   8 - 10
FR
   A.R. & Co.
      Girl Sitting on Her Hat   10 - 12   12 - 15
F.W.
   H.M. Co.
      Series 141   15 - 18   18 - 22
      "Sambo Getteh Mixed Up With Brethren"
      "Sambo Serenadeth His Lady Love"
FERNEL (F in Circle) (France) (UndB)
   "Cake Walk"
      Man in Tails and Girl with Umbrella   40 - 45   45 - 50
FERREL, MARY
   White City, 1906   8 - 10   10 - 12
FRANK, E.
   Blacks-Whites   10 - 12   12 - 15
FUL
   M.M. Munk Series 242 (6)   22 - 25   25 - 28

Fernel, Anonymous French Publisher
"Cake Walk"

FYCH, C. D.
Valentine & Sons   8 - 10   10 - 12
G.F.C. (GEORGE F. CHRISTIE)
International Art Pub. Co.
    "Will Gentleman in Black..."   10 - 12   12 - 15
GASSAWAY, KATHERINE
Rotograph Co.
    F.L. 105 "I Scared I'll Get Sunburned"   12 - 15   15 - 18
    F.L. 123 "I Wish I was in Dixie"
    F.L. 124 "Thought I Heer'd de Boss Comin"
    F.L. 193 "New Orleans"
Raphael Tuck
    Series 6666
    "Help" Black Baby/White baby   12 - 15   15 - 18
GILSON, T.
E. J. Hey & Co.
    Series 262   12 - 15   15 - 18
    Series 378
        "After Dinner Rest Awhile"
        "Ha! Ha! Ha!"
        "He's Coming Home on Furlough"
        "I Wonder if all White Gals..."
        "Wall Flowers"
    Series 410
        Mama and Child
        "A Broken Melody"
        "During the Raid"

K. Gassaway, Rotograph Co.
F.L. 124, "Thought I heard de ..."

K. Gassaway, Rotograph Co.
F.L. 123, "I wish I was in Dixie"

"Everything is Thumbs Up"		
Series 474	12 - 14	14 - 16
"A Black Affair"		
"Black & Blue"		
Ludgate		
201 "Rats"	10 - 12	12 - 15
"During the Raid"		
"A Game of Skill"		
325A "The Question of the Day!"		
626 "He's Coming Home on Furlough"	15 - 18	18 - 22
627 "Three of the Best"	10 - 12	12 - 15
627X "Good Luck in the New Year"		
816 "We are all up a Tree"		
0145 "Friday"		
1081 "A Blot on a Clean Sheet"		
J. Salmon		
Series 2571	10 - 12	12 - 14
Series 2580 "If dems what you use..."	10 - 12	12 - 15
British Manufacture Series	8 - 10	10 - 12
952 "And this is what HE calls LOVE!"		
"Blimey, I'm Tired"	8 - 10	10 - 12

GOSSETT
  U.S.S. Post Card Co., 1905
      "Way Down South in Dixie"   10 - 12   12 - 15
GREINER, MAGNUS
  International Art Pub. Co. (7)   22 - 25   25 - 28
       701 "A Darktown Trip"
       702 "The Serenade"
       704 "A Lad and a Ladder"
       707 "A Darktown Idyl"
       708 "A Feast"
       709 "A Darktown Lover"
       710 "A Darktown Philosopher"
     Series 780 Valentines
       "Ah'll Twang De Banjo..."   15 - 18   18 - 22
GRELLIER, H. HARLEY
     "A General Upset"   8 - 10   10 - 12
     "The Walking Craze"
HB
  Roth & Langley
     "Chicken? Whar He?"   8 - 10   10 - 12
     "Dis Sutinly Looks Good to Me"
H.B.G. or H. B. Griggs
  L & E
     Series 2217 Blacks on Big Hearts   18 - 22   22 - 25
       "Golly but you's got a tough ole' Heart..."
       "Honey You'se done busted a Hole..."
       "Honey When I See You Smile..."
       "Ma Heart's Dat Full ob Laughin..." (Uns.)
       "Yo' Heart is Dat Cold..."
       "Yo' Heart is so Hard..."
     Series 2224
       "A Bright and Merry Christmas"   15 - 18   18 - 22
       Woman with Pudding
       Others
H.U.S.
  Hildesheimer
     5268 "Teeter Totter"   12 - 15   15 - 18
HANSON (B&W)   5 - 6   6 - 7
HARLOW, GRACE
  R. L. Wells Children
     "An Automobile Ride"   10 - 12   12 - 15
     "Dar Ain't Gwine to be no Rine"
     "Good Night"
     "Rivals"

M. Greiner, Int. Art Pub. Co. 707
"A Darktown Idyl"

M. Greiner, Int. Art Pub. Co. 708
"A Feast"

M. Greiner, Int. Art Pub. Co. 709
"A Darktown Lover"

M. Greiner, Int. Art Pub. Co. 710
"A Darktown Philosopher"

H.B.G., L&E Series 2217
"My heart is full ob honey ..."

H.B.G., L&E Series 2217
"My Heart's dat full ob ..."

"Way Down in My Heart..."
Croquet - "You aint a gwine..."

HARTMAN, E. VON

   E. Nister

      3478 "Ah Wants Yo' Mah Honey"   18 - 22   22 - 25

      "Be Mah Valentine"

      "My Gal am like de Honeysuckle..."

HASSAL

      Poems Illustrated   8 - 10   10 - 12

HEICH

   American Litho

      "A raise in the South"   8 - 10   10 - 12

HERZIOS, E.   8 - 10   10 - 12

HALLOWAY

   A. Liebel & Co.

      Series 4239

      "I'm Black But I'm Comely"   12 - 15   15 - 18

H.H. (H. HORINA)

   J. I. Austin Co. (Sepia)

      A-269 "A Dream of Paradise"   15 - 18   18 - 22

      A-273 "The Line's Busy"   10 - 12   12 - 15

Halloway, A. Liebel & Co.
4239, "I'm Black But I'm Comely"

E. von Hartmann, E. Nister 3482
"Mah girl am like de honey ..."

E. von Hartmann, E. Nister 3478
"Ah want yo' mah honey, ..."

H.H. (Horina), Ullman, 208, "Gin"
"Favorite Drinks" Series 103

Bamforth Co.
    2190 "Extremes Meet"   8 - 10   10 - 12
White City Art Co.
    Series 234
        "Rollerskating"   15 - 18   18 - 22
        "Golly, It's Good"
Ullman Mfg. Co.
    Series 85 "Thanksgiving"
        1988 "For Thanksgiving"   15 - 18   18 - 22
    Series 103 "Favorite Drink"
        2082 "Gin"   22 - 25   25 - 28
    Series 106 "In the Colored Swim" (4)
        2095 "We're Off"   18 - 22   22 - 25
        2096 "We're Out"
        2097 "We're In"
        2098 "We're Safe"
    Series 109 "The National Game"
        2152 "A Slide for Second"   30 - 35   35 - 40
        2153 "Out on a Fly"
        2154 "A Foul Ball"
        2155 "Making a Home Run"
    Series 116 Skaters
        2189 "Help"   20 - 22   22 - 25
        2190 "Extremes Meet"
        2191 "Her First Lesson"
        2192 "So Easy"
HUTAF, AUGUST
Ullman Mfg. Co.
    Series 113 "Blacktown Babies"   20 - 22   22 - 25
        2174 "Two Beauties"
        2175 "Don't Wake the Babies"
        2177 "Pleasant Anticipation"
        2180 "The Cake Walk"
Rotograph Co.
    Doublefold Mechanical   60 - 65   65 - 75
HYDE, GRAHAM
Raphael Tuck
    Series 9094 "Coons Motoring" (6)   20 - 25   25 - 28
        Run Away Wagon
        Running from Mammy
        Others
    Series 9542 "Coon Studies" (6)
IBANEZ, J.
    Series 596 Children   6 - 8   8 - 10

H.H. (Horina), Ullman Ser. 109
2152, "A Slide for Second"

H.H. (Horina), Ullman Ser. 109
2153, "Out on a Fly"

H.H. (Horina), Ullman Ser. 109
2154, "A Foul Ball"

H.H. (Horina), Ullman Ser. 109
2155, "Making a Home Run"

H.H. (Horina), Ullman 106
2095, "We're Off"

H.H. (Horina), Ullman 106
2096, "We're Out"

H.H. (Horina), Ullman 106
2097, "We're In"

H.H. (Horina), Ullman 106
2098, "We're Safe"

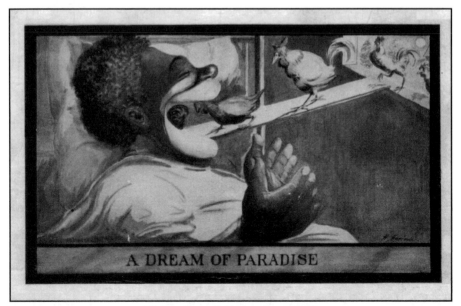

H. Horina, J. I. Austin, A269
"A Dream of Paradise"

August Hutaf, Ullman Series 113
2175, "Don't Wake the Babies"

IRBY (L)
  Asheville Post Card Co.
    GC422 "Air Raid and Blackout"   4 - 5   5 - 6
J.C.T.
  Anonymous   5 - 7   7 - 8

August Hutaf, Ullman Series 113
2180, "The Cake Walk"

Graham Hyde, R. Tuck, "Coons Motoring"
Series 9094 (No Caption)

JERVIS, G.
> Button Family
>> Black Face in Button   60 - 70   70 - 80

JOTTER
>> "Put me among the girls"   10 - 12   12 - 15

K.V.
> **L.P.**
>> Series 205 Black-White Kewpies   12 - 15   15 - 18
>> Series 206 Black-White Kewpies
>> Series 210 Black Kewpies   10 - 12   12 - 15
>> Series 224 Black-White Boxers
>> Series 227 Black-White Kewpies
> **KVKV**
>> Series 340 (6) Black-White Kewpies   10 - 12   12 - 15
>> Series 341 (6) Black-White Kewpies   12 - 15   15 - 18

KARCH, PAT (C)
> **S.V.**
>> "You were missed Sunday"   5 - 8   8 - 12

KEMBLE, E. B.
> **Detroit Pub. Co.**
>> "Kemble's Coontown" (10) (B&W) (UndB)
>>> 14159 "Miss Snowball, Yo ain't much..."   28 - 32   32 - 35
>>> 14160 "Look heah, Rufus Jackson..."
>>> 14161 "Will half a fried chicken..."
>>> 14162 "Doan' try to insult me..."
>>> 14163 "I notice you seem sprized..."
>>> 14164 "Why doan' you' fader raise melons?"

Irby, Asheville P.C. Company
GC422, "Air Raid and Blackout"

K.V., L.P. 210/4 (Foreign)
Black and White Kewpies

Na svatebni cestĕ

14165 "Well, Chile, what lesson..."
14166 "Why yo' use dat ol' cannon foh..."
14167 "Now we'll see ef dat sawed off..."
14168 "Not gwine ter meetin dis mornin..."

Fairman (B&W)   8 - 10 10 - 12

"Ah jes wish I had a girl"
"Ah sho would love to get er line..." Uns.
"Ain't yer got a few cherrin words..."
"Ain't yo nebber gwine to let me..."
"Honey yo sho has me fascinated" Uns.
"I'se bin er waiten, an er waiten..."
"I'se feelin prime an mah appetite's fine"

Gibson Art

"Honey, Yo Sho Does Make..." (B&W) 8 - 10 10 - 12
"If Ah Little Affection Am..." (B&W)

KENNEDY, T. R., TRK (G.B.)

A. M. Davis Co.

"Little Darkies" Series 521 (6) 15 - 18 18 - 22
"Dis-Am-Fine"
"Dis am Susan"
"For-my-Lady-Lub"
"The Little Beggar"

"She-Lubs-Anodder"
"Some-Little-Darkie-Gal"
Gale & Polden
Series 2143 (6)   15 - 18   18 - 22
W.B.
475 "Yes we have no bananas"   10 - 12   12 - 15
KINSELLA, E. P.
Langsdorf & Co.
Series 713 (6) "Diabolo"   25 - 30   30 - 35
"I Can Do Dis All Day"
"I'm De Coloured Champion"
"Dis Am De Cake Walk Movement"
"Dis Am Easy"
"Got It! On The Brain"
"Now For De Catch"
KOBER
B.K.W.I., Austria
Series 63406 Blacks Dancing (6)   15 - 20   20 - 25
Series 2966 (6)   15 - 18   18 - 22
KORLE
AR&CiB (6)
Black Boy-White Girl   10 - 12   12 - 15
LAMBERT, HGC MARSH
A. M. Davis & Co.
Golliwogs Series 501   15 - 18   18 - 22
"I'll play, I think, with Sambo..."
"At nine my breakfast is over..."
"Oh Dear! How quickly six has come..."
"Children of the Empire" Series 562   15 - 18   18 - 22
"Jamaica"
"New Zealand"
"South Africa"
LEVI, C.
Ullman Mfg. Co.
"Kute Koon" Series 165   12 - 15   15 - 18
2913 "A Study in Black & White"
2915 "A Little Black Washing"
2916 "Two Souls with but a..."
Series 210
3308 "Suffragette"   30 - 35   35 - 40
LEWIN, F. G. (G.B.)
Inter-Art Co.
"Artisque" Series   12 - 15   15 - 18
"De Temperature am gettin..."

"Dis-am-Fine."   "The Little Beggar."   "She-Lubs-Anodder."

"Some-Little-Darkie-Gal."   "For-my-Lady-Lub."   "Dis am Susan."

T. R. Kennedy, "Little Darkies" Series 521
Published by A. M. Davis & Company, London

2517 "Do you Balf dis morning?"
"Fancy Meeting You"
"I don't want no Sugar"
2258 "It am not de place, it's de company"
2259 "I's Sweet Nuff..."
2262 "Honey, Dat 'Brella am de wrong..."
"I Guess Somebody's Welcome"   10 - 12   12 - 15
"I've a Little Hut..."

South Africa, she sends us gold
And lustrous diamonds too,
And feathers from her ostriches,—
(You've seen them at the Zoo.)

Jamaica is an Island famed
For many lovely fruits.
Tobacco, too, is also grown,—
— Coffee, and ginger roots.

H.G.C. Marsh Lambert
A.M. Davis Co., 562, "S. Africa"

H.G.C. Marsh Lambert
A.M. Davis Co., 562, "Jamaica"

"Just Room for Two"   10 - 12   12 - 15
"Marfa, You sure am de Better Half"
2158 "Women & Children First, Rastus"
2578 "Something is coming your way"
"I Hab Lost One..."
6912 "I Ain't Taking on no Followers"
6916 "When you says go way..."

W. E. Mack
2238 "Bobbed!"   10 - 12   12 - 15
"Something's Coming"
"Things am a Bit Upside Down"
Others

J. Salmon
1286 "Yes! We have no bananas..." (Uns.)   10 - 12   12 - 15
1837
1840 "Come and Take Pot Luck..."
"May Your Troubles Be Small Ones"
1841 "Ain't it about time..."
1928 "Love will find a way."
1930 "Life's Just One Darn Thing..."
2257 "Rastus always is de pufec' gentleman!"
2260 "We Don't Talk, We Does Things"

H.G.C. Marsh Lambert, A.M. Davis Co., "Round the Clock" Series 501
"Oh dear! How quickly Six has come, My toys I put away, -- ..."

H.G.C. Marsh Lambert, A.M. Davis Co., "Round the Clock" Series 501
"I'll play, I think, with Sambo, And with Teddy-bear till Ten, ..."

C. Levi, Ullman 2913
"A Study in Black and White"

F. G. Lewin, E. W. Savory 515
"Saturday Night"

2519 "It will take...to make you white"   10 - 12   12 - 15
2575 "Must be Heaven"
2583 "I's is jus' nuts on you"
2584 "Jus' Room for..."
2595 "After you wid de ball Marfa"
2756 "A Little Light on a Dark Subject"
"Come and see us"
"I'm having my annual..."
"I's a Waiting For You"
"Life's just one darn..."
"Love Will Find a Way"
"Nigger: For we married..."
"Your lips are berry Lubly"
Boy with flowers for Pickaninny Girl
2920 "Honey! d'you like Black Chicken?"
2974 "You Am De Honeysuckle..."
3421 "You should be a little boulder..."
3545 "I'm looking after de younguns..."
3881 "If we weren't in de Boat..."
4059 Girl Making Phone Call"
   (Also with Belgian Caption)
4071 "Bed & Brekfus" Sign on Tree

Bamforth Co.
    "Nigger Kid" Series

61 "E's Naughty and I'm Impressin..."	8 - 10	10 - 12
"Black Kid Comics"		
178 "The Outlook Here is Good"	10 - 12	12 - 15
182 "Course I'se Mad. You'd be Mad..."		
727 "Honey - Next to Myself..." (Uns.)		
729 "Wont you be my Chocolet Drop?"		
1561 "You is De One I'm Fondest of..."	8 - 10	10 - 12
1564 "Alone At Last"		
"Dis Mus Be Heaven"		
2047 "Here's a quaint Coon, with..." (Uns.)		
13592 "Just We Two - in Our Little Canoe"		
13594 "I Love the Sea When You Are In It"		
13593 "I's Just Bilin' Ober..."	6 - 8	8 - 10
"Piccaninny Comics"		
1939 "Honey-Next to Myself I Love You"	10 - 12	12 - 15

Florence House
  "Artisque" Series

2516 "Honey! I'se 'fraid the real pinch..."	10 - 12	12 - 15

L.N.S. (Dutch Publisher)

Dutch Captions	8 - 10	10 - 12

E. W. Savory, Bristol
  Series 515

"Saturday Night"	18 - 22	22 - 25
2278 "The Honeymoon"		
Series 443 "The Nigger Series"		
"There's No Place Like Home"		
Series 737		
"The Last Little Nigger Boy..."		
N512 "An unwanted bath"		

LEWIS
  Inter-Art

2401 Nurse and Soldier	8 - 10	10 - 12

  Ullman Mfg. Co.
    Series 165 "Cute Koon Kids"

2913 "A Study in Black"	12 - 15	15 - 18
2914 "A Study of Black Bawl"		

LINDAU	6 - 8	8 - 10

LILLO, R.
  P. Sander
    Series 503

9 "View of a Pessimist all Dark..."	12 - 15	15 - 18

F. G. Lewin, W. E. Mack, 2238
"Bobbed!"

F. G. Lewin, Bamforth Co., 1564
"Alone at Last!"

F. G. Lewin, J. Salmon, Ltd., 2974
"You am de honeysuckle, I am de Bee!"

LONG, F. C. (U.S.A.)
  Kaufmann & Strauss 1904 (UndB)

49 The prisoner, with Ball and Chain	18 - 20	20 - 25
50 "It Just Struck My Mind"		
55 Boy with Very Big Razor	20 - 25	25 - 30
56 "The Very First Time"		
Others		
1904 Boy Kicks Watermelon		
Series 60 Valentines	18 - 20	20 - 25
1940 Boy Eats Big Watermelon		

M.D.S.
  Ullman Mfg. Co.

Series 81 "Happy Day"		
1913 "I'se Right In It"	12 - 15	15 - 18
1914 "Waiting at the Church"		

  American Post Card Co.

Series 160 (Sepia)		
"Who's Baby is OO?" *	6 - 8	8 - 10
"Kute Koon Kids" Series 165		
2665 "Life is Just One..."	8 - 10	10 - 12
2666 "Stand Still"		

  * Although this is signed M.D.S., it is
    really a Bernhardt Wall image.

MAC

J. Amiard	10 - 12	12 - 15

MMS
  G.K. Prince & Co.

376 "A Bit of Song"	10 - 12	12 - 15
1261 "Dar' Aint No Use A Hurrying"		
1507 "W'en Trouble Come to..."		

MACH

Girl in Bonnet	8 - 10	10 - 12
1768 "Dat Gal's a Guine to be Mine"		

MALLET, BEATRICE (G.B.)
  R C

Series 55659	10 - 12	12 - 15

MARQUIS (France)
  IMP American Series 14

"Black and White" Nursing Black Baby	35 - 40	40 - 50

MARSJEAN

"Comique" Series 811		
"Alligator Tears"	6 - 8	8 - 10
"Hatching Snakes"	6 - 8	8 - 10

F. G. Lewin, Bamforth Co., 13594
"I Love the Sea When You Are ..."

F. G. Lewin, Bamforth Co., 13593
"I'se jus' bilin' ober wid lub ..."

F. G. Lewin, E. W. Savory, 2278
"The Honeymoon."

MAURICE, REG (G.B.)
   D. Regent
      Series 4137 (6)   12 - 14   14 - 18
        "Can't eat nothing..."
        "Can't send you..."
        "Cut dat sob stuff..."
        "Dat Louie Stuff makes me sick"
McGILL, DONALD (G.B.)
   J. Asher & Co.
      1093 "If Cleanliness am Next to..."   10 - 12   12 - 14
      A1168 "I Send You This Sunflower..."   12 - 15   15 - 18
      A1176 "Who Said C-C-Cookie Spanked...?" 10 - 12   12 - 14
      A1177 "Wash My Face"
      A1178 ""Dat's Burglars..."
   Inter-Art Co.
      "I Can't Hide..."   10 - 12   12 - 14
      4638 "T'se Awful Lonesome..."
      2138 "We're Rather Crowded..."
      4636 "Oh Honey! How I Loves..."
      4637 "Why Don't a Certain Party..."
   Bamforth Co.
      5 "If Dat Chile Doan Soon Change Color" 12 - 15   15 - 18
      174 "We're Rather Crowded..."   10 - 12   12 - 14
MINNS, B. E. (G.B./Australia)
   Carlton Publishing Co.
      "Glad Eye" Series (6)   15 - 18   18 - 22
      "Glad I'se Alive"
MORGAN
   Raphael Tuck
      Series 8497 "Some Clothes"   18 - 22   22 - 25
      "I Spect His Clothes Done It"
      "S'pose I'd Better Start Dressing"
      "You'se Hiding..."
MORRIE (C)
   Mike Roberts
      Continental Size
      27949 "How, Paleface"   1 - 2   2 - 3
      27950 "It's Brotherhood Week"
      27951 "Wow Chitlins, Blackeye Peas..."
      27952 "I Told You We Shouldn't..."
MUNSON, WALT (L) (C)
   Colourpicture (Tichnor Bros.)
      21 "If You Want a Nice Dark Tan..." (Uns.) 5 - 6   6 - 8
      119 "Big Blow Out!"

F. C. Long, Kaufmann & Strauss
49, "Valentine Greetings"

F. C. Long, Kaufmann & Strauss
55, "Valentine Greetings"

200 "I'm Prepared in Case..."	5 - 6	6 - 8
204 "Silly Goose" (Uns.)		
205 "Sure We're Cuckoo..." (Uns.)		
206 "Can You Tie This One?" (Uns.)		
208 "I'm Not Saying, You're..." (Uns.)		
209 "Boy! How you can throw it!" (Uns.)	4 - 5	5 - 7
253 "I Ain't Worried About No Sugar..."		
257 "Blackout! I'm on Home Defense Now"		

M.D.S., Ullman, 165
2666, "Stand Still!"

Marquis, I.M.P.
American Series
14, "Black and White."

MMS, G. K. Prince
376, "A Bit of Song."

D. McGill, Bamforth Art Comic
5, "If dat chile doan soon ..."

D. McGill, Jos. Asher Co., A1168
"I send you this Sunflower..."

N.U.
   American Post Card Co.
      Series 160 (Sepia)

2531 "Deed I dun Eat no Chicken"	10 - 12	12 - 14

NEIGHBORS, HILLARY
   Pen Drawings, 1942

"Narcissus!"	5 - 6	6 - 8

O.V.
   Trenkler & Co. (6) (UndB)   12 - 15   15 - 18

O'NEILL, ROSE
   Raphael Tuck
   "Pickings from Puck"
   Series 2482 "High Society in Coontown"

"A Misunderstanding" (Uns.)	80 - 100	100 - 110
Series 2483 "Pickings from Puck"	70 - 80	80 - 90

      "A Brain Worker"
      "Better than a Sermon"
      "Ne Plus Ultra"
      "One View"

Series 9411 "High Society in Coontown" (6)	100 - 110	110 - 120

      "A Matrimonial Alliance"
      "A Misunderstanding"

Walt Munson (Uns.), Tichnor
69421, "Sure We're Cuckoo ..."

Walt Munson (Uns.), Tichnor
69268, "Boy! How You Can ..."

Walt Munson (Uns.), Tichnor
69508, "I'm Not Saying You're ..."

Walt Munson (Uns.), Tichnor
69422, "Can You Tie This One?"

Walt Munson (Uns.), Asheville P.C. Company, 21
"If You Want a Nice Dark Tan Come and Join Us ..."

Walt Munson, Colourpicture, 200
"I'm Prepared in Case You Git Fresh.....and I Have 'ta Git Out ..."

"A Provisional Finance"
"All that was Necessary"
"Finis"
"His Limited Provisioning Capacity"
Series 9412 "Coontown Kids" *   35 - 45   45 - 55
* Reprinting of Series 2483

Rose O'Neill (Unsigned), R. Tuck, "High Society in Coontown"
2482, "A Misunderstanding"

Rose O'Neill (Unsigned), R. Tuck, "Coontown Kids" Series 912
9412, "A Brain Worker"

OUTCAULT, RICHARD F.
I. H. Blanchard Co.

"Buster Brown & His Bubble" *   28 - 32   32 - 35
    3 "Black or White"
    6 "A Good Bump"
    8 "A Bit of Smooth Road"
*Same series also by Souvenir P.C. Co.

J. Ottoman	12 - 15	15 - 20
Ullman Mfg. Co.		
Series 76 "Darktown"	22 - 25	25 - 30
1889 "Koontown Kids"		
1890 "Deed, I dun eat no Chickun"		
1891 "Darktown Doctors"		
1892 "Darkytown Dames"		
American P.C. Co. (also did Series 76)	22 - 25	25 - 30
H. H. Tammen		
Buster Brown Series 1001 (Emb.)		
"Got no time..." (With Watermelon)	16 - 20	20 - 25
Raphael Tuck		
Undivided Back Valentines		
"I dreams erbout yo' every night..."	15 - 18	18 - 22
Series 1001		
Buster Brown and His Bubble (3, 6 & 8)	25 - 30	30 - 35
Hildesheimer & Co.		
Series 5268 (No Captions)	15 - 18	18 - 22
PARKINSON, ETHEL		
B. Dondorf Series 517	15 - 18	18 - 22
"The Lovers"		
Pelican Eating Swimmer's Clothes		
PAT		
Colourpicture (L)		
"I'se Pinnin a Lot of Hopes..."	3 - 4	4 - 5

R. F. Outcault, Ullman, "Darktown" Series 76
1889, "Koontown Kids"

R. F. Outcault, Ullman, "Darktown" Series 76
1892, "Darkytown Dames"

Asheville Postcard Co. (Uns.) (L)
    110 "Enee, Menee, Minee Moe ..."   3 - 4   4 - 5
PATERSON, VERA
   Regent Publishing Co.
     "A' Don't Want Nothin', Not Nobody..."   12 - 15   15 - 20
PETERSON, HANNES   10 - 12   12 - 15

R. F. Outcault, "Buster Brown and His Bubble" -- 3
Souvenir Post Card Co., "Black or White"

*R. F. Outcault, Ullman Mfg. Co., "Darktown" Series 76
1890, "Deed, I Dun Eat No Chickun"*

*E. Parkinson, B. Dondorf
Series 517, No Caption*

*E. Parkinson, B. Dondorf
Series 518, German Caption*

Vera Paterson, Regent Pub. Co.
285, "A' Don't Want Nothin, ..."

Pippo, Anonymous Italian
Series 3124, No. 8

Pippo, Anonymous Italian
Series 124, No. 7

Pippo, Anonymous Italian
Series 3124, No. 5

Pat, Asheville-Colourpicture, 287
"T'se Pinnin' a Lot of Hopes ..."

Pat (Uns.), Asheville P.C. Co.
110, "Enee, Menee, Minee Moe ..."

A. Richardson, Photochrom Co.
554, "My Curly-Headed Babby"

Mary Russell, Rischar (Russian)
371, "Alte Liebe"

A. Richardson, R. Tuck, 8688
"I'm down here with the Family"

C. Ryan, Winsch Back, A103
"A Cinch Party"

C. Ryan, Winsch Back, A104
"A Trick in Hearts"

PHIFER, L. C.
Theo Eismann

Illustrating Song Series, 1820, Baseball	40 - 50	50 - 60

    "Eve stole first and Adam second"
    "Goliath was struck out by David"
    "Rebecca went to the well with a pitcher"
    "The Prodigal Son made a Home Run"

De Witt C. Wheeler
    Same Series with Light Blue Borders   35 - 40   45 - 50
    Note: These Were Also Issued in Strip Form. 25 - 30   30 - 35
PIPPO, France
    3124-5 Black Man Ogles White Girl   20 - 25   25 - 28
    3124-6 Black Man Ogles White Girl
    3124-8 Black Man Ogles White Girl
PUVASIO
  AR
    Black Man Playing Accordion   18 - 20   20 - 25
R.J.W.
  M. Munk, Vienna
    Series 363
    Black Southern Wooden Doll Caricatures 22 - 25   25 - 30
RICHARDSON, AGNES (G.B.)
  Photochrome
  "Celesque" Series
    554 "My Curley-Headed Babby"   18 - 22   22 - 25
    555 "So Shy"
    557 "Well I Never"
    558 "I Loves Yo, Ma Honey..."
    635 "Twas Ever Thus"
    1720 "A Dusky Cavalier"
  Raphael Tuck
  Golliwogs
    Series 1232 "Rescued" (6)   22 - 25   25 - 30
    Series 1262 "Art" (6)
    Series 1281 "Art" (6)
    Series 1397 (6)
    Card C1420 "Little Snowflakes..."   22 - 25   25 - 28
    Card C1421 "My Greeting is Loving..." 18 - 22   22 - 25
    Card 8688 "I'm down here with the..." 25 - 30   30 - 35
  Valentine & Sons
  Golliwogs
    Series C2006 (6)   18 - 22   22 - 26
ROBINSON, F. A.
    "Free from Care"   10 - 12   12 - 15
ROBY (France) 1940's   5 - 8   8 - 10
ROSE, MABEL
    Series 46   10 - 12   12 - 15
    "Like de Orange Blossom Better"
ROSELAND, HARRY
    "The Teacup's Fortune Telling"   6 - 8   8 - 10

Sandford, R. Tuck & Sons
"Curly Coons"
9093, No Caption

Sandford, R. Tuck & Sons
"Happy Little Coons"
9049, "Quarrelsome Coons"

Sandford, R. Tuck, "Happy Little Coons"
9299, "Buried Treasure"

Sandford, R. Tuck & Sons
"Happy Little Coons"
9299, "Beauty on the Beach."

Xavier Sager, 519
No Caption

RUSSELL, MARY L.
  Rischar (Russian)
      371 "Alte Liebe"   15 - 20   20 - 25
RYAN, C.
  Winsch Backs
      A100 "Two Souls with but a single..."   20 - 25   25 - 30
      A104 "A Trick in Hearts"
      A103 "A Cinch Party"
      Boxers "Fake"
SAGER, XAVIER
  B. M., Paris
      519 Black Lady Beckons White Man (no cap.)   30 - 35   35 - 40
      568 "Noir garanti bon teink" (At the Bath)   15 - 20   20 - 25
SANDFORD, H. DIX, H.D. or H.D.S.
  Raphael Tuck
      Series 6891 "Happy Little Coons"   18 - 22   22 - 25
      Series 8457 "Happy Little Coons"
        "We Likes You"
        "We Four Little Topsies"
      Series 9003   18 - 22   22 - 25
      Series 9048 "Happy Little Coons" (6)   18 - 22   22 - 25
        "Go it Dinah"

"Great Sport"
"Quarrelsome Coons"
"Quite the Lady"
"Sweethearts"
"Sweets to the Sweet"
Series 9049 "Happy Little Coons" (6)   18 - 22   22 - 25
  "Quite the Lady"
  "Quarrelsome Coons"
  "Sweethearts"
Series 9050 "Happy Little Coons" (6)   18 - 22   22 - 25
  "Down by the Riverside"
  "Fishing"
  "Mermaids"
  "Nice Cool Coons"
  "Sand Coons"
  "In the Smart Set"
Series 9093 "Curley Coons" (6)   20 - 25   25 - 28
  Girl, Close-up, Large Eyes, Facing Right
  Profile of Boy in White Shirt and Hat
  Full Face of Girl in Bonnet
  Young Boy Smoking
  Young Boy Crying
  Girl in Orange Dress with Beads
Series 9227 "Happy Little Coons" (6)   18 - 22   22 - 25
  All are not signed.
  "A Man"
  "Mixed Bathing" (Uns.)
  "My Turn Next"
  "Racing the Waves"
  "The Swimming Lesson" (Uns.)
  "Too Cold"
Series 9228 "Happy Little Coons" (6)   18 - 22   22 - 25
Series 9229 "Happy Little Coons" (6)
  "A Young Preacher"
  "Dearest Friend"
  "In Polite Society"
  "Me and My Dog"
  "Saturday Night"
  "Up a Tree"
Series 9299 "Happy Little Coons" (6)   22 - 25   25 - 28
  "Beauty on the Beach"
  "Buried Treasure"
  "The Catch of the Season"
  "Just as the Sun Goes Down"

Unsigned Schmucker??, John Winsch, 1912
"Thanksgiving Day in the South"

W. Schwering, M.M.B. 606
"Black and White"

"Lost"
"Tired Out"
Series 9318 "Seaside Coons" (6)   18 - 22   22 - 25
  "After the Dip"
  "Come on, It's Lubly"
  "Dem White Niggers Very Funny"

MY GAL'S A HIGHBORN LADY

I LUB A LUBLY GAL I DO ! SON IDÉAL !

G. S. Shepheard, R. Tuck & Sons
9068 "Coons Cooning"
"My Gal's a Highborn ..."

G. S. Shepheard, R. Tuck & Sons
9068, "Coons Cooning"
"I Lub a Lubly Gal ..."

"Disturbers of the Peace"		
"So Polite"		
"When the Tide Comes In"		
Series 9819 "Seaside Coons" (6)	18 - 22	22 - 25
Series 9427 "More Coons" (6)	18 - 22	22 - 25
"A Difficult Choice"	15 - 18	18 - 22
"A Friend in Need"		
Man Golfing, Children Watch	25 - 28	28 - 32
"Our Motor"	15 - 18	18 - 22
"When Mudder Wash Our Clo's"	15 - 18	18 - 22
Series 9428 "Dark Girls & Black Boys" (6)	18 - 22	22 - 25
Series 9429 "Dark Girls & Black Boys" (6)		
Series 9457 "Happy Little Coons" (6)	15 - 18	18 - 22
"The Camel Race"		
"Hold Tight" Kids Ride Alligator		
"A Friend in Need"		
"The Latest Thing in Feathers"		
"The Price of a Ride"		
Series 9489 "Dark Girls & Black Boys" (6)	18 - 22	22 - 25
"Won't Go to Bed"		
"The Barrel-Organ"		
Others		

Series 9791 (6)   18 - 22   22 - 25
Series 9968 "Seaside Coons" (6)   18 - 22   22 - 25
Series 9969 "Seaside Coons" (6)   18 - 22   22 - 25
  "Buried Treasure"
  Others
Hildesheimer & Co.
Series 5268 "Negroes"   18 - 22   22 - 25
  Children Do Cake Walk
  Others
E.H.S. (Ellen H. Saunders)
M.A. Sheehan   8 - 10   10 - 12
SCHMUCKER, S. L. (Uns.??)
John Winsch, 1912 Thanksgiving
  "Thanksgiving Day in the South"
  Pappy, Mammy, Boy w/Coon & White Girl   100 - 120   120 - 140
SCHOENPFLUG
B.K.W.I.
Black-White Boxers   12 - 15   15 - 20
SCHWERING, W.
M.M.B.
606 "Black and White" Black/White Kiss   25 - 30   30 - 40
SHEPHEARD, GEORGE E. (G.B.)
Raphael Tuck
Series 9068 "Coons Cooning" (6)   22 - 25   25 - 30
  "The Cake Walk"
  "Come and Kiss Your Honey"
  "I Lub a Lubly Gal I Do"
  "I Want You Ma Honey"
  "My Gal's a Highborn Lady"
  "You Honey Boy"
Series 9297 "Among the Darkies" (6)   22 - 25   25 - 30
  "Conspirators"
  "Enough for Two"
  "My Face is My Fortune"
  "The Sleeping Beauty" 1 man
  "The Sleeping Beauty"
  "Under the Bamboo Tree"
Series 9536 "Coons Cooning" (6)   22 - 25   25 - 30
Series 740, French (6)
SHINN, COBB (U.S.A.)
T.P. & Co.
Series 790 (B&W)
  "Parson is dar a dog heaven"   8 - 10   10 - 12

F. Spurgin, Inter-Art, 154
"Like the Germans I'm Coming ..."

Suze (France), C&B Series 50
"Hier e' etail moi ..."

SIL, MIKE (L)
  Metropolitan Pub. Co.

396-6 "What a Palm-Garden..."	3 - 4	4 - 5

SMITH, LARRY (L)
  Asheville Post Card Co.

GC84 "O.K. Big Boy, You Furnish..."	3 - 4	4 - 5
SMITH, SID	8 - 10	10 - 12

M. SOWERBY

"Negro Children of North America"	18 - 22	22- 25
"Out of Reach"		

SPARKUHL and SPARKY
  AVM

Series 636 Blacks-Whites	12 - 15	15 - 18
628 "Smooching"		
629 "Reading the Paper"		
645 "The Beloved of His Heart"		
SPURGEON (France)	6 - 8	8 - 10

SPURGIN, FRED (Latvia/G.B.)
  J & A Co.

"Coon Series" 405	12 - 15	15 - 18
"Am My Nose Still Shiny?"		
"Golly! You are looking Pale"		
"Things are looking Black"		

Suze (France), C&B Series 50
"C'est elle qui l'a- voulu..."

D. Tempest, Bamforth, 2047
"Here's a Quaint Coon, ..."

D. Tempest, Bamforth, 132
"Look Me Over, Buddy ..."

D. Tempest, Bamforth, 807
"Oh, Honey! If Things Seem ..."

Others	12 - 15	15 - 18
Inter-Art Co.		
Series "One-Four-Nine"		
154 "Like the Germans I'm Coming out..."	12 - 15	15 - 18
STERNBERT, V. W.		
Regent Publishing Co.		
Series 1747 "Thinking of You - I Think..."	6 - 8	8 - 10
SUZE		
Cathblain and Bartrim, Paris		
Series 50 Pebbled paper		
Girl with Finger at Lips	18 - 22	22 - 26
Girl Painting Herself White		
TAYLOR, A. or A.T.		
Bamforth Co.		
"Vacation Comics"		
50 "No, This Isn't Me!"	6 - 8	8 - 10
"Kid Comics"		
174 "We're Rather Crowded Here"	6 - 8	8 - 10
"Black Kid Comics"		
"Somebody's Little Sweetheart" (Uns.)	6 - 8	8 - 10
13565 "Two Loving Hearts"	6 - 8	8 - 10
TEMPEST, DOUGLAS (G.B.)		
Bamforth Co.		
"Nigger Kids" Series		
127 "Am I Tanned? You'd Be Surprised"	8 - 10	10 - 12
K-15 "I Just Dassn't Look Around..."		
425 "Why Don't You Come Down..."	6 - 8	8 - 10
7041 "There's a Great Opening For You..."		
"Black looks never got..."	8 - 10	10 - 12
"Kiddy Comics"		
132 "Look me over, buddy... I'm a real..."	10 - 12	12 - 15
807 "Oh, Honey! If things seem black.."		
67-B "I'se Black all over..."	8 - 10	10 - 12
13553 Same		
675 "Let's Kiss and Be Friends"		
"Full on top...cooler than riding inside!"		
"I Dassn't Look Around"		
2047 "Here's a Quaint Coon"		
"Comic" Series 2249		
"Inside Only. Full on Top"	8 - 10	10 - 12
"Black Kids"		
7036 "The Florida Pelican - Very Fond..."	8 - 10	10 - 12
"Nigger Comic"		
868 "Why Don't you Come Down?"	8 - 10	10 - 12

THIELE, ARTHUR (Germany)
  FED

Series 306 Head Studies (6)	30 - 35	35 - 40

  Theo Stroefer

Series 871 Sports Series (6) *	30 - 35	35 - 40
Auto Driving		
Cycling		
The Jockey		
Rowing		
Soccer		
Tennis	35 - 40	40 - 45

  * Same 871 Series Without Stroefer Byline

  German-American Novelty Co.
    Series 871

Duplication of Theo Stroefer Series Above	30 - 35	35 - 40

  Carl Garte, Leipzig
    1897 Sachs. Thur-Ausstellung, Leipzig

"Gruss aus Ost-Afrika"	50 - 60	60 - 75

TIMMONS, JR. (L)
  Colourpicture & Asheville P.C.

1153 "Get a Load of This!"	4 - 5	5 - 6

TRODE
  A.S., St. L. (Adolph Selige)

Arth. Thiele, Carl Garte, 1897 Sachs. Thur-Ausstellung, Leipsig
"Gruss aus Ost-Afrika"

Arth. Thiele, F.E.D. Series 306
No Caption

Arth. Thiele, G.A. Art Series 871
No Caption

Arth. Thiele, Anon. Publisher
Series 871, No Caption

Arth. Thiele, F.E.D. Series 306
No Caption

"I Take Delight...dropping" 5 - 6 6 - 8
TWELVETREES, CHARLES (U.S.A.)
  Bergman Co.
    "Is Yo' Fond of Blackberries...?" 8 - 10 10 - 12
  Edward Gross*
    6 "Ah may be fond of chickens..." 10 - 12 12 - 15
    7 "Does yo' want a little honey"
    14 "I'se a Brunette"
    44 "I'se not light-headed..."
    61 "Does yo' tink dat smelly cabbage..."
    65 "Some Elegant Chocolate Screams"
    69 "Does anybody know where there's a..."
    107 "Henry! I jus lubs every corner of yo..."
    110 "Assorted Chocolates" 6 - 8 8 - 10
    128 "Ah Suttan Party am Gonna..." 10 - 12 12 - 15
    151 "She do, she don't"
    185 "Dey all looks fo' me..."
    310 "Kiss Me Honey I'm Starvin"
    429 "I'm Awful Blue..." 8 - 10 10 - 12
    713 "Woman - Kiss me while yo is able" 10 - 12 12 - 15
    864 Two Boys in Basket 8 - 10 10 - 12
    "Henry, I Jus Lubs..." 8 - 10 10 - 12
    "I May Be Fond of Chicken..."

Timmons, Jr., Asheville Post Card Company
1153, "Get a Load of This!"

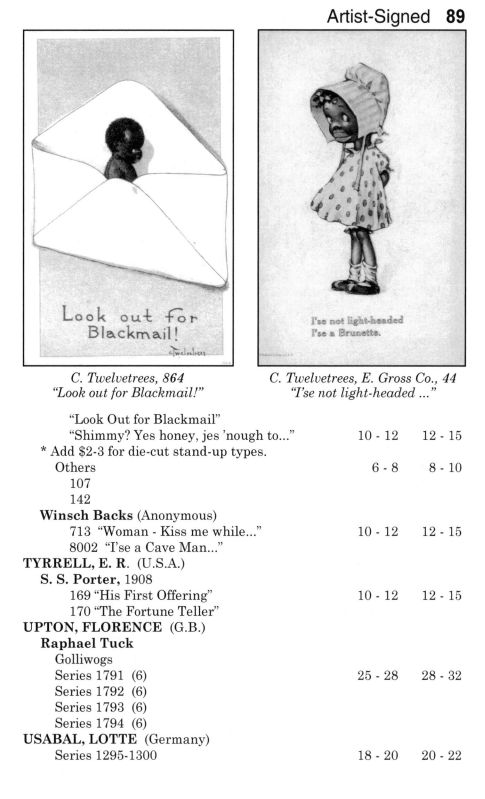

C. Twelvetrees, 864
"Look out for Blackmail!"

C. Twelvetrees, E. Gross Co., 44
"T'se not light-headed ..."

"Look Out for Blackmail"		
"Shimmy? Yes honey, jes 'nough to..."	10 - 12	12 - 15
* Add $2-3 for die-cut stand-up types.		
Others	6 - 8	8 - 10
107		
142		
Winsch Backs (Anonymous)		
713 "Woman - Kiss me while..."	10 - 12	12 - 15
8002 "I'se a Cave Man..."		
TYRRELL, E. R. (U.S.A.)		
S. S. Porter, 1908		
169 "His First Offering"	10 - 12	12 - 15
170 "The Fortune Teller"		
UPTON, FLORENCE (G.B.)		
Raphael Tuck		
Golliwogs		
Series 1791 (6)	25 - 28	28 - 32
Series 1792 (6)		
Series 1793 (6)		
Series 1794 (6)		
USABAL, LOTTE (Germany)		
Series 1295-1300	18 - 20	20 - 22

E. R. Tyrrell, S. S. Porter, 170
"The Fortune Teller"

E. R. Tyrrell, S. S. Porter, 169,
"His First Offering"

Bernhardt Wall, Bamforth, 316
"I'm Your MELON Honey"

Bernhardt Wall, Ullman, 1661
"Deed, I Did'n't Steal Um!"

V.W.S.
  Regent
    Series 2372
      "We Can't Help Being Happy"   6 - 8   8 - 10
VOIGHT, C. A.
  Kidville Ball Team Series 12
    "The Water Boy"   12 - 14   14 - 18
WS
  Novitas Series 865 Children   10 - 12   12 - 15
F.W.
  A.S.W. "Little Minstrels" Series   12 - 15   15 - 18
WALL, BERNHARDT (U.S.A.)
  Bamforth Co. (Back)
    "I'm Your Melon Honey"   20 - 25   25 - 30
  Bergman Co.
    850 "I'se got mu eyes on yo'"   8 - 10   10 - 12
    6500 "I Don't Like Dark September Morn"   8 - 10   10 - 12
    8800 "Fade Away September..."
    "Go 'long White Man, I Ain't..."
  Ullman Mfg. Co.
    548 "Christmas"   10 - 12   12 - 15
    Series 59 "Little Coons"   10 - 12   12 - 15
      1660 "You all can hab de Rine"
      1661 "Deed, I didn't steal um"
      1662 "Who's dat say chicken?"
      1663 "Just two Coons"
    Series 70 "Cute Coons"   10 - 12   12 - 15
      1852 "A Chip O' the Old Block"
      1853 "Whose Baby is OO?"
      1854 "He lubs me"
      1855 "I's so happy" (Uns.)
    Series 81 "Happy Day"
      1601 "A Quiet Smoke"   10 - 12   12 - 15
    Series 143 Black Halloween
      2414 "Who Is OO?"   20 - 25   25 - 30
    Series 173
      2703 "Here is a Man Who Never Drinks"   8 - 10   10 - 12
    Thanksgiving Series 127
      238 "For Thanksgiving"   10 - 12   12 - 15
      Others
    Automobile Series 155
      2483 "Lawd a Massy!"   10 - 12   12 - 15
      1383 "Comparing Notes"
      1384 "No Race Suicide"

Bernhardt Wall, Ullman, Halloween Series 143
2414, "Who Is OO?"

WAY
> "Dangerous Neighbors" Black-White Babies   6 - 8   8 - 10

WEIDERSEIM, GRACE (Uns.)
Hand-made of Blacks and White; U.S. Postal   50 - 60   60 - 75

WELLMAN, WALTER
Manhattan Postcard Co. (Uns.)
> Art Deco Types of 1920's-30's; Some Are Linen
> C-9 "Mah Face am Mah Fortune..."   8 - 10   10 - 12
> C-12 "Ah Calls Her Mah Big Moment..."
> C-22 "Lay Off Yo' Peekin..."
> C-32 "Oh Mammy! Is We Havin' A..."
> C-38 "Honey, Yo' Sho is Got Wot it Takes"
> C-45 "So Yo' Lubs Me F'om De Bottom..."
> C-46 "Ah's Askin' Yer - Is Ah Got..."
> C-82 "Mah New Boy Friend is..."

Colourpicture (Tichnor) (L)
> 235 "Ah Takes After My Pappy..." (Signed)

WHITE, E. L. (L)
Asheville Post Card Co.
> C-215 "Hope You Drop In Soon!"   3 - 4   4 - 5

Manhattan P.C. Co.
Comic Series 12
> 1053 "This place is a palm-garden"

WHITE, FLORA (G.B.)
J. Salmon
> 1902 "I'se so Lonely"   10 - 12   12 - 15

W. Wellman (Uns.) Manhattan
C9, "Mah Face Am Mah ..."

W. Wellman (Uns.) Manhattan
C45, "So Yo' Lubs Me F'om ..."

W. Wellman (Uns.), Manhattan
C38, "Honey, Yo' Sho' Is ..."

W. Wellman (Uns.), Manhattan
C46, "Ah's Askin' Yer -- ..."

Walter Wellman, Colourpicture
235, "Ah Takes After Mah Pappy--An' Mah Pappy Takes After ..."

E. L. White, Asheville Post Card Co.
C-215, "Hope You'll Drop In Soon!"

"No Sir"
WITT
Series 2002
"I ain't mad at nobody..."   6 - 8   8 - 10
"I'se gwine to be yo' sugar lump..."

Grace Weiderseim (Unsigned)
Hand-Made on U.S. Government Postal

WOOD, L.
  Valentine Co.
    1 "Flirtation"   12 - 15   15 - 18
WUYTS, A. (Austria)
  A. Noyer
    Series 76 (6)   10 - 12   12 - 14
      "A Little"
      "Do you Love Me?"
      "Neither do I, then!"
      "Not at all"
      "Passionately!"
      "Very Much"
YOUNG, HAYWARD
  Photochrom Co.
    1367 "De gems mus' be pure!"   10 - 12   12 - 15
    1370 "In dese hard times!"
ZA, NINO (Italy)
  E. Zacchelli
    A74 Josephine Baker
      Continental Size, Color   120 - 130 130 - 150
ZAHL
    Anonymous Poster Series   12 - 14   14 - 16
      "Othello"
      "Be's Jst Du?"
    Black Boys Court White Girls (6)   12 - 14   14 - 16

Hayward Young, Photochrom Co.
1370, "In dese hard times!"

Hayward Young, Photochrom Co.
1367, "De gems mus' be pure!"

ZARCHE	6 - 8	8 - 10
ZIM	6 - 8	.8 - 10

To the Collectors and Readers of this Publication

This reference has been a tremendous undertaking, and would have been impossible without the great effort and contributions of many collectors, dealers and postcard historians. We hope this book will fill the need for everyone in the hobby. We know, however, that the listings here are incomplete. In order to make the second edition even more comprehensive, we request that you send us any additions to checklists or publishers' listings that we have missed.

J. L. Mashburn, COLONIAL HOUSE
P. O. Box 609, Enka, NC 28728 (704-667-1427)

Nino Za (Italy), Zacchelli e C.
"Josephine Baker"

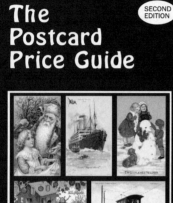

UNSIGNED ARTISTS, BY PUBLISHER

Occasionally, collectors will find black postcards that are not signed by the artists who originally drew or painted them. Therefore, they cannot be identified in the usual manner in which artists' works are listed and must be categorized by the name of the publisher who produced them.

There are several reasons for an artist's work to be issued on postcards without his initials or signature. The predominant one is the possibility that when an image of a painting or watercolor is reduced down from the normal 16" x 20", or larger size, the signature is cropped off. Also, many signatures may be very small on the original and when they are reduced to postcard size they become invisible in the reproduction.

A third reason is that many artists, feeling that early postcards were just a passing fancy and demeaning to their talents, just refused to sign any they produced for the trade. This was not the norm in later years of the golden age of postcards, however, as many artists became famous (or more famous) by the tremendous popularity of the picture postcard.

Experienced collectors can usually identify the works of many artists although they are unsigned because they "resemble" known signed pieces, and sometimes by knowing that the artist worked with a certain publisher. Painters of many beautiful single cards, as well as large numbers of sets and series, remain unidentified and are not as collectible or in as much demand as those that are signed.

Highlights among some of the unsigned works are a set of six World War I cards published in Paris by George W. Didd, Series 001, illustrating the war life of a black soldier and his final safe return to his home and family in the South; several great fantasy series by B.K.W.I. of Vienna; a wonderful and colorful embossed Series 131 by E. Nash of a girl participating in various activities and sports; and a red background Series N-26, of dancers, by M.W. Taggart.

Curt Teich's undivided back "Courting and Marriage" Series of 10 is a classic, and their linen "Jitterbug Comics" series is one of the most relished of that era. Last, but not least, are the many fine series produced by Raphael Tuck, the most prolific of all publishers of fine art.

In this section, the publisher is listed in bold capital letters, and the series, the series number, card number and card caption, if known, are listed. In most listings, only the publisher and a value are listed. The value would be a relative value for any card the publisher produced, whether a single card or a complete series. When possible, and if available, a card number and identifying caption is listed. This listing does not mean that it is the only card(s) in the set or series. If no value is listed for a card or series, refer to the listing just above it and the price would be the same.

	VG	EX
A-H		
"Keep a Stiff Upper Lip"	22 - 25	25 - 28
"If the Man in the Moon were a Coon"		
"Songs & Their Singers" Series	25 - 30	30 - 35
"After The Ball"		
ALBERTYPE CO.		
Children Comics (B&W)	12 - 15	15 - 18
ALPHASIA PUBLISHING CO., London		
4502 "Quo Vadis"	6 - 8	8 - 10
4502-A "The Mighty Atom"		
AMAG		
Series 0260, Blacks Courting White Girls	15 - 18	18 - 22
Black Band Plays As Whites Dance	12 - 15	15 - 18
A.M.P. CO.		
"Cute Coons" Series 70	12 - 15	15 - 18

A.M. & B.
Series 564, "Frolic and Dance"

"1854 "He Lubs Me"

A. M. & B.

564 Frolic and Dance	18 - 22	22 - 25

AMERICAN ART CO.

"September Night"	8 - 10	10 - 12

AMERICAN EXAMINER

"Love Drop" Fortune Teller	6 - 8	8 - 10

AMERICAN POSTCARD CO.

"Happy Day" Series 81	6 - 8	8 - 10

A. R. & CO.

Series 1677

Children	8 - 10	10 - 12

ASW

Little Minstrels	15 - 18	18 - 22

ASHER, JOSEPH & CO.

A1678 "Two Blacks don't make a White"	25 - 30	30 - 35

ASHEVILLE POST CARD CO. (L)

B. L. & P. Co.

68087 "Yo' Jus' Haunts Me Honey!"	4 - 5	5 - 6
828 "Sam? He's Down De Creek..."	5 - 7	7 - 9

Colourpicture (Tichnor Bros.)

10 "Just a Line to Say..."	3 - 4	4 - 5
11 "Carbon Copies"		
21 "If You Want a Nice Dark Tan"	5 - 7	7 - 9
99 "The Fountain of Youth"		
110 "Enee, Menee, Minee, Moe..."	3 - 4	4 - 6

A-H, "Songs and Their Singers"
"After the Ball"

AMAG, Series 0260
No Caption

Joseph Asher & Company, A1678
"Two Blacks Dont Make a White"

B.K.W.I., 4105-2
No Caption

128 "The Three Bares"		
253 "I Ain't Worried About..."	5 - 7	7 - 9
287 "I'se Pinnin' a Lot of Hopes..."	4 - 5	5 - 7
360 "Just a Little 'Local Color' to..."		
523 "Who's in There...?"		
927 I May Be a "Little Shaver..."	5 - 7	7 - 9
6927 "Silly Goose"		
Metrocraft, Everett, Ma.		
C200 "Two Loving Hearts"	3 - 4	4 - 5
C240 "Kiss Me, Honey, I'se Starvin!"	4 - 5	5 - 6
C310 "Oh Boy! Can You Throw It!!"	4 - 5	5 - 7
Curt Teich		
C-15 "Alligator Bait"	4 - 5	5 - 7
C-18 "Blackout Tonight!"		
C-46 "Be My Blackout Sweetheart"		
C-47 "Accidental Blackout"		
C-49 "I Like to Paddle You In..."		
C-51 "Brother, If These Dice Are Loaded..."		
C-53 "Blackout Blues"		
E-5452 "Drop us a Line" Fishing	2 - 3	3 - 4
K-205 "Silly Goose" (Chrome)	2 - 3	3 - 4
K-828 "What Would You Have Done?"	1 - 2	2 - 3
AUSTIN, J. I.		
No No. "The Sport"	15 - 18	18 - 22
No No. "A True Citizen"		
203 "Go Way Youse"		
205 "Something Doing"		

Bamforth, London Opinion 3
"The Sea-(in)-side smile."

B&S (Barton & Spooner), CS495
"I lubs mah watermelon but ..."

B&S (Barton & Spooner), CS528
"You're brighter dan de white ..."

B.B., London, Series X296
"To greet you with Loving ..."

206 "The Executioner"
207 "Happy Days"   15 - 18   18 - 22
208 "A True Citizen"
209 "Rag Time Member"
210 "Who's De're?"
211 "Dinner in Sight"
212 "Caddie" Boy with Golf Clubs   22 - 25   25 - 28
213 "Ain't going to be none left"   15 - 18   18 - 22
246 "Dat am Fine"
298 "A True Citizen"
324 "A Southern Exposure" (UndB)
426 "The Watch on the Rine"
946 "I'm going to be an Elk" (Sepia)   10 - 12   12 - 15

B.B., London **(BIRN BROTHERS)**
  Golliwogs - Silver Background
    Courting Series with Stick Girl   25 - 28   28 - 32
      At the Beach
      In the Row Boat
      In the Automobile
      On the Park Bench
      Playing Cards
      The Family Outing
    Series X296 Christmas Greetings
      "To greet you with Loving Wishes"

B.K.W.I.
  Fantasy
    355 "Follow Thou My Choice"   22 - 25   25 - 28
    Series 634 "Dancing"
      3 Two Men and One Girl Dancing
    Series 4105 (6)
      Jockey Rides Rooster
      2 Driver in Wagon Pulled by Chicks
    Series 4126 (6)
      Fantasy Easter Animals and Blacks

BPC
  Series 226 "Thanksgiving"   10 - 12   12 - 15

BAMFORTH CO.
  Series 3 from *London Opinion*
    "The Sea-(in)-side smile"   30 - 35   35 - 40
    "Ever Loving Thoughts..."   10 - 12   12 - 15
    38 "A Little Light on a Dark Subject"
    "Stay in Your Own Back Yard"
    178 "The Outlook Here is Good"
    359 "May I Leave the Room Teacher?"

*B.B., London (Birn Brothers)
Golliwogs, No Caption*

*B.B., London (Birn Brothers)
Golliwogs, No Caption*

*B.B., London (Birn Brothers), Golliwogs
"Keep off the Grass"*

*Birn Brothers' Golliwog and Stick Girl -- Meeting, Courtship and
Marriage Series. These are three of the cards in the six-card series.*

727 "Honey, Next to Myself..."
729 "Won't You Be My Chocolate Drop?"
930 "Another Little Study in Black & White"
1418 "How'd You Like a Box of Chocolates?"
1425 "Here's Some Assorted Chocolates"
1876 "Instead of Rock I'm sending a couple..."
2008 "Somebody's Little Sweetheart"
2040 "But Where is the Car..."
2047 "Here's A Quaint Coon..."
2507 "Here's Some Assorted Chocolates"
7039 "There's A Dark Man Acoming..."
7041 "There's A Great Opening..."

BARDELEBEN, F. von

704 "In the Slot Machine" | 8 - 10 | 10 - 12

BARTON & SPOONER

Series 142

"Ah Lub Sweet Things..." | 10 - 12 | 12 - 15
"Dis Yere Would Be Heaben..."
"Gee! Ah Thinks Ah'll Turn Chicken..."
"Gee!! Dat Sho' Wuz Some Sweet Kiss"

Series 495

"I Done Brung a Bokay Wif My Love"
"I Lubs Mah Watermelon but..."
"Nobody Gwine ter Fool Roun My Gal..."

Series CS528

"I'se Mighty Interested in You, Honey!"
"You're a Bright Spot in a Dark Day..."
"You're Brighter dan de White Moonlight"
"Ah faces my duty like a man"
"Oh, Honey, It's Heaben to be wid you!"
"Watermilyun Ain't in it wif You..."

Series 6505

"Ah Honey! don' turn yo back on me"
"When is Yo Gwine to Pucker..."

BERGMAN CO.

"Always Pick a Soft Place to Fall" | 10 - 12 | 12 - 15
6342 "Oh Lardy, Mah Heart's Full..."
6343 "Ah Lubs Turkey and Turkey-trottin"
6500 "I Don't Like A Dark September..."
6505 "I Don't Want a Million..."
6505 "Ah lubs to go down de avenyu..."
8803 Golfer "Wanted. Someone to play..." | 18 - 22 | 22 - 25
Series 9015 New Year's | 10 - 12 | 12 - 15
"Wishin' I'se Heap Happy..."

Bergman Co., 6343
"Ah lubs turkey an' turkey-..."

Bergman Co., 8803
"Wanted. Some One to Play ..."

"A Heap O' De Best Fing's..."
"What My Heart Does Fink...
"May Yu Life Be Filled Wif Honey"
Series 2200 Valentines Day
"Ah Habs Sumpin Fer Yu..."
"Mah Heart am Workin' Obertime"
6509 "Lawd A Massy' Dis Am Some..."
Valentine Series (B&W)

"Lub yo' Sweetheart"	6 - 8	8 - 10

BICKNELL MFG. CO. (B&W)

"I'm Enjoying the Good Things..."	6 - 8	8 - 10

"Thou Art So Near and Yet So Far"

BIEN, JULIUS
"Comic Series"

13 "Whose is Whose?"	12 - 15	15 - 18

15 "Get Up"
26 "I am Completely in the Dark"
37 "Expect Us Down Soon"
44 "Don't Come in Your Glad Rags"
45 "A Low Down Trick"

1203 "I'm So Glad This is Leap Year"	15 - 18	18 - 22

Bergman Co.
"Lub yo' sweetheart as yu lub ..."

Julius Bien, 1203
"I'm so glad this is Leap Year ..."

Julius Bien, Comic Series 45
"A Low-Down Trick"

Julius Bien, Lincoln Series 78
7800, "The great Emancipator"

Julius Bien, Thanksgiving Series 930
No Caption

Series 930 Thanksgiving (Gold B.G.)
    8300 Black Lady with Serving Tray   12 - 15   15 - 18
    8301 Boy/Girl, Lady Carving Turkey
    8302 Boy/Girl at Table/Lady's Hand Raised
    8303 Boy/Girl w/Straw, Lady Standing
    8304 Boy/Girl Help Lady w/Tray
    8305 Boy/Girl Asleep at Table
Lincoln: 7800 "The Great Emancipator"   15 - 18   18 - 22

C M B   (1930's)
"Cupidos" Series 6
    Black Boys Court White Girls   10 - 12   12 - 15

CELLARO   (1930's) (Possibly S/**A. Richardson**)
"Dolly Series"
    Little Girl, Deco Dress, Red Bow   15 - 18   18 - 22
    Boy/Girl
    Two Girls, One Wearing Red Hat,
       Holding Dog

CLIFTON
Series 2165 Comical Blacks   10 - 12   12 - 15

COLE BOOK CO.
    "Sambo in a Watermelon..."   12 - 15   15 - 18
    "Gr. From Sunny S. - Old Black Mammy"   10 - 12   12 - 15
    "A Little Alabama Coon in Dixieland"
    A Little Pickaninny in Cotton Boll
    "Uncle Remus Brings Greetings..."

COLOURPICTURE   (Tichnor) (L)
    Enjoying the "Blackout Here"   4 - 5   5 - 6
    "Water Sports - The Fountain of Youth"   5 - 6   6 - 8
    10 "Just a Line to Say We..."   3 - 4   4 - 5
    11 "I'm Doing Things Here on a..."
    36 "Stewed Again!"
    63 "I'm All Set For the Big Blowout"   4 - 5   5 - 6
    72 "Honey I Hope's You're..."
    108 "That Remind's Me..."
    191 Enjoying the "Blackout Here"   5 - 6   6 - 8
    204 "Silly Goose" (Uns./Walt Munson)
    205 "Sure We're Cuckoo..." (Uns/Munson)
    206 "Can You Tie This One" (Uns./Munson)
    208 "I'm Not Saying You're..." (Uns./Munson)
    209 "Boy Can You Throw..." (Uns./Munson)
    307 "Madame, Could I Interest You..."
    541 "Don't Give Me any Lip..."
    558 "You Oughta See How They Dip..."
    599 "Wish You Were Close to..."   4 - 5   5 - 6

Crest Trading Company
"How kin yo' doubt"

Colourpicture, 541
"Dont Give Me Any Of Your Lip!"

625 "Yo' Used to be My Pin-up..."
626 "I Broadcast When I's in the Mood..."
629 "I's Goin' Right to Pot..."
676 "The Point We're Trying to Make..."
762 "Here's a Little Tip For You..."

CORNISH, GEORGE B.

"I love my Chicken, but oh you Turkey"	10 - 12	12 - 15

CREST TRADING (UndB) (B&W)

"We's Lookin' Fo'ward wid much..."	25 - 30	30 - 40
"How Kin Yo' Doubt"		

D. F. & CO.

416 "Stage Artists: The Cake Walk"	20 - 25	25 - 30

DAVIS, A. M.

"Little Darkies" Series 521	12 - 15	15 - 18
"For My Lady Lub"		
"Little Beggar"		

DAY & CO.

850 "Quo Vadis"	6 - 8	8 - 10

DIDD, GEORGE, Paris

WWI Series 001

"At the Second Sedan"	40 - 50	50 - 60
"Back in Dixie"	60 - 70	70 - 80
"Brothers in War"	40 - 50	50 - 60
"Fraternal Salute"		
"O'er the Top"		
"My Boche"		

DONA PANCHA

Series 596 Girl in Pink Sunbonnet	10 - 12	12 - 15

DUNBAR

366 "Our Flag"	10 - 12	12 - 15

DUTTON, E. P.

High Quality Comics	18 - 22	22 - 25

EMNA

Series 6, Dutch captions, 1930's	6 - 8	8 - 10

E. B. & E. CO. (L)

504 "Bill" (L.L.)	3 - 4	4 - 6
"I Got My Eye on You"	5 - 6	6 - 8
"I'm Living High"		

EASTERN PHOTO LITHO (L)

E-6174 "You Don't Know Sunshine..."	2 - 3	3 - 4

EISMANN, THEO., New York

Series 1321

31 "The Great White Hope"	25 - 30	30 - 35

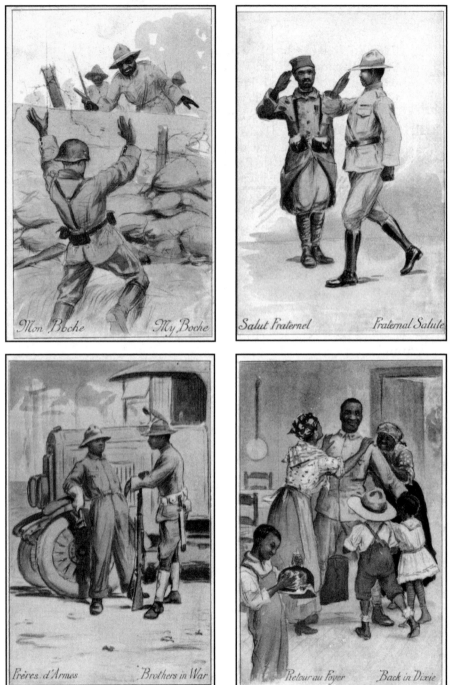

Four cards from the anonymous six-card World War I Series 001 published by George Didd of a Black Soldier serving in France, and his triumphant return to his family in the South.

Forman & Sons
1002, "A Happy Thought!"

EPSTEIN & CO.
 "A Black Cupid" (B&W)   4 - 5   5 - 6
F.E.D.
 Portrait Types
 Series 306   12 - 15   15 - 18
FAIRMAN CO., Cincinnati
 "Black Kids" Series 127 (B&W)   6 - 8   8 - 10
 Series 159   Baseball   (B&W)
  "Ah sho would love to get a liner..."   15 - 18   18 - 22
  'I'se jes' makin er short stop here"
  "I'se makin' er slide fo home..."
  "A Sho Would Love to Get Er..."
  "Ain't You Nebber Gwin..."
  "Honey, Yo Sho Was He Fasinated..."
  "I's Feelin Prime and Mah Appetite..."
  'I'se jes makin short stop here"
FORMAN & SONS,   1904
 1002 "A Happy Thought!"   12 - 15   15 - 18
FREY, E.
 Cake Walk Series   15 - 18   18 - 22
GAM
 Series 1827   Black Doll   15 - 18   18 - 22
GARTNER & BENDER (G&B)
 "He Loves Me, He Loves Me Not" (B&W) 8 - 10   10 - 12
 "If Dat Don't Fetch Her..." (B&W)

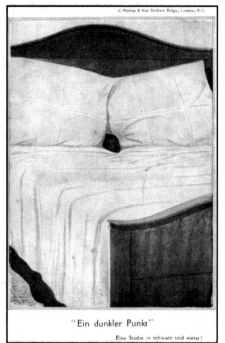

Theo Eismann, Series 1321-31
"The White Hope.--"

J. Harrap, "Ein dunkler Punkt"
(Study in Black and White)

GIBSON ART CO.
　　"Honey, Yo Sho Does Make..." (B&W)　　8 - 10　　10 - 12
　　"If Ah Little Affection Am..." (B&W)
G. B. CO.
　　Husband & Wife Series 404 (6) (Emb.)　22 - 25　　25 - 28
GAILLE
　　"I Got My Eye on You"　　　　　　　　6 - 8　　8 - 10
GORDON, P.
　　"Beware of Cupid"　　　　　　　　　　8 - 10　　10 - 12
GOTTSCHALK & DREYFUS
　　Song Series 2032 (Gold Borders)
　　"In Dixie Land"　　　　　　　　　　15 - 18　　18 - 22
　　"My Old Kentucky Home"
　　"Old Folks at Home"
GRAPHIC POST CARDS CO.
　　A-17 "The Little Black Behind" (B&W)　6 - 8　　8 - 10
H.I.R.
　　317 "Yoos Ma Honey Chile"　　　　　8 - 10　　10 - 12
　　669 "Life is Just one D..."
HAHN, ALBERT
　　"The Regimental Mascot"　　　　　　8 - 10　　10 - 12

"Lead Us Not Into Temptation"
""You Can't Steal No Kiss...""

HAMMON, V. O.

29 "Life Ain't Worth Living..."	8 - 10	10 - 12

HB, Germany

401 Black Playing Saxophone	15 - 18	18 - 22

HWB

Series 2830 (6)	12 - 15	15 - 18

HARRAP & SONS, London

With English Captions

"Far From the Madding Crowd"	12 - 15	15 - 18

Novitas Series 638 W/German Captions
  "Ein Dunkler Punkt" (One Study in B&W)
  Others

HARTMAN CARD CO. (L)

153 "Two Staple Products" Down in Sunny..."	4 - 5	5 - 6

HELLER'S ORIGINALS

Golliwogs

"Just a line from..."	22 - 25	25 - 28

  Others

HEININGER, H. CO.

32 "No Sah, I'se not hyphenated..."	12 - 15	15 - 18
33 "I am an American, same as you..."	18 - 22	22 - 25

Gottschalk & Dreyfus, 2032 Song Series
"In Dixie's Land"

Hellier's Originals, 21056
"Just a line from ..."

Illustrated Postcard Company, "Old Songs Re-sung" Series
8, "Thou art so near and yet so far"

HEY, E. J. & CO.
"A Little Study in Black & Fright" 12 - 15 15 - 18
Series 282
"Black Children" 8 - 10 10 - 12
HILDESHEIMER, S. 8 - 10 10 - 12
J.R.H.
"Disturbing the Peace" (Watermelon) 6 - 8 8 - 10

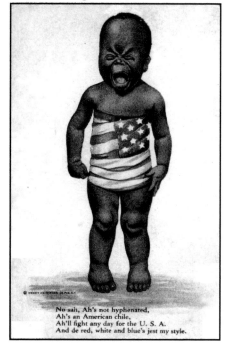

HB, 401
No Caption

Henry Heininger, 32
"No sah, Ah's not hyphenated ..."

HOT SPRINGS NOVELTY CO.
"In the Swim at Hot Springs"	6 - 8	8 - 10

HOWE, J. RAYMOND CO., Chicago
731-8 "I Want to Hear From You" (DB)	8 - 10	10 - 12
1283-Y "Dis am Heben"	12 - 15	15 - 18
"A Regular Cut-up"		
"Disturbing the Peace" (DB)		
"Go Long White Man, I Ain't..."	10 - 12	12 - 15
"My Li'l Baby Lamb..."		
"Just Arrived"	10 - 12	12 - 15
"Ole Mammy"		
"Open and Above Board"		
"You Should Be Stocking Up"		
"Who's a Niggar?"	18 - 22	22 - 25

ILLUSTRATED POST CARD CO., N.Y.
"Old Songs Re-Sung" Series		
8 "Thou art so near and yet so far"	12 - 15	15 - 18
Series 5 Invitation Series		
"You are cordially invited..."	8 - 10	10 - 12

ILLUSTRATED P. C. & NOVELTY CO.
Thanksgiving Series	10 - 12	12 - 15
"A Merry Christmas" Series		

*Henry Heininger, 33, "I'm
an American, same as you ..."*

*International Art Pub. Co.
Black Cherubs*

*V. O. Hammon, Copyright 1908 (M.S.P.)
"Life Ain't Worth Living When Your Broke."*

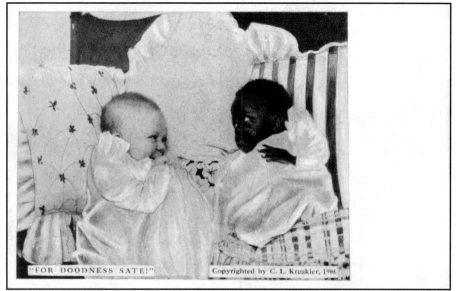

"FOR DOODNESS SATE!"   Copyrighted by C. L. Kreakler, 1906

C. L. Kreakler, 1906
"For Doodness Sate!"

INTER-ART, London
    Quaint Kid Series 256
        "I'm Afraid of the Dark"   10 - 12   12 - 15
        "A little light on a dark subject"
    Coon Series
        625 "Go 'long White Man..."
INTERNATIONAL ART PUB. CO.
    Black Cherubs (UndB)
        Chromolithographs   22 - 25   25 - 28
        "Lincoln and the Contrabands" (Emb.)   15 - 18   18 - 22
    See Ellen Clapsaddle and M. Greiner
KOEHLER, A.
    601 Comical   10 - 12   12 - 15
P.C.K. (PAUL C. KOBER)
    S.52 "Old Black Joe" (UndB)   12 - 15   15 - 18
    S.52.2 "Yours Truly"
    Series 104   18 - 22   22 - 25
        "Our Fancy Cake Walk"
        "Dinner in Sight"
KOELLING & KLAPPENBACH, Chicago
    Three Golliwogs (UndB)   15 - 18   18 - 22
    Others
KREAKLER, C. L. 1906
    "For Doodness Sate!"   20 - 25   25 - 30

E. C. Kropp, 1321
"Dere's No Flies On This Gal"

E. C. Kropp, 15130
"Honey, I'se Waitin' Fo' You ..."

PCK (Paul C. Kober)
"Yours truly"

Arthur Livingston
919, "Dis-Pos-Zess Means Move"

KROPP, E. C., Milwaukee
    1 "Watermelon Days"   12 - 15   15 - 18
    2 "Who Says I Want Chicken"
    3 "A Study in Black and White"
    4 "A Blackmailer"
    5 "Memories of by-gone Days"
    32 "Solid Comfort
  Comic Series (UndB)
    380 "Watermelon Days"   12 - 15   15 - 18
    381 "Who Says I Wants Chickens?"
    383 "A Black Mailer"
    384 "A Foul proceeding"
    385 "Memories of Days Gone By"
    389 "A Study in Black and Red"
    449 "Delicious"
    450 "Mammy"
    452 "Pickaninnies"
    1320 "The Hottest Coons in Dixie"
    1321 "Dere's no Flies on this Gal"
    1322 "Dat's My Gal" (L)   5 - 6   6 - 8
    15130 "Honey, I'se Waitin' Fo' You"
L & P CO.
    "Lincoln and the Contrabands"   15 - 18   18 - 22
LIVERMORE & KNIGHT (See Topicals)
    "No Ma'am, I ain't seen no stray rooster..."   18 - 22   22 - 25

Fred Lounsbury, Thanksgiving Series 2088
3, "After the Bird is Dressed ..."

J. J. Marks
175, "A Strong Temptation"

M. & S. (Misch & Stock), 48
238 "A Strict Vegetarian"

LIVINGSTON, ARTHUR 1905
   Black Comics (UndB)   10 - 12   12 - 15
     Weather Forecast "Another Squall"
     919 "Dis-Pos-Zess Means Move"
     "Give My Regards to Broadway"
     686 Old Aunt Liz "I Reckon I's a Hundred"
LOLLESGARD SPECIALTIES
     "Mammy! A Blitzkreig!!"   6 - 8   8 - 10
LOUNSBURY, FRED C.
     "Trite Sayings Illustrated"
     9 "Black as Coal"   15 - 18   18 - 22
     "Thanksgiving" Series 2088 (Emb.)
     3 "After the Bird is Dressed"   12 - 15   15 - 18
M.S.P. (1908)
     "I'd Like to Be an Angel"   10 - 12   12 - 14
     "I've Got My Eyes on You"
MAJESTIC PUBLISHING CO.
     "Howdy Kid" Series
     "De Less You Talks About it..."   8 - 10   10 - 12
     "Howdy - I'm Munst'ous Peart..."
     "My But You's a Runnin' Wile"
     "You's a Cautio'n Now For True"
MANHATTAN POST CARD CO. (1920's-30's)
  Unsigned Walter Wellman
     C-9 "Mah Face am Mah Fortune..."   10 - 12   12 - 15
     C-12 "Ah Calls Her Mah Big Moment..."
     C-22 "Lay Off Yo' Peekin..."
     C-32 "Oh Mammy! Is We Havin' A..."
     C-45 "So Yo' Lubs Me F'om De Bottom..."
     C-46 "Ah's Askin' Yer--Is Ah Got..."
     C-82 "Mah New Boy Friend is..."
   Linens
     615-12 "Man - Yo' Shud See De Sights"   4 - 5   5 - 6
     34796 "Two Lovin Hearts"
     43229 "Yas Suh! Coconuts Sho is Mah Meat"
MARKS, J. J.
     175 "A Strong Temptation" (Sepia)   10 - 12   12 - 15
McCARTHEY, HELEN
     "I'se Mammy's Valentine"   10 - 12   12 - 15
McLAUGHLIN BROS. (UndB)
     "Dar's Nobody Looking..."   12 - 15   15 - 18
     "Dar's Something About You..."
     "Gee, Why Leave..."
     "Go Way, Leave Me Alone"

Moore & Gibson
26, "The whole Black family"

Moore & Gibson
2, "Evolution of a coon"

"Honey, You're My Turtle Dove"
"Just Pack Your Clothes and Go"
"Under the Bamboo Tree"
"Just Pack Your Clothes and Go"
MILLER, GEORGE V. (L)
"Don't Yo Lub Me Honey!"   4 - 5   5 - 6

MILLAR & LANG
"National Series" 1395   15 - 18   18 - 22
MILLS NOVELTY CO.
  "Where are you going my pretty maid?"   8 - 10   10 - 12
M. & S. (MISCH & STOCK) (UndB)
  Series 48
    238 "A Strict Vegetarian"   15 - 18   18 - 22
  Series 49
    230 "Up to Date"
MITCHELL, EDWARD H.
    610 "One of the Good Things..."   10 - 12   12 - 15
    Same in B&W   8 - 10   10 - 12
    1831 "Dixie Blossoms"
MOORE & GIBSON, New York
    15 "Brushing Up On Acquaintance"   12 - 15   15 - 18
    26 "The Whole Black Family"   20 - 25   25 - 30
    31 "A Southern Bird Fancier"   15 - 18   18 - 22
    32 "I Take This Opportunity"
    34 "The pearly gates ajar"
    35 "It's The Little Things in Life..."
    36 "A Sudden Rise in Wool"
  Evolution Comic
    2 "Evolution of a Coon"   90 - 100   100 - 120
MORRISON, H. M. CO.
  "Chocolate Drops"   8 - 10   10 - 12
  "Don't You Get Gay With Me"
  "Es You Looking For Me?"
  "Race Suicide Down South"   12 - 15   15 - 18
MOSS, F. A.
    6386 Large Heads   6 - 8   8 - 10
    6549 "I May Look Like a Coon but I Aint"   15 - 18   18 - 22
    6539 Large Heads   6 - 8   8 - 10
MUNK, M., Vienna
  Series 416 (6)   15 - 18   18 - 22
MWM COLOR LITHO
    BP706 "Air Raid - Black Out" B.P. Card   3 - 4   4 - 5
NASH, E.
  Sporting Girl Series 131 (Emb.)
    "Baseball Girl"   25 - 30   30 - 35
    "Chorus Girl"   20 - 25   25 - 30
    "Football Girl"   25 - 30   30 - 35
    "Yachting Girl"   20 - 25   25 - 30
    Others

E. Nash, Series 131
"The Baseball Girl"

E. Nash, Series 131
"The Football Girl"

E. Nister, Series 1270
"Darkie gal, I lub so well, ..."

E. Nister, Series 1280
"To My Valentine"

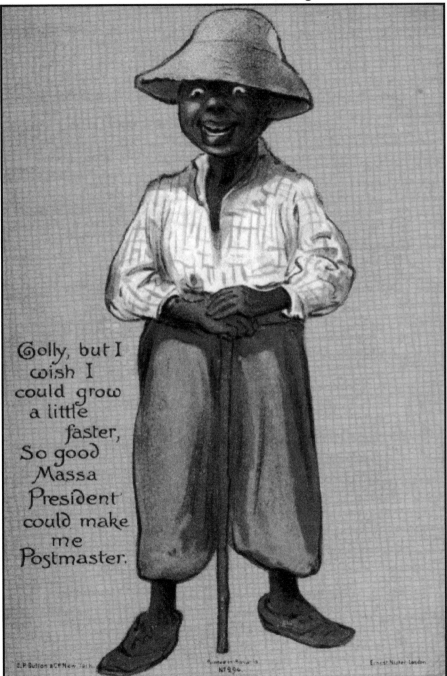

E. Nister, No. 294
"Golly, but I wish I could grow a little faster,
So good Massa President could make me Postmaster."

Thanksgiving Series 875 (Emb.)

875-3 Black Chef and Turkey   12 - 15   15 - 18

NATIONAL ART CO.

3668 "Just Another"   10 - 12   12 - 15

NATIONAL POSTKARTEN

Series 17 (UndB)

"Amerikanische Neger"   22 - 25   25 - 28

NEWMAN, P. C. CO.

"Far from the Madding Crowd"   12 - 15   15 - 18

NISTER, ERNEST (See B or Bonte)

294 "Golly, but I wish I could grow ..."   40 - 50   50 - 60

297 "Why do folks call me Jim Crow..."

303 "I See Mr. Possum up de Tree..."   25 - 30   30 - 35

304 "Watermellons Juicy and Ham is..."

Quality Valentines

Series 1270   20 - 25   25 - 28

Girl sits on big heart "...Your Coon"

"Darkie Gal I Lub So Well..."

1280 Valentine Series

Boy and Girl Embrace on Tree Limb

NOVITAS (N)

Series 50575   12 - 15   15 - 18

OPF

High Quality, 1904 (6)

Elegantly Dressed Ladies and Gentlemen   30 - 35   35 - 40

Man Dancing, Stepping High

Lady Dancing, Stepping High

OGILVIE, J. S. PUB. CO.

"Am expecting to have my hands full"   8 - 10   10 - 12

"Way down in my heart I've a..."

PFB (Paul Finkenrath, Berlin)

Series 7179 (Emb.) (6)   22 - 25   25 - 28

"Dere! Enery Clay Can't Stand Up..."

"Dere is no Doubt, Sah..."

"If dat don't fetch her..."

"If Sambo doesn't Love Me..."

"Oh, De Rudeness of De Men..."

"That Strain Again!"

Series 7942 New Year's (6) (Emb.)

Boy with Pipe   22 - 25   25 - 28

Boy with Flowers

Boy Holding Big Flower Pot

Girl with Letter

Girl/Boy Yell Happy New Year

OPF, 1904, The Cake Walk
No Caption, Brown "tow sack like" Background

OPF, 1904, The Cake Walk
No Caption, Brown "tow sack like" Background

Children
PLATINACHROME
2016 "Glad You Came"   10 - 12   12 - 15
PORTER, S. S., Chicago, 1907
171 "The Rivals"   8 - 10   10 - 12
"His First Offering"

PFB, Series 7942
"A Prosperous New Year"

PFB, Series 7179
"That Strain Again"

Charles Rose Co., Song Series 11
15, "The Old Cabin Home"

The Rose Company, "No. 1--
The Latest Thing in Hats."

*Regent Publishing Company, Series 1220
11, "Lots of little Nigger Boys ..."*

PRINCE, C. D.
    Comics   8 - 10   10 - 12

RKM
    Series 108
        Comical Black with Tears Flowing   40 - 50   50 - 60

R. I. POSTCARD CO., Rock Island, Il.
    "The Attractions Here are Great" (UndB)   8 - 10   10 - 12

REINTHAL & NEWMAN, N.Y.
    216 "Far From the Madding Crowd..."   12 - 15   15 - 18
    706 "Blackmail"

RIEDER, M., Los Angeles
    Comics   12 - 15   15 - 18
        169 "Something Doing" Thief
        170 "The Executioner" With Chicken
        171 "Happy Days" With Banjo
        172 "True Citizens" With Flag
        173 "Ragtime Member" Most Happy
        174 With Golf Clubs
        175 "Dinner in Sight" Chases Chicken
        177 "Ain't Gonna be none Left" (Watermelon)

REGENT PUBLISHING CO.
    "I Sent them because I Knew..."   12 - 15   15 - 18
    1220-11 "Lots of Little Nigger Boys"   15 - 18   18 - 22

ROBBINS, H. I.
    Embossed Series
        "Go Way"   8 - 10   10 - 12

S&M, Series 1415
No Caption

S&M, Series 1415
No Caption

S&M, Series 1415
No Caption

Santway, Series 034
"Poor old Joe!"

Schlesinger Brothers
"Jes' de banjo, an' de moon, ..."

Schlesinger Brothers
"Yo' sholy takes de cake wid ..."

ROSE, CHARLES, CO.
    Song Cards
        Series 11
            12 "Dixie Land"   15 - 18   18 - 22
            15 "The Old Cabin Home"
            22 "Way Down Upon the Swanee River"
            24 "Old Black Joe"
THE ROSE CO.
    "No. 1 -- The Latest Thing in Hats"   12 - 15   15 - 18
ROSSETTI
    "The Serenade"   10 - 12   12 - 15
ROTH & LANGLEY
    "Great Heavens! I'll Fire the..."   8 - 10   10 - 12
    "Chicken? Whar He?" (S/HB)
S In diamond (SANTWAY)
    Series 034 Embossed
        "Poor Old Joe"   18 - 22   22 - 26
SB
    Thanksgiving - Scared Blacks & Big Turkeys   12 - 15   15 - 18
        C5495 "Nobody gwine to fool roun' my gal"   10 - 12   12 - 15

Adolph Selige, "Good Luck" Ser.
11 "Dis Am Sho Good Luck"

M. W. Taggart, Series T.F. 607
"Thanksgiving Greetings"

S&M
Possibly by **Donadini, Jr.,** Dresden
Series 1415

Man Pulls Another's Tooth with Rope	25 - 28	28 - 32
Man and Woman Under Umbrella	25 - 28	28 - 32
Tall Man Eats Watermelon		
Woman Kicks Little Man in Teeth		

SWSB
Beach Comics

Blacks-Whites	10 - 12	12 - 15

SALMON, J.

1707 "Lend us Yo' Jumper"	10 - 12	12 - 15
3421 "You Should Be a Little..." S/Lewin		
1651 "To Greet You - I've Just Arrived"	8 - 10	10 - 12

SAMPLINER, H. S. (L) (Colourpicture)

99 "Water Sports, Fountain of Youth"	5 - 6	6 - 8

SAVORY, E. W. LTD.
Series 551

"We'll Walk an' Talk My Honey"	8 - 10	10 - 12
68 "We'll Hab a Little Tiff Lub..."		

M. W. Taggart, Series N-24
"There's Something Doing"

M. W. Taggart, Series N-24
"Oh You Kid"

SCHLESINGER BROS.
    Children Comics (B&W)
        "Go 'long, yo' sassy niggah..."   10 - 12   12 - 15
        "Golly! don' I wish I Wuz a yaller pup!"
        "Jes de' Banjo, an' de Moon"
        "What Fo' Yo' Eat Dat Snowball, Lily?"
        "Yo' sholy takes de cake wid me!"
SELIGE, ADOLPH, St. Louis
    "Good Luck" Series 11
        "Dis am Sho Good Luck"   8 - 10   10 - 12
    Comics
        "I take delight in dropping"   6 - 8   8 - 10
        "A Day in the Cottonfields"
SEXICHROME (C)
    17806 "Possum and De Coon"   2 - 3   3 - 4
SHEAHAN, M. T.
    "Little Peter Pie and His Dog Fido" (Sepia)   6 - 8   8 - 10
    361 "A Study in Black and White" (Sepia)
SHELDON PRESS
    42 "A Nigger From Cork"   12 - 15   15 - 18
STROEFER, THEO Nuremburg, (T.S.N.)
    Series 440 (6) Classical Blacks   25 - 30   30 - 35

T. P. CO., New York
  Series 562

    "Who am Champion Now"   12 - 15   15 - 18

T. R. CO.

  "The Latest Thing in Hats"   15 - 18   18 - 22

TAGGART, M. W.

  Series N-24 (6)

  Red Background   25 - 30   30 - 35

    "A Soul Kiss"

    "I'm Sending you a Pair of Black Kids"

    "Now What's Up?"

    "Oh You Kid"

    "There's Something Doing"

    "You Ain't Mad, Are You?"

  Series 607 Feather Border

  Thanksgiving (6) 1909   12 - 15   15 - 18

  Series 608 1909

  Thanksgiving (6)   10 - 12   12 - 15

TAMMEN, H. H. Denver

  904 "Everything Comes to Him..."   8 - 10   10 - 12

  926 "I Certainly do miss the Children" 8 - 10   10 - 12

  975 "I'se Got a Feeling For You"   6 - 8   8 - 10

  6362 "I wuz Going to Write, But..."

  6663 "Will Start Soon..." (**F.A. Moss**)

TEICH, CURT Chicago

  Courting and Marriage Series (10) (UndB)

    1 "The Flirtation"   25 - 28   28 - 32

    2 "Introduction to the Twins"

    3 "Courting"

    4 "The Proposal"

    5 "The Duel"

    6 "The Wedding"

    7 "The Wedding Feast"

    8 "Return from the Honeymoon Tour"

    9 "Coming Events"

    10. "The Event or where two pair is better
        than four of a kind"

  Child in Tree Reading ABC Book.   12 - 15   15 - 18

  C. T. Art Colourtone (L)

    2B-H591 "Lawsey Me! What a Peculiar..."

    C-46 "Be My Blackout Sweetheart"   4 - 5   5 - 8

    C-49 "I'd Like to Paddle You In..."

    C-51 "Brother, If These Dice are Loaded..."

    C-62 "Look What I Got For Two Meat..."

C-84 "I'se Quittin'. This Kitchen..."	5 - 6	6 - 8
C-112 "Shut Yo' Mouth and Mammy Will..."		
C-796 "My Tale is Told" (Busy Persons)	3 - 4	4 - 5
C-816 "That Model Stands Far Out Front..."	5 - 6	6 - 8

JITTERBUG COMICS *

"C.T. Jitterbug Comics" (10) (L)

C-1191 "Come On You Killer-Dillers..."	25 - 30	30 - 35

C-1192 When Suzie "Goes To Town"
C-1193 "Hop! Hop! The Lindy Hop..."
C-1194 "Boogie Woogie"
C-1195 "Pa and Ma You Better Look Out"
C-1196 "Little Doodle Bug..."
C-1197 "Killer! Diller!"
C-1198 "In a Swig-Mid-Swank Ingle Nook"
C-1199 "This Little Alligator..."
C-1200 "I'm Comin, I'm Comin..."

* Numbers listed are on front of cards.

"C.T. Chocolate Drop Comics"

C-241 "When de golden moon..."	5 - 6	6 - 8

C-248 "I is busy, 'scuse de view..."

Curt Teich, 6C-K1396
"Oh - I Is Not! ..."

Curt Teich, 0B-H1150
"Big Blow Out!"

In a swig-mid-swank ingle nook
There was such a "jam" we could hardly move,
But we found two gut bucket brigadiers
Who really went truckin' down the groove.

Curt Teich, "Jitterbug Comics"
"In a swig-mid-swank ..."

I'm comin', I'm comin',
For the alligators are swingin' low
I hear the dipsey-doodle callin'
Old black Joe.

Curt Teich, "Jitterbug Comics"
"I'm comin', I'm comin', ..."

Come on you killer-dillers jive session
This is a
Swing-G Shag-G Susie Q-Q
There won't be a recession.

Curt Teich, "Jitterbug Comics"
"Come on you killer-dillers. This is a jive session ..."

"C.T. Pickaninny Comics, Etc."

2B-H580 "It's Not a Secret Anymore..."	3 - 5	5 - 7
2B-H591 "Lawsey Me! What a Peculiar Boy"	3 - 4	4 - 5
2B-H643 "Honey Come on Down..."		
2CH413 "That Model Stands Far Out..."		
4B-H1019 "All's Peaceful Along the Suwanee..."		
5A-H1555 "I'm on the Move"		
6B-H712 "They Gave Us Quite a Blowout"	5 - 6	6 - 8
6B-H1151 "Pot Luck"		
6B-H1153 "Two of a Kind"		
6B-H1155 "Surprised to Hear From Me?"		
6B-H1157 "It Won't Be Long Now"		
6B-H1158 "I Can't Hold Back any longer"		
6B-H1159 "A Pair of Loaded Dice"		
6B-H1160 "You'll Be Hearin' From Me"		
6B-H1876 "My Tale is Told" (Busy Person)		
7B-H2601 "Which?"		
8A-H 2223 See "Jitterbug Comics"		
9A-H "The Darkey Preacher in Florida"		
OB-H788 "A Darkey's Prayer"		
OB-H1150 "Big Blow Out"		
OB-H1403 "I is Busy 'Scuse de view..."		
OB-H1407 "You all can see without a guess"		
Curteichrom & Curteichcolor		
P-178 "Oh - I is Not..."	1 - 2	2 - 3
P-219 "It's Amen Not Yeah Man!"		
9C-K2755 "It's Amen Not Yeah Man!"		

TICHNOR BROS. (Colourpicture) (L)

66260 "I'm Prepared in Case You..."	4 - 5	5 - 7
68087 "Yo' Jus Haunts Me Honey!"		
69187 "Gone With The Wind!"		
69421 "Sure We're Cuckoo-But Happy"	5 - 7	7 - 9
69422 "Can You Tie This One?"	4 - 5	5 - 7
69267 "Silly Goose"	5 - 7	7 - 9
69508 "I'm Not Saying You're All Wet..."		
69498 "Remember-I'll Stand For None..."		
69499 "If Things Look Dark to You..."		
72119 "Madam, Could I Interest You..."	4 - 5	5 - 7
73897 "Cotton Blossoms in Dixieland"		
74295 "Well, Fry Mah Hide!"		
74911 "You Oughta See How They..."	5 - 7	7 - 9
74914 "Who All Sed Dis Here is A..."	4 - 5	5 - 7
75824 "Yo' Used to be My Pin-Up Gal..."		
75827 "Lady Could I Interest You in..."		

Tichnor Brothers, 74911
"You Oughta See How They Dip Chocolates Down Here!"

75829 "What'll You Have Gracie..."
77084 "If Things Look Dark..." (Busy Person)
78835 "Blacks near Ferry"
80539 "Fishing is Good in Dixie"
82378 "A Darkie's Prayer, Florida"
84032 "Watermelon Time in Dixieland"
84031 "Dixie" (L.L.)

TITHFIELD

Series 316 "She's Black, but Comely"	18 - 22	22 - 25

TUCK, RAPHAEL

Series 100 "Love Songs"		
"Honey. I'm Waitin"	22 - 25	25 - 30
Series 115 "Little Wooers"	15 - 18	18 - 22
Series 368M-French		
"Le Cake-Walk"	22 - 25	25 - 28
"Bonne Annee"		
Series 891P - French		
Boy Smokes Cigarette	10 - 12	12 - 15
Series 970 (UndB)		
"Write Away" Minstrel Series		
"It has just occurred to me..."	22 - 25	25 - 28
"Yes-I Do! I Want"		
"You'll hardly believe"		
Series 1043 "Calendar" (6)	22 - 25	25 - 30

Tichnor Brothers, 72119
"Madame, Could I Interest You in a Pair of White Kids?"

Tichnor Brothers, 75824
"Yo' Used to be My Pin-Up-Gal Honey, An' Yo' Still Is!"

Couples Sitting at the Dance
Children Cake Walk Behind Mammy
Series 1794 "Write Away"
    Boy/Girl Do Cake Walk   25 - 28   28 - 32
    "I Want You Ma Honey, Yes I Do"

"Wishing you a Merry Christmas"
Series 1819 (6)
Christmas "Cake Walk"   22 - 25   25 - 28
Series 2087 "Coon Studies" (6)   18 - 22   22 - 25
Series 2088 "Coon Studies" (6)
Series 6696 (6) "Dusky Belles"
   "Queen of the Cake Walk"
Series 6706 (6)   25 - 28   28 - 32
"Humorous" Series "The Cake Walk"
   Black Man and Four Dogs Walk Left
Series 6813 "Humorous" Series
   Sophisticated, Well Dressed Blacks (6)
   "Yes! And I Mean to Stick to It"   18 - 22   22 - 25
Series 6891 (6)
"Happy Little Coons" (Uns./Sandford?)   15 - 18   18 - 22
Series 6909 "Art"
Negro Melodies
   "Way down upon de Swanee ribber..."   15 - 18   18 - 22
Series 6950 "In Dahomey"
   "Full Dress"   10 - 12   12 - 15
Series 7494
   Write Away "I Want You Honey!"   15 - 18   18 - 22
Series 8200 "Christmas"
   Loving Couples   20 - 22   22 - 25
Series 8438 (6)
"Happy Little Coons" (Uns./Sandford?)   20 - 22   22 - 25
   "Is Dat a White Bogey?"
   "We Wants Mammy to..."
Series 8869 (6)
   "Dere go My Civies" (WWI)   15 - 18   18 - 22
Series 9094 (6)
"Coon Studies" (Uns./Sandford?)   18 - 22   22 - 25
   Runaway Wagon
Series 9270 "Dusky Smiles" (6)   18 - 22   22 - 26
Series 9281 "Gentle Art of Making Love"
Series 9285 "Gentle Art of Making Love"
   Boy with cane gives flowers to girl
Leatherette Christmas Series 1825 (6)   10 - 12   12 - 15
   The Butler
   "We All Has Many..."

TULLY, J.
   "Honey, You's Worth Waitin Fo!"   10 - 12   12 - 15
   "Have a Smile With Me"
   271 "I'll Call For You..."
   280 "We're Out on Bail"

R. Tuck, 6909 Series
"Negro Melodies" (Swanee)

R. Tuck, "Love Songs" Series 100
"Honey, I'm Waitin'"

R. Tuck, "Humorous" Series 6706
"The Cake Walk"

Raphael Tuck, "Calendar" Series 1043
No Caption

Raphael Tuck, "Christmas" Series 1819
"The Christmas Cake-Walk"

Raphael Tuck, Series 1794
"Wishing you a Merry Christmas"

Boy with Sack Watches Chicken

ULLMAN MFG. CO.

"Affinity"	12 - 15	15 - 18
"One Touch of..."		
586 "The Gamblers"	10 - 12	12 - 15
1503 "The Blackbird" Habitat--Coonland	22 - 25	25 - 28
Valentine Series		

Ullman, 1503, "The
Blackbird" Habitat--Coonland

Ullman, "Happy Days" Ser. 81
1913, "I'se Right in it."

1582 Girl's Face in Watermelon	12 - 15	15 - 18
Valentine "Happy Days" Series 81		
Girl in Watermelon		
Boy in Watermelon, "I'se Right in it"		
"Kute Koon Kids" Series 165	15 - 18	18 - 22
"Affinity"		
"One Touch of..."		
2912 "Black undressed Kid"		
2913 "A Study in Black and White"		
2914 "A Case of Black Bowl"		
2915 "A Little Black Washing"		
2916 "Two Souls with but a single thought"		
2919 "Jesh wait til we grow up!"		
Series 210 Suffrage		
3308 "De Suffre-Jet"	25 - 30	30 - 35
VALENTINE AND SONS (also Valentine's)		
"Christmas in Coon Land"		
"We've Come to Meet Yo' Massa Santy..."	70 - 80	80 - 90
"Nautical Terms"		
"A Heavy Swell from the South"	22 - 25	25 - 28
"I Want Yer, Ma Honey" (W/Verse)	12 - 15	15 - 18
1 "Flirtation - Doan' Git De Hump..."		

Valentine and Sons
"Two Blacks don't make a white."

Valentine and Sons, "Nautical Terms" -- "A Heavy Swell ..."

Valentine and Sons, "Christmas in Coonland: We've come to meet yo', Massa Santy Claws!"

Note: Black Santas are extremely rare and much in demand!

"Little Nigger" Series (6)	12 - 15	15 - 18
"5 Little Niggers"		
"6 Little Niggers"		
"7 Little Niggers"		
"8 Little Niggers"		
"9 Little Niggers"		
"10 Little Niggers"		
Negro Minstrels	10 - 12	12 - 15
"Flirtation Series"	12 - 15	15 - 18
"Doan Git de Hump"		
Black Series 6-10		
Variation of "Ten Little Indians"	12 - 15	15 - 18
Series 602		
Black Santa w/White & Black Children	175 - 200	200 - 225
Coon Series 508		
"Strangers Yet"	12 - 15	15 - 18
"In the Gloaming"		
"Uncle Tom's Cabin" (UndB)		
"The Death of Eva"	15 - 18	18 - 22
"Topsy and Miss Ophelia"		
"The Death of Uncle Tom"		
"Uncle Tom Bought by the Cruel Legree"		
"Two Blacks Don't Make a White"	18 - 22	22 - 25
WK (possibly Wildt & Kray)		
Large Heads	12 - 15	15 - 18
"How long does an Ostrich take to hatch?"	10 - 12	12 - 15
WARD, E. C. 1906		
"Heads in Cotton" Series		
"Cotton Blooms Tomorrow, Today..."	8 - 10	10 - 12
"Topsy and Uncle Tom"		
WARNER PRESS		
Sunday School (S/**Doug Hall**)		
"Celebrate Christmas at Sunday School"	6 - 8	8 - 10
"Join the Bunch at Sunday School"		
WARWICK		
FL160 "The Cigarette Fiend"	10 - 12	12 - 15
WATKINS & KRACKE		
Series 16	12 - 15	15 - 18
WATLING MFG. CO.		
"I Take Delight in Dropping" (B&W)	6 - 8	8 - 10
WELLS, R. L.		
"The Whole Damm Black Family"	8 - 10	10 - 12
"The Hook For You"		
WHITE CITY ART CO.		

Watkins & Kracke, "Infantastic"
Series 16, "She's Black, but ..."

White City Art Co., 235
"Aint I yo' Honey?"

Some are signed H.A.		
233 "Gosh! Why Hain't I Got Three..."	22 - 25	25 - 28
235 "Aint I Yo' Honey?"		
236 "Trunned Down"		
238 Boy Holding Rabbit		
240 Boy/Girl Waist Up Under Umbrella		
WHITNEY, GEO. C.		
Halloween		
"The Goblins Will Get You..."	20 - 25	25 - 30
WILDT & KRAY		
Series 1836	12 - 15	15 - 18
WILLIAMSON & HAFFNER	6 - 8	8 - 10
WINSCH, JOHN		
Unsigned **S. L. Schmucker (?)**		
Thanksgiving, 1912		
"Thanksgiving Day in the South"	90 - 95	95 - 100
Christmas, 1911		
Little Girls and Golliwog	20 - 22	22 - 25
WOOLWORTH, F. W. (L)		
17811 "A Lucky Nigger"	4 - 6	6 - 8
YERKES, A.		
"He Winked the Other Eye"	8 - 10	10 - 12

John Winsch, 1911
"Best Christmas Wishes"

ZIMMERMAN, H. G.
"Fishing is Great Here"   5 - 6   6 - 8

ANONYMOUS

Cards listed in this section are unidentified. They have no publisher byline and have not been signed by the artists who painted them. Those listed, unless a postcard Era (Pioneer, PMC, L or C) is noted, are cards issued from 1902 to 1930 and are in color. Many cards were produced in this manner, and it is impossible to list them all. However, identification and pricing of similar cards are possible by noting the pricing of individual cards below.

BABIES
  "A Study in Black and Red" (Watermelon) 10 - 12 12 - 15
BIRTHDAY GREETINGS
  Series 686 "Greetin's" 10 - 12 12 - 15
BLACK & WHITE
  "The Shan't Tickle'er" Black versus White 15 - 18 18 - 22
BOXING BABIES
  "Who's Champion Now?" 12 - 15 15 - 18
CAKE WALK
 Black Man and Dogs Cake Walk Left 22 - 25 25 - 30
  This card also by Raphael Tuck, 6706.
  "The Champion Cakewalkers" Steel Pier 18 - 22 22 - 25
CHILDREN
 Boy with Banjo "To Greet My Love" (Emb.) 15 - 18 18 - 22

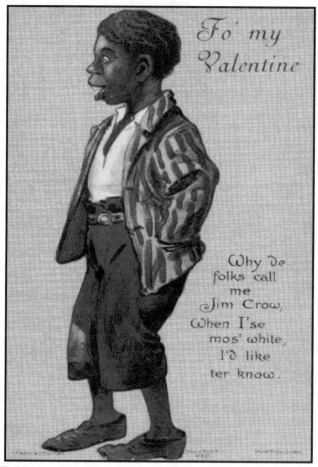

E. Nister, No. 297, "Why do folks call me Jim Crow,
When I'se mos' white, I'd like ter know."

Jim Crow Law -- The state of Tennessee was the first to enact laws against intermarriage and was also first to adopt the "Jim Crow" law in 1875. It resulted in the separation of blacks and whites on trains, in depots, and on wharves. The Supreme Court voted in 1883 to outlaw the Civil Rights Acts of 1875, and blacks were banned from white hotels, barbershops, restaurants, and theaters. By 1885, most Southern states passed laws requiring separate schools. It was said that the Jim Crow law forced blacks to "be kept in their place" -- to use separate and inferior facilities in public accommodations such as bath rooms and drinking fountains; sitting in "the back of the bus" or the Negro car on trains; Negro grandstands; theater sections, etc. The law practically guaranteed segregation as a social system in the United States.

Series 397 (UndB)		
Little Girl with Flowers	12 - 15	15 - 18
Little Boy with Flowers		
CHRISTMAS		
Printed in Germany		
Airplane Interrupts Blacks' Party	22 - 25	25 - 28
Frolicking Blacks Greet Airplane		
DOLLS	15 - 18	18 - 22
EVOLUTION		
Evolution Series 977		
"Watermelon to Coon"	100 - 120	120 - 140
Anonymous, 1909		
Handmade "Watermelon to Coon"	70 - 80	80 - 90
GOLLIWOGS		
"To Wish You a Merry Birthday"	18 - 22	22 - 25
HALLOWEEN		
Anonymous		
6505 "Strange sights are seen"	25 - 28	28 - 32
6508 "You would laugh too"		
POLITICAL		
Black Man Kicks Teddy Roosevelt's Hat		
"You Aught'a Quit Kickin that Hat..."	40 - 50	50 - 60
SANTAS (See Topicals for More Santas)		
Series 10 (UndB)		

"The Champion Cakewalkers"
"Steel Pier"

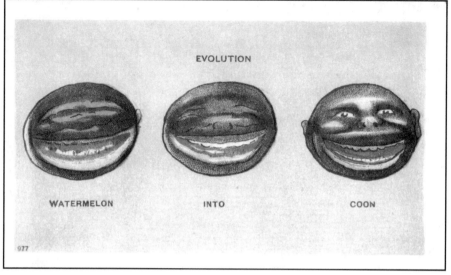

Anonymous, #977, 1909, Evolution
"Watermelon into Coon!!"

Golliwog, "To Wish You a Merry Birthday"

"Though Oft Repeated..."	50 - 60	60 - 70
Others (Not Silhouettes)	50 - 60	60 - 70

SONG CARDS

Words Only

1106 "Old Black Joe"	15 - 18	18 - 22
1107 "Darling Nellie Gray"		
1107 Same Card but Different Back		

415, Lovers Under Red Umbrella

Boy with Banjo
"To Greet My Love."

STEREOTYPES

2112 "You doun want none ob my lip, hey?"	22 - 25	25 - 30

THANKSGIVING

Series 4045, Germany (6)	15 - 18	18 - 22
Big Turkey Frightens Boy		
Boy Riding Turkey		
Two Black and One White Boy w/Turkey		

THANKSGIVING

High Class Embossed, Germany		
Blacks and Turkeys	15 - 18	18 - 22
Turkey Series 706 (Emb.)	10 - 15	15 - 20
Black Chef in White - with Turkey		
Two Boys Taunting Turkey		
Two Boys Taunting Two Turkeys		
Series 226 (6) (Emb.) B in diamond	15 - 18	18 - 22
Man in Uncle Sam Clothing Brings Turkey		
Man in Uncle Sam Clothing Cutting Turkey		
Man with Gun, Turkey and Family at Table		

UMBRELLA

Black Man with Umbrella	10 - 15	15 - 18
415 Stereotypes, Man/Woman Under		
Umbrella	25 - 28	28 - 32

German Valentine, "Love's Offering" (The Kiss)

VALENTINE'S DAY
Comic Heart Faces Series   4 - 6   6- 8
    "Do You Care for Chocolates"
    "Honey - I'se Willin to Share..."
    "Won't You be My Honey..."
    Others
Series 034, German (Embossed)
    "De Spider and De Fly"   18 - 22   22 - 26

German Valentine, "Love's Token" (The Same Kiss)

Valentine Greetings
"Ef yo' will only be ma wife ..."

Valentine Greetings
"Ma auto-car for yo an ready, ..."

Valentine Greetings
"Here ah stan, a pore lone ..."

Valentine Greetings
"Pretty chocolate colored Sal, ..."

2112, "You doun want none ob my lip hey?"

Series 310 Valentines		
12 designs		
"Kiss me honey I's starvin"	8 - 10	10 - 12
Valentine's Day (UndB) Chromolithographs		
"Ef yo' will only be ma wife..."	22 - 25	25 - 28
"Here I stan, a pore lone Coon..."		
"Ma Auto-Car for yo an ready"		
"Pretty Chocolate Colored Sal"		
Printed in Germany		
Valentine's Day		
Little Girl with Sunflower	18 - 22	22 - 25
The Kiss "Loves Offering"		
The Same Kiss, Larger Image "Love's Token"		
Series 415 (Embossed)		
Man Pulls Another's Tooth with Rope	25 - 28	28 - 32
WHOLE BLACK FAMILY (DB) (Embossed)		
521 "The Whole Black Family"	18 - 22	22 - 25
Baby: "Nothing Like This in Our Family"	10 - 12	12 - 15
Boy-Girl: "I Lubs two kinds ob Chicken - You and Fried"		
Black Satire: "Keep a Stiff Upper Lip"	12 - 15	15 - 18
SAMBO: "If Sambo Doesn't Love Me..."	12 - 15	15 - 18
SPIRITUALS ILLUSTRATED		
1106 "Old Black Joe"		
1107 "Darling Neyyie Gray"		

Halloween, 6508
"You would laugh, too, if you ..."

German Valentine
"To my Valentine"

Halloween, 6505, "Strange sights are seen on Halloween"

521, "The Whole Black Family."

686, "Birthday Greetings"
"Greetin's, I suttinly wishes ..."

Christmas, Germany
"A Merry Christmas"

Christmas, Germany
"A Merry Christmas"

Anon., Thanksgiving, Series 4045
"Thanksgiving Greetings"

Boy with Flowers, Series 397   *Girl with Flowers, Series 397*

WATERMELONS
　　40 "You can plainly see how Miserable..."　　8 - 10　　10 - 12
　　Baby in wood auto "I've a longing..."
　　Boy w/2 watermelons "I am pleased..."
WHOLE BLACK FAMILY
　　No. 521 "Ebony Black, Mrs. Black, ..."　　18 - 22　　22 - 25
YMCA WW1 COMICS (B&W)　　8 - 10　　10 - 12
OTHERS
　　"A Pair of Shines" (A Gross Couple)　　15 - 18　　18 - 22

IMPORTANT NOTE

Re:　Price Quotations for Cards Listed in This Price Guide

For a card, or cards, that have no values listed, please refer to the entry just above.

Wings King Size Cigarettes
Continental Size, Published in The Netherlands, 1950's

Advertising postcards are those which list the name of a company, the name of one of the products it sells, or the service it renders. Their primary use is to get the attention of a potential customer and then to eventually sell him the product or service. These can be printed on the front or back, but the most desired types have the product or service shown on the front of the card.

Advertising cards relating to blacks have always been a prime target of postcard collectors. Their scarcity is caused by the large numbers of avid collectors in several different hobby groups... postcard col- lectors, Black Ephemera and Memorabilia collectors, plus paper advertising collectors. The early black cards seemed to focus on products that reflected the use of strong hands and bodies to apply them and make them work, and also for those doing various types of laborious tasks. A good example of this is the great series of cards of the always busy and industrious Gold Dust Twins, the most well known of the product type.

Real photo types, as with other topicals, lead this field as far as collectibility and value are concerned. Issues showing tires or anything automotive, shoes, drinks, and minstrel shows are in great demand. One issue that has become very popular in recent years is Roadside America advertising of black-owned hotels, tourist courts, and other businesses. Many of these were printed on linen and chrome cards. The cards of "Coon Chicken Inn," for instance, have reached prices in the $200-250 range.

	VG	EX
AFTON VILLA		
Eagle Post Card Views		
St. Francisville, La. (B&W)		
Aunt "Shug" the Praline Maker	12 - 15	15 - 18
ALZORIA & JOHANNA VARIETY SHOW		
Coney Island, 1940's		
Dwarfs	22 - 25	25 - 30
AMERICAN BLOWER CO.		
Black Man with Watermelon	20 - 25	25 - 30
AMERICAN MINSTRELS		
The German Times - Advertising:		
"Mamie"	70 - 80	80 - 90
"Lam, Lam, Lam"		
"A Side Talk to the Crowd" and Others		
ANGOLA FAIR		
Great Angola Fair, Sept. 21-24, "You'll be		
Tickled" (R.P.)	40 - 50	50 - 60
JOHN ASCUAGA'S "NUGGET" (C)		
Pearl Bailey	12 - 15	15 - 18
Others		
AUBURNDALE HARDWARE, Toledo		
Sheriff Holding Gun on Two Black Men	15 - 18	18 - 22

American Minstrels, The German Times
"A Side Talk to the Crowd" and Others

American Minstrels, The German Times, "Mamie"

American Minstrels, The German Times, "Lam, Lam, Lam..."

BARLOW HOTEL, Hope, Arkansas
   Curt Teich
      4A-H1071 Boy with Huge Watermelon   18 - 22   22 - 26
BARNUM AND BAILEY
   "Zipp" Posing with Giant (R.P.)   70 - 80   80 - 90

"Hotel Barlow--Hope, Arkansas"
CT 4AH1071

AZO, "Drink Cel-I-Ko"
Real Photo of Shoe Shine Boy

"Pearl Bailey"- M. Roberts
SC15265 John Ascuaga's Nugget

"Use Black Beauty Axle Grease"
National Refining Co.

"Candee Rubbers," by Goodyear
"A Well Balanced Rubber"

Metrocraft, 1585
"Hot Springs National Park Ark."

"You'll be Tickled ... With the many amusement features of the
Great Angola Fair, Sept. 21-24"

"Coon Chicken Inn" -- Portland, Oregon
C.T. 1B-H2641

BARTLETT, J.B.L., Real Estate
"Typical Negro Home, Turpentine..."   18 - 22   22 - 26
BERRY BROTHERS VARNISHES
A. E. Weidner
"Spare the Varnish, Spoil the Finish"   30 - 40   40 - 50
BILTMORE HOTEL, Durham, N.C.
O. M. Styron (W. Border)
"America's Finest Colored Hotel"   22 - 26   26 - 30
BLACK BEAUTY AXLE GREASE
National Refining Co.
Man on Donkey, with Axle Grease Sign   40 - 50   50 - 60
"Seeing is Believing"   30 - 35   35 - 40
BOWSER SHOES
Simplicity Co.   15 - 18   18 - 22
BUTTERNUT BREAD
Kaufmann-Strauss, S/F. C. Long
55 Boy with Razor   25 - 30   30 - 35
CANDEE RUBBERS, by Goodyear
"A Well Balanced Rubber"
Black Boy With Rubber Shoes   100 - 125   125 - 150
CAFE SOCIETY
Josh White (B&W)   12 - 15   15 - 18
THE CHATHAM KIND
H. M. Doty (B&W)
"Fast Black, Warranted Not to Fade"   15 - 20   20 - 25

"The DeRue Brothers, Ideal Ministries"
Sepia, Undivided Back

"Do-Nut Dinette, Orlando, Fla."
"It's Always Chicken Time*"

CEL-I-KO SODA (R.P.)

   Shoe Shine boy with sign:

"Drink Cel-I-Ko" - 5 Cents	150 - 175	175 - 200

CHERRY BLOSSOM CALENDAR CARDS

S/**Remy** (12) Brown/Blue	20 - 25	25 - 30

CHICKEN SHACK

   Harvey Advertising Co.

14934 Interior with Large Chef	20 - 25	25 - 30

CONTINENTAL-TENNIS BALL

Blacks Playing Tennis	70 - 80	80 - 100

COON CHICKEN INN, Portland, Ore. (L)

Curt Teich 1B-H2641	175 - 200	200 - 250
There are two other views of this restaurant.	175 - 200	200 - 250

COTTON STATES EXPOSITION, 1895

Negro Building, Regular Size	200 - 225	225 - 250
Negro Building, Large Card	350 - 375	375 - 400

CRACKER JACK BEARS

No. 8 "Away to southward they flew..."	40 - 45	45 - 50

CRADDOCK TERRY SHOES

Jamestown Exposition, 1907 (B&W)	20 - 25	25 - 30

CREST MINSTRELS 1906

Advertising Traveling Minstrels (12) (B&W)	25 - 30	30 - 40

"Duke Ellington and His Famous Orchestra In Concert ..."
Government Postal

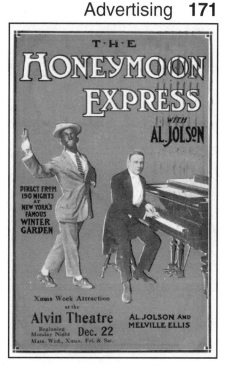

Fisk Tires
"Time to Re-tire -- Get a Fisk"

"The Honeymoon Express"
1913, Al Jolson

"Green River Whiskey"
She was Bred in Old Kentucky"
(1899, Owned by J. W. McCulloch, Owensboro, Ky.)

"Gold Dust Twins"
"A word to the <u>WIFE</u> is sufficient ..."

"Gold Dust Twins"
"I am scouring the earth for my affinity. Are you interested?"

	25 - 30	30 - 40
1 "Dere's no use denyin'"		
2 "I'se anticipatin' de pleasure"		
3 "I'se holdin' my own"		
4 "Le' me say right yere"		
5 "We's lookin' fo'ward wid much pleasure"		
6 "No use a kickin'"		
7 "Taint no use argufy"		

"Gold Dust Twins"
"There's a washout on the line --- Walking home."

"Gold Dust Twins"
"How would you like to skate with me?"

The Gold Dust Twins, probably the most well-known of all black advertising postcards, were used by the Fairbanks Company to make their washing powders the No. 1 product in the field. This set of four by E. W. Kemble (unsigned) was followed by cards showing the Gold Dust Twins dressed as Santas and one with a Thanksgiving motif. Because of their rarity, these have surpassed the original four in value.

"Said Mammy to me-- ..."

"Maw, whar's your politeness? ..."

"Gran'pa done say dat his ..."

"I'se a going to be de whole ..."

"It aint a bit o' use to talk ..."

"Susie done thought she'd ..."

The H-O Co., Buffalo, N.Y. issued two "Jocular Jinks" advertising cards (backs shown above) that offered a series of six "darkey" cards if the recipient would cut out and send to them "the man and boy picture" from two packages of "Korn-Kinks," plus 4 cents postage.

*"Korn-Kinks" -- 5¢ on
Cabin and No Print-
ing on Driveway.*

*"Korn-Kinks" -- No
5¢ on Cabin; Caption,
"You Smash Dem
Kinks, I'll Spoil You'
Face Chile."*

*"Korn-Kinks" Advertising Cards, H-O Co., Buffalo, N.Y.
Illustrating Two Printing Variations*

*"National Casket Co." -- Jamestown Exposition Ground, Va.
Jamestown A & V Company, 1907*

8 "Jes as I was sayin"
9 "How kin yo' doubt"
10 "I hab de honor"
11 "Dere'll be considerable doin'"
12 "De point am dis"
"Don't Miss the Big Minstrel Show"
"I'se Anticipating De Pleasure"

JIMMY DALY ATTRACTIONS
"Harry Watkins, Song Stylist" 1950's   20 - 25   25 - 30
DeRUE BROTHERS IDEAL MINSTRELS
Ad for Touring Minstrel Show (Und/B) (Sepia)   40 - 50   50 - 60
DINAH BLACK ENAMEL
Blacks Painting   40 - 50   50 - 60
DO-NUT DINETTE, Orlando, Fla. (1950's)
"It's Always Chicken Time" (Oversized)   20 - 25   25 - 30
DUKE ELLINGTON CONCERT
Advertises Upcoming Show   75 - 85   85 - 100
FISK TIRES
"Time to Re-Tire - Get a Fisk"   50 - 60   60 - 70
FOSTER ROBE & TANNING CO.
"We Tan Coonskins"   40 - 50   50 - 60
"We Can Tan Your Cowhide"
GOLD DUST CLEANSER
Gold Dust Twins (4)
(Unsigned **E. B. Kemble**)
"A Word to the Wife..."   40 - 50   50 - 60
"How Would You Like to Skate..."
"I am Scouring the Earth..."
"There's a Washout on the line..."
GOLD DUST FAIRBANKS CLEANSER
Gold Dust Twins Dressed as Black Santas
"Yuletide"   100 - 110 110 - 120
Thanksgiving (Fairbanks Cleaner)
"Be Thankful"   50 - 60   60 - 70
Real-Photos
Black-face Children W/Gold Dust Costumes   150 - 175 175 - 200
Black-face Children W/Gold Dust Products
GREAT WESTERN COMICS
"Children"   18 - 22   22 - 26
GREEN HEART TABASCO SAUCE
Blacks Picking Peppers   20 - 25   25 - 30
GREEN RIVER WHISKEY
Black Man and Horse with Whiskey Keg
"She Was Bred in Old Kentucky"   60 - 70   70 - 80

"The Lewis Plantation and Turpentine Still -- Brooksville, Fla."
Real Photo by EKC

"Langford's Band & Revue, 1944"
Cole Bros. Circus, Real Photo by EKC

GREENVILLE LUMBER CO., S.C.

    "Give us a Trial!"   15 - 18   18 - 22

GUTSCHLUCK BEER

    K & S, Signed by **F. C. Long**   35 - 40   40 - 50

HARPERS WEEKLY

    Black Man Reading **Harpers Weekly**   70 - 80   80 - 90

HEARST'S BOSTON SUN-AMERICAN
No. No. "Love Drop"   10 - 15   15 - 20
HENRY ROSENBURG CLOTHIERS
Black Man Dressed in Fine Clothing   30 - 40   40 - 50
HONEYMOON EXPRESS
Dana P. Bennett Co., 1913
Al Jolson Black-Face Show Ad   120 - 130 130 - 150
HORN'S PAVILION
Souvenir Post Card Co.
"A Flock of Blackbirds"   20 - 25   25 - 35
HOT SPRINGS BATH
Triple-Fold Card, Black Washing Man's Foot   25 - 30   30 - 40
Metrocraft, 1585
"Hot Springs National Park Ark."   20 - 25   25 - 30
HUYLER'S CHOCOLATES   20 - 25   25 - 30
'THE JAZZ SINGER"
Featuring Al Jolson, Black-Face   120 - 130 130 - 150
KORN KINKS
H-O Co. "Jocular Jinks of Kornelia Kinks"
Series A (6)   28 - 32   32 - 36
1 "Said Mammy to Me..."
2 "Maw, Whar's Your Politeness..."
3. "Grandpa Don Say Dat..."
4. "I'se a Going to Be De Whole Town..."
5. "It Ain't a Bit O' Use to Talk..."
6. "Suzie Done Thought' She'd a Voice..."
The Korn Kinks Advertising Cards (2)
Souvenir Card Back   30 - 35   35 - 40
"Jocular Jinks of Kornelia Kinks"   30 - 32   32 - 35
There are 4 printing variations of ad cards.
Captions are in different type fonts, the logs are varied sizes. (1) Has
5 cents on left side of cabin, kite in air, and little girl wears a print
dress. (2) Has 5 cents on right side of cabin, kite on ground, little girl
wears white dress. (3) Has no 5 cents on cabin, kite on ground, little
girl wears white dress. (4) The rarest variation shows the kite in the
air and no 5 cents on the cabin.
Rare Var. - Kite in Air; No "5 cents" on Cabin   50 - 60   60 - 70

KRAMER AUTO SERVICE, Savannah, GA
Wrecker with Black Mechanic (R.P.)   120 - 130 130 - 150
LACKAWANNA RAILROAD
"The Phoebe Snow Drift" Black Porter   20 - 25   25 - 30
LANGFORD'S BAND AND REVUE, 1944
Cole Bros. Circus (R.P.)   200 - 225 225 - 250

LEWIS PLANTATION, Brooksville, Fla.
    Turpentine Still (R.P.)   25 - 30   30 - 40
LITHGOW'S VAUDEVILLE CONCERT CO.
    Advertising "Fun Show"   30 - 40   40 - 50
LONGWEAR SHOES
    Old Slave in Shoe Shop   25 - 30   30 - 35
MARINE TERRACE HOTEL, Miami Beach
    L. L. Cook   M-396 (R.P.)
    "Dining Room and Kitchen Staff"   25 - 30   30 - 40
MECCA SLIPPERS
    "Black Man with Guitar" (B&W)   18 - 22   22 - 26
MINSTRELS   "Old Plantation Minstrels" (R.P.) 120-140 140-160
MITCHLER CLOTHIER
    "A Nigger in the Pink of Condition"   30 - 35   35 - 45
NAGEL GROVES
    Daniel Ferrigno
    61168 (Dextone)   6 - 8   8 - 12
NATIONAL CASKET CO.
    Jamestown Exposition, 1907   60 - 80   80 - 110
NESTLE'S FOOD
    Henri Nestle Cupid's Advice
    "Give the Babies Nestle's Food"   18 - 22   22 - 26

"Old Plantation Minstrels"
Real Photo -- 1909 Era

Nestle's Food, Henri Nestle, 1910
"Give the Babies Nestle's Food"

Read House, Chattanooga, TN
H. Brown, 1A2453

O'Brien's Restaurant, Waverly, New York, Curt Teich 7B-82142
Tuskegee Institute Students Working Part-Time

Ross Avenue Motel, Dallas -- "The South's Finest Colored Motel"
Nationwide Postcard Co., Arlington

"Sugar Ray's Cafe ... The Show Place of Harlem"
Eagle Postcard View Company

"Trublpruf" Tires, "Wet or Dry"
Lambert Tire & Rubber Co.
Real Photo by AZO

1939 N.Y. World's Fair
Tichnor 66053
"Here's a Tip for Yo-All! ..."

NORFOLD ROXITE PAINT
Blacks Painting, 1950's .... 15 - 20 .... 20 - 25
O'BRIEN'S RESTAURANT
 "Tuskegee Students as Chefs & Waiters" (R.P.) .. 40 - 50 .... 50 - 60
 Curt Teich, 7B-82142 (L)
 Tuskegee Students Working Part-Time .... 20 - 25 .... 25 - 28
O'BRIEN'S CHOCOLATES
 Children in Candy Box .... 15 - 20 .... 20 - 25
ORIGINAL DIXIE RAMBLERS
 11 Piece Colored Orchestra (B&W)
 "Red Perkins and His Orig. Dixie Ramblers" .... 20 - 25 .... 25 - 30
PIEDMONT HOTEL
 Piedmont Hotel, Atlanta, Ga.
 "An Old Timer" .... 25 - 30 .... 30 - 35
RCA RADIO CORP. OF AMERICA
 Duke Ellington .... 20 - 30 .... 30 - 40
 Lena Horne
 Thomas (Fats) Waller
READ HOUSE
 H. Brown
 1A2453, "M...is wanted at the Read House" .... 20 - 25 .... 25 - 30

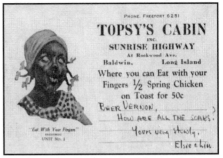

Topsy's Cabin, Baldwin, L.I.
"Eat With Your Fingers"

Livermore & Knight, Applique
Basket with Adv. Pull-out of
Schamberg Rattan Furniture

Curt Teich, R-65788
Thomas Drugstore
Hot Springs, Arkansas

"Steel Pier" Mail Card, Atlantic City
"Cake Walks: Mondays, Wednesdays and Saturdays"

Walk-Over Shoes, Signed Frank Vinnie Smith
"The Mammy"

RED STAR LINE
Black Man in Top Hat Looks at Ship   30 - 35   35 - 45
RINGLING BROS. (C)
Barnum & Bailey Circus
"Wizards on Wheels"   8 - 10   10 - 12
ROCHESTER PACKING CO.
The Arpea Ko Minstrels   30 - 35   35 - 45
ROSS AVENUE MOTEL, Dallas (L)   20 - 25   25 - 30
Nationwide P. C. Co., Arlington
"The South's Finest Colored Motel"
ROYAL TAILORS
S/F. C. Long   25 - 30   30 - 35
SANDERS MINERAL WATER
World Fair, St. Louis 1904   40 - 50   50 - 60
SCHAMBERG, F. & CO. (Oversize)
Mechanical Pull-out Adv. Rattan Furniture
Lady with Large Basket   50 - 60   60 - 70
SCHMIDT & CO.
Tea
Black Servant Serving Tea   25 - 30   30 - 35
SOUTHERN RAILWAY
Commercialchrome (White Border)
"Strawberries for Northern Markets"   20 - 25   25 - 30
STEEL PIER
Atlantic City Mailing Card
"Cake Walks - Monday, Wed., and Sat."   30 - 40   40 - 50

SUGAR RAY'S CAFE, 1950's		
Eagle Postcard View Co.		
Sugar Ray Robinson		
"Showplace of Harlem" (B&W)	30 - 40	40 - 50
THOMAS DRUGSTORE, Hot Springs, Arkansas		
Curt Teich, R-65788	50 - 60	60 - 70
TIPTOP LAUNDRY		
Starchroom Pub. Co.		
"If it is a Question of Clean Linen"	25 - 30	30 - 35
TOPSY'S CABIN, 1933 (Sepia)		
Restaurant Offering a Menu of Chicken	40 - 50	50 - 60
TOPSY HOSIERY		
Souvenir Postal #1 (B&W)		
White and Black Girls	20 - 25	25 - 30
"TRUBLPRUF" Wet or Dry Tires		
Lambert Tire & Rubber Co., Akron		
Real Photo with Little Black Boy (AZO)	150 - 175	175 - 200
WALKER THEATRICAL AGENCY		
"Gladys Bentley" (1950's)	20 - 25	25 - 30
WALK-OVER SHOES		
"Weighing Cotton"	12 - 15	15 - 20
Topsy Hosiery (B&W)	15 - 18	18 - 22
S/**Frank Vinnie Smith**		
"Going to the Ball"	20 - 25	25 - 30
"The Mammy"		
WARREN'S AMUSEMENT CO.		
Ad for Black Minstrel Show	30 - 40	40 - 50
WINGS KING SIZE CIGARETTES		
Published in Netherlands (Blacks Dancing)	75 - 85	85 - 100
WORLD'S FAIR, NEW YORK, 1939		
Tichnor Bros. 66053 "Here's a Tip for Yo-all!"	10 - 15	15 - 20

ABBREVIATIONS USED IN THIS BOOK

(B.P.)	Busy Persons
(B&W)	Black and White
(C)	Chromes
(Emb.)	Embossed or Raised Printing
(L)	Linen Finish
(L.L.)	Large Letter Cards, Usually States
(PMC)	Private Mailing Cards
(R.P.)	Real Photo Type
(UndB)	Undivided Backs
(Uns.)	Unsigned

S. Langsdorf & Co., N.Y.
"Greetings from the Sunny South," 5642, "Old Uncle Joe"

Real-life postcards, basically, are those that have resulted from pictures taken of real people with a camera. These fall into several categories and, ultimately, they will be classified to include real photos, colored (or tinted), and black & white images. Artist-signed (or artist-unsigned) are just the opposite, and all were derived from the pen or brush of the artist or illustrator.

1. To classify a card (or sets and series of a group of cards) so that it can be easily identified and valued, the collector must first decide whether it is in the real-life category or artist-signed.

2. Look for the publisher's name which is usually listed on the reverse, or address side of the card. Publishers' names in this section are listed alphabetically in bold letters. If there is no date or era listed after the publisher's name, the card would be from the 1904 - 1930 era. This is explained in Chapter 1, Introduction.

3. If the card is a part of a series, the series number will also be listed on the reverse side; e.g., "Series 1" or "Baby Series." Normally, there are 4, 6, or 8 cards in a set or series. However, in some instances there may be many more.

4. The caption, which usually describes the image on the picture side, may also have a card number preceding it.

5. Values are listed as VG (Very Good) and EX (Excellent) condition for each card, whether a single card or for all cards in the series.

6. Anonymous cards, which have no publisher, are listed separately at the end of this section.

	VG	EX
AH CO. (Albert Hahn)		
"Sambo" Old Man (B&W) (UndB)	12 - 15	15 - 18
A-W DISTRIBUTORS (C)		
32885-2 "Texas Oil Fields-Old Days..."	1 - 2	2 - 3
ABINGDON		
Sunday School		
330939 "Happy Birthday from Sunday School Class"	8 - 10	10 - 12
330904 "We Need You. You Need Us"		
330920 "Come to Revival - Bring Family"		
32324X Happy Birthday		
ACMEGRAPH CO., Chicago		
4991 "A Plantation Shack"	15 - 20	20 - 25
4992 "A Southern Cotton Plantation"		
4994 "Down Where the Cotton Blossoms..."		
5056 "Wash Day on the Old Plantation"		

A-H Company
"Sambo"

Albertype Co., "I'se ready to caddy
for you." (Greensboro, NC)

Albertype Co. (PMC) -- "Greetings from Savannah"
"Georgia Cake Walk"

Albertype Co. (PMC)
"Greetings from the Sunny South"

5116 "Two of a Kind"	15 - 20	20 - 25
5117 "A Joy Ride in Dixie"		
6257 "Rapid Transit"		
6262 "River Lamp on the Mississippi"		
6264 "The Old Slave Block in St. Louis"	8 - 10	10 - 12

The Albertype Co. (By E. C. Eddy)
"A Fruitful Long Leaf Pine. Southern Pines, N.C."

ADAMS SPECIALTY CO. (C)

    P5418 "Old Black Joe at Old Kent..." (Koppel)   1 - 2   2 - 3

ALABAMA POSTCARD CO. (L)

    43239 "Picking Cotton in the South"   3 - 4   4 - 6

    "Crystal Caverns Park, Clay, Ala."

    62286 "Oakwood College"

    73682 "Father Charles G. Hayes, Chicago"

    C12377 "Greetings from Alabama" Map, Etc.

ALBERTYPE CO.

  Pioneers with "Souvenir Card" Backs

    Series 12   35 - 40   45 - 50

    "Aunt Charlotte"

    "Cotton Picking"

    "I'se Born Tired"

    "Come Seben, Come Eleben"

    "Come and Play With Me"

    "On the St. John's River"

  "Greetings from Savannah" PMC

    "Georgia Cake Walk" (B&W)   30 - 35   35 - 40

  "Greetings from the Sunny South" (12) (PMC)   30 - 35   35 - 40

    Boy in Straw Hat

    Three Boys

    Three Boys Eating Watermelon

    Boy in Round Felt Hat

    Old Man with Beard

    Many Boys Eating Watermelon

    Boy's Face

Old Cabin
Vegetable Vendor
Man Eating Watermelon
Other PMC (B&W)
    5 Old Man with Beard and Stick in Hand   30 - 35   35 - 40
Others
    "Ned's Farm, Southern Pines"   22 - 25   25 - 28
    "Two Pickaninnies"   18 - 22   22 - 25
    "Georgia Cake Walk"
    Oxford, Pa. "Billy"
  "Greetings from the Sunny South"
    Man Picking Cotton
    "Come Seven Come Eleven"
    "Uncle Remus and the Little Boy"*
    "This is the Life" 2 Boys on Donkey
  * Hand-Colored
  Pinehurst, Southern Pines, N.C. Series

The great photographic works of E. C. Eddy are featured on the early cards of the Pinehurst and Southern Pines areas. They are very scarce and are in great demand by collectors. His real photo cards of some of those listed here are considered to be gems and command very high prices. Please refer to the REAL PHOTO section for the listing on Eddy.

    "A Fruitful Long Leaf Pine ..."   22 - 25   25 - 28
    "Woman's Exchange, Pinehurst, N.C."*
    "Uncle Tom's Cabin" (E. C. Eddy)*
    "Ned's Cabin" (E. C. Eddy)*
    "Ned's Family, Sou. Pines" (E. C. Eddy)*
    "Cotton Picking Time" (E. C. Eddy)*
    "By the Sand Road" (E. C. Eddy)*
    "From Grand-daddy down" (E. C. Eddy)*
    "The Life Saving Crew at 10th Hole"
    No 3 Course, Pinehurst" (E. C. Eddy)*   25 - 30   30 - 35
    "The Berry Sch. Band, Mt. Berry, Ga." (B&W)   18 - 22   22 - 25
    "I Love My Chicken, but O' You..." (B&W)   10 - 12   12 - 15
    "Kitchen Yard of Gov. Palace"   8 - 10   10 - 12
    "Students Passing..." Hampton Inst. (B&W)   10 - 12   12 - 15
    "Midshipmen's Mess Hall" Annapolis (B&W)   10 - 12   12 - 15
  * E. C. Eddy cards are hand-colored types.
  HISTORICAL (Sepia)
    Dr. J. Kinney & B. T. Washington, Souvenir
    of Nat. Med. Assoc. at Tuskegee, Ala.   110 - 120   120 - 140

Asheville P. C. Co., 46737
"Old Black Joe"

Asheville P. C. Co., E-5412
"Uncle Tom"

Asheville P. C. Co., 16246
"Dem Cotton Boll"

Asheville P. C. Co., 46738
"A Good Wool Crop in ..."

252 A COON TREES A POSSUM IN DIXIELAND

D. 154

The Darkey Preacher

"Listen Sistern and Bredren,
You must give up your devilish
  way
Give up all your wickedness,
Or de good Lawd'll make you
  pay

Stop drinking dat mean corn
  likker.
Dat makes you crazy to fight.
Stop rolling dose "Galloping
  dominoes"
Dat makes you stay up all
  night.

Sisters, don't let your tongues
  wag too much.
Stop putting on all dat paint.
And don't use dat bleach and
  powder,
Dat makes you look white when
  you ain't.

Before we dismiss, we'll jine
  in prayer
De deacons will now pass the
  plates aroun',
And if you don't help out de
  collection,
St. Peter will mos likely turn
  you down."

VERSE COPYRIGHTED BY ASHEVILLE POST CARD CO.   46089

Asheville P. C. Co., E-5618
"A Coon Trees a Possum in ..."
(Also published as a DB card by
the Hugh C. Leighton Co.)

Asheville P. C. Co., 46089
"The Darkey Preacher"

"Success" B. T. Washington and Emmett Scott		80 - 90	90 - 100
B. T. Washington "Useful Living"		80 - 90	90 - 100
ALLGOOD, SUSIE W.			
Taft Possum Series, 1909 (32)		20 - 25	25 - 28

"A barnyard gathering in Possum Land"
"Around the cabin door"
"Coming events cast their shadows..."
"Daddy dats a fine one"
"The end of the washin"
"Expectation"
"Her day's washing begun"
"Hundred and five and raised on Possum"
"I'll wah you chiluns out"
"I'se waitin to cook dem Possum"
"Luncheon"
"Mandy, bake dem taters right"
"The Pickaninnies play time"
"Possum and Taters waitin for three"
"The Real Thing"

A Barnyard Gathering in Possum Land

Susie W. Allgood, Taft Possum Series B-23
"A Barnyard Gathering in Possum Land"

"Return from the Hunt"
"Stringing the Banjo"
"Taint no Sin to eat Possum"
"Wash you Chiluns"
"Way down South in the Land of Cotton"
"Worth County Hunt"
"Yassum, I'se cotched twenty a night..."
Others

AMERICAN NEWS CO.

"Cotton Being Taken to Steamers"	10 - 12	12 - 15
Watching Minstrel Show Wagon	15 - 20	20 - 25
C642 "Scene on the Wabash River"	8 - 10	10 - 12
C1293 "Negro Rapid Transit in Sunny South"	10 - 12	12 - 15

AMERICAN OPINION (C)

CR2 "Highland Folk School" (B&W)	2 - 3	3 - 4

AMERICAN POSTCARD CO. (C) (Continental)

Art by Gary Johnson, Deckle Edge

1419 "Typical Scene in the Deep South"	10 - 12	12 - 15

ANY

Series 6085

"Praline Seller, New Orleans"	12 - 15	15 - 18

ARKANSAS HERITAGE (Dexter)

24425-D "Mustered Out Black Volunteers"	2 - 3	3 - 4

ARMY Y.M.C.A. (B&W)

"Colored Recruits Drilling Camp Jackson"	18 - 22	22 - 25

Asheville P. C. Co., E-5453
"Sittin' Soft" in Dixie Land

ART PHOTO GREETINGS, Elizabeth, N.J. (B/W)

Bloom Bros. Department Store	3 - 4	4 - 6
Auctioning Tobacco, Lumberton, N.C.	2 - 3	3 - 4
Watermelon Season, Laurinburg, N.C.	3 - 4	4 - 5

ARTVUE POST CARD CO.

"Football, Camp Atwater, Mass."	12 - 15	15 - 18
"Church Rectory & Hall, St. Gabriel's	15 - 18	18 - 22
Mission for Colored" Greenville, S.C. (Sepia)		

ASHEVILLE POSTCARD CO.

The Asheville Postcard Co. was the largest distributor of postcards south of Washington, D.C., and was in business from 1916 until 1977. Therefore, they were one of the principal distributors of blacks on postcards for many U.S. and foreign publishers for over a half century.

Although Curt Teich was their major publisher, they also distributed for many other firms. The author was fortunate to have been a frequent visitor and customer of the Asheville Postcard Co. during the last five years it was in business. I was allowed to roam through their three large warehouses and search through boxes, some of which had been there since 1916. Through the years, as unsold cards were returned by salesmen from all over the southeast, the employees placed them in the backs of boxes where new stock was being withdrawn. Consequently, it was commonplace to find complete sets and series of cards of all descriptions, and especially those of early blacks of the 1905 to 1920 era.

In the linen era from 1930 to 1948, the Asheville Postcard Co. accumulated stocks of over 200 different linen-finish cards showing images of blacks, both real life and comics. These black postcards, according to Mr. LeCompte, the owner, were his best sellers to drug stores and to S. H. Kress, Newberrys, Woolworth, and other five and dime stores throughout the ten southeastern states he serviced. Because of terrific sales, he placed large orders with publishers and accumulated large stocks of the cards during the years of World War II. The bubble burst, as he explained, when the NAACP complained, and Kress, Newberrys, and others took them off their shelves and refused to sell them. The loss of these sales, plus the end of their tremendous WWII comics sales, brought about the slow demise of the once flourishing business of the Asheville Postcard Co.

"COLOURPICTURE" (TICHNOR)

16245 "I Love That Cotton"	4 - 5	5 - 6
16246 "Dem Cotton Boll"		
16247 "The Payoff"		
16557 "Greetings From N.C." (L.L.)	3 - 5	5 - 6
A-299 "The Old North State"	3 - 5	5 - 7

METROCRAFT (L)

43074 "A Darkey's Prayer"	4 - 6	6 - 9
43075 "Honey, Come Down..."		
45760 "A Busy Day in a Cottonfield..."	3 - 4	4 - 6
46089 "The Darkey Preacher"	5 - 7	7 - 9
46733 "Three of a Kind in Dixieland"		
46734 "An Old-Fashioned Negro Mammy"		
46735 "The Old Folks at Home"		
46737 "Old Black Joe"		
46738 "A Good Wool Crop..." (Haircut)		
46827 "Who Said Watermelon?"		
46828 "Three of a Kind"		
48032 "Bales of Cotton Ready for..."	4 - 5	5 - 7

CURT TEICH

"C.T. American Art"

White Border and Linens Included

17253C "A Busy Day in the Cotton Field"	4 - 6	6 - 8
12851-C "The Darkey Preacher"	6 - 8	8 - 10
17811-C "Nine Coons, Count 'em..."	6 - 8	8 - 10
21051 "Dipping and Scraping Pine..."	3 - 4	4 - 5

Curt Teich, 2C-1492 (One of a Series)
"Looking Thru Glass-Bottom Boat into 80 Feet of Water
Paradise Park on Silver River near Ocala, Florida

Curt Teich, OB-H36
"Dixie Express"

21449 "Waiting for a Bite in..."	4 - 5	5 - 7
35216 "Romeo and Juliet..."	4 - 6	6 - 9
· 5399C "The Old North State"		
60676 "A Coon Trees a Possum..."	6 - 8	8 - 10
63766 "The Home Stretch"	4 - 6	6 - 9
72475 "Come On Down, I'se Waiting..."		

75667 "Honey come down. I'm waiting..."		
88672 "Pet Deer at Children's Zoo..."	2 - 3	3 - 5
93434 "Sugar Cane Grinding..."	4 - 6	6 - 9
94199 "View of Atlantic Ocean"	2 - 3	3 - 5
94297 "A Narrow Escape in Florida"		
94471 "Alligator Bait"	4 - 6	6 - 9
104820 "Wash Day in Dixie"		
R94260 "Alligator and Child in Palm..."		
A94261 "A Darkey's Prayer"		
A94771 "Alligator Bait"		
E-4967 "Southern Products"	4 - 6	6 - 9
E-5319 "Southern Products" (Timesaver)		
E-5405 "Seven Up" in Dixieland		
E-5406 "Give us De Rine..."		
E-5408 "Cotton Pickers at Work..."	2 - 3	3 - 5
E-5409 "Old Folks at Home"	4 - 6	6 - 9
E-5412 "Uncle Tom..."	6 - 8	8 - 10
E-5419 Negro "Heben"	4 - 6	6 - 9
E-5453 "Sittin' Soft" in Dixieland		
E-5467 "De Cabin Home in..."		
E-5468 "A Busy Day in a Cotton..."		
E-5469 "Cotton Pickers at Work..."	2 - 3	3 - 5
E-5556 "Old Black Joe in Cotton F..."	4 - 6	6 - 9
E-5557 "A Happy Pair in Dixieland"		
E-5613 "Romeo & Juliet in Dixieland"		
E-5614 "Yes-Suh! Some Punkins..."		
E-5618 "A Coon Trees a Possum in..."	8 - 10	10 - 12
E-5739 "Working Hard for the Family..."	4 - 6	6 - 9
E-6577 "The Darkey Preacher"		
E-6695 "A Cotton Picker on a..."	2 - 3	3 - 5
E-7428 "A Native of Dixieland..."	4 - 6	6 - 9
E-7431 "Grand-Pap Embarrassed"		
E-8796 "Gr. From Dixieland" (L.L.)	3 - 5	5 - 7
E-9639 "Nebber Min' Me Mr. Gator..."	4 - 6	6 - 9
104820 "Wash Day in Dixie"		
104821 "Lollypops and Chocolate Drops..."		
105349 "Old Black Joe" in a Southern...		
105350 "De Cabin Home in..."		
105355 "Sho Do Love Melons"		
2C-1492 "Looking Thru Glass-Bottom Boat ..."	15 - 20	20 - 25
Others in Series		
4A-H1234 "Yes Suh! Some Punkins..."	4 - 6	6 - 9
6A-H448 "Listening to the Master's Word"		
6A-H451 "Getting Ready For a Feast"		

6A-H455 "The Blackville Serenade"
6B-H1919 "All's Peaceful Along the..."
7A-H2993 "A Happy Pair in Dixieland"
8A-H2568 "Greetings From N. Carolina" (L.L.)   3 - 4   4 - 5
9A-H897 "Alabama" Multi. View With Verse   3 - 4   4 - 5
9A-H1635 "The Darkey Preacher" W/Verse
CG12525 "Old Fashioned Southern Ki..."
Chromes
    AC23 "A Busy Day in the Cotton Field"   2 - 3   3 - 4
AUSTIN, J. I. CO.
    Real-life comic "Don't Butt In" (Sepia)   5 - 6   6 - 8
    56 "Cotton Plantation Scene near Rome, Ga."   4 - 5   5 - 6
    56 "Out on the Miss. Cotton Plantation"
BARNHILL, E. G.
    "A Darkey's Mansion and Autymobile"   10 - 12   12 - 15
BEDOU, A. P. (Sepia and B&W)
    Booker T. Washington and Dr. John Kenney"
    "Souvenir - National Medical Association"*   50 - 55   55 - 60
    Booker T. Washington
    "Useful Living" Verse (Sepia)*   40 - 50   50 - 60
    Booker T. Washington and Emmett Scott
    "Success" Verse by B.T.W.*   45 - 50   55 - 60
  * Cards printed earlier by **Albertype Co.**
    Tuskegee Institute
    "Booker T. Washington, Residence"
    Tuskegee Institute, Alabama"   15 - 18   18 - 22
    "John A. Andrew Memorial Hospital,
      Tuskegee Institute"
    "White Hall, Girls Dormitory" (B&W)   12 - 15   15 - 18
    "Machine Division" (B&W)
    105 "Trade Building" (B&W)
    118 "Tatum Hall" (Sepia)
    120 "Dorothy Hall" (B&W)
    122 "Rockefeller Hall" (B&W)
    123 "Office Building" (B&W)
    125 "Williston Square" (B&W)
    127 "Court Square" (B&W)
BLACKMON DIST. CO. (L) (C. Teich)
    15286-C-N "Negro Baptizing Scene in
      Greeneville, Miss."   7 - 8   8 - 10
BLUFF CITY NEWS, Memphis (C. Teich) (L) (C)
    1B-H2099 "Greetings From Memphis..."   3 - 4   4 - 5
    2A-H928 "Levee Scene and Waterfront"
    3B-H450 "Cotton Ginning in Memphis"

A. P. Bedou, Booker T. Washington
"Useful Living"

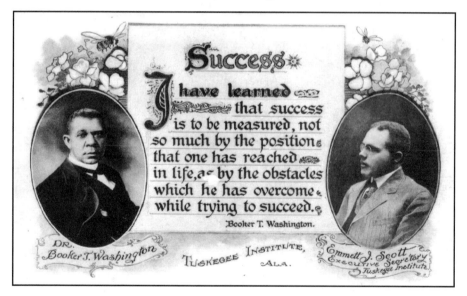

A. P. Bedou, Booker T. Washington and Emmett J. Scott
Tuskegee Institute, Ala., "Success"

5A-H1451 "Field of Cotton in Bloom"		
6A-H4447 "Black and White Symphony"	5 - 6	6 - 8
SK3918 "Roll That Cotton Bale..."	1 - 2	2 - 3
P19674 "A Typical Scene, Memphis"		
P38841 "Cotton Pickin' Time"		

P77844 "W. C. Handy Statue, Memphis"
BLUMENTHAL & BECKER, Murfreesboro
08 724 "Turkey Killing at Murfreesboro"   15 - 18   18 - 22

BOOKER T. WASHINGTON *

Booker T. Washington was a graduate of Hampton Institute and also taught there. In 1881 he was chosen to head a Negro Normal School at Tuskegee, Alabama. Beginning from a small shanty having 40 students, he built the school into a famous institution with more than 100 buildings. By the time of his death in 1915 the Institute owned 2000 acres, had an endowment of almost $2,000,000, and an annual budget of $290,000. There were 197 faculty members and 1,357 Negro students. Tuskegee students, who were taught a number of trades and professions as well as academic subjects, proved to be hardworking, humble and courteous, and attained a high standing in the minds of whites in the area.

Washington's speech at the Cotton States and International Expo in Atlanta in 1895 gained him much acclaim and recognition as the leading Negro in the country. He believed in using humility, a slow and even approach, flattery, politeness and restraint to try to end racial discrimination. By taking this approach, he gained enthusiastic approval in the South as well as from the industrialists and politicians of the North. Many blacks, however, opposed him because they felt that he had not pushed hard enough for equality for them. His high standing earned him an invitation to dinner at the White House in 1901 with the newly elected Theodore Roosevelt.

He received one of the greatest honors ever bestowed on an American educator in 1912 by the National Medical Association which held their annual meeting at Tuskegee Institute. Souvenir postcards of him being honored were designed by A. P. Bedou of New Orleans and published by The Albertype Co. Copies of these cards are extremely rare and command very high prices. Bedou later republished the cards using his own byline.

* *Excerpts from "A History of Negro Americans," 3rd Edition, by John Hope Franklin, and published by Alfred A. Knopf, New York.*

BOSSELMAN, A. C.
3221 "Street View in Old Jacksonville"   6 - 8   8 - 10
9632 "Christ Church, Alexandria"
BOURNE, A. E., Hamilton (B&W)
26 "Three Native Minstrels, Bermuda"   12 - 15   15 - 18

A. P. Bedou, 120
"Dorothy Hall (Girls' Trades Building)" -- Tuskegee Institute, Ala.

A. P. Bedou, 122
"Rockefeller Hall" -- Tuskegee Institute, Ala.

BROADMAN SUPPLIES

"Sunday School" (C)

42 "Come Back Next Sunday"	8 - 10	10 - 12
43 "Come Join us in Sunday School"	8 - 10	10 - 12
75 "Our Adult VBS Group Needs You"		
"Our Adult VBS Group Needs You"		

Blumenthal & Becker, Murfreesboro
08 724, "Turkey Killing at Murfreesboro"

CARNISH, GEORGE B., 1907 (B&W)		
"I'se Glad I Came to Oklahoma"	10 - 12	12 - 15
CAROLINA CARD CO., Asheville, N.C.		
10724 "In A Southern Hemp Field"	8 - 10	10 - 12
CHAMBERLIN, J. N.		
R-24116 "Orange Grove, Miami, Florida"	6 - 8	8 - 10
Same, White Border	4 - 5	5 - 6
R-69013 "Home Sweet Home Down in Dixie"	8 - 10	10 - 12
CHARLESTON POST CARD CO. (C)		
75382B "Old Slave Mart Museum"	1 - 2	2 - 3
28083D "Basketmakers, Charleston"		
33112-D "Flower Woman, Charleston"		
CHESSLER CO., Baltimore		
"From Field to Wagon"	6 - 8	8 - 10
"Mammy"	12 - 15	15 - 18
CHILTON PRINTING CO.		
"Chipping the Pine Tree..."	6 - 8	8 - 10
CHISHOLM BROS., 1903		
"Coon Trees a Possum"	12 - 15	15 - 18
CHRISTIAN STANDARD		
Children Singing from Song Books	12 - 15	15 - 18
CLARK, P. S. (American News Co.)		
"Colored Baptist Church, Darien, Ga."	12 - 15	15 - 18
CLINE CO., W. M. (C) (R.P.)		
1-K-12 "Molasses Time in Dixie" Men	5 - 6	6 - 8
1-K-13 "Molasses Time in Dixie" Women		

Chessler Co.
"Mammy"

George Cornish
"I'se Glad I Came to Oklahoma"

1-K-30 "Southern Cotton"
1-K-45 "Yum! Yum!"
Chromes

39249 "Uncle Alfred"	1 - 2	2 - 3
66131 "Uncle Remus Museum"		
M40181 "Old Black Joe" Diorama		
ICS-2980-8 "Florida State Song" Diorama		
ICS-2979-9 "Kentucky State Song"		
ICS-17524-7 "The Glendy Burk"		
ICS-45981-7 "Old Folks at Home"		

COASTAL NEWS CO.

"Old Slave Huts at Hermitage"	4 - 5	5 - 6

COCHRANE CO. (L)

12822 "Waiting For the Circus"	5 - 6	6 - 9
R26708 "Grape Fruit, a Heavy Load..."	4 - 5	5 - 6
A31607 "Alligator Bait"	5 - 6	6 - 9
A-64394 "Study in Black and White..."		

COLEM

"Patsy and Jim Crow"	12 - 15	15 - 18

COLLOTYPE CO.

Stratford Hall, Va. Views (B&W)	4 - 5	5 - 6
"Uncle Wess" at Stratford Hall (B&W)	6 - 8	8 - 10
"Harvesting Sugar Cane in Louisiana" (B&W)	8 - 10	10 - 12

School for Colored People, New Albany, Ind.

Connor Drugs
"School for Colored People," New Albany, Ind.

Coral-Lee, 1984 -- Aviator Lt. Robert Goodman
(with Pres. Reagan, Jesse Jackson, etc.) after Release from Syria

COLOURPICTURE (TICHNOR BROS.) (L)

16245 "I Love That Cotton"   3 - 4   4 - 6
16246 "Dem Cotton Boll"
16247 "The Payoff"
16509 "Greetings From Alabama" (L.L.)

16551 "Greetings From Louisiana" (L.L.)
16555 "Greetings From Georgia" (L.L.)
16557 "Greetings From N. Carolina" (L.L.)

A96506 "Signal Taxi - Fairmont Hotel..."	4 - 6	6 - 8

Chromes

P22324 "Monument - Booker T. Washington..."	2 - 3	3 - 4
P23898 "Greetings From Down South..."	3 - 4	4 - 6

P23899 "Gathering Pine Gum or Resin..."
P3331 "Friends"
P13830 "Ole King Cotton"
P31756 "Cotton Picking Hands"

COLUMBUS NEWS
Ft. Benning, Ga.

"Training at Grenade Throwing"	12 - 15	15 - 18

Infantry OCS, "Classroom..."

COOK, L. L., Milwaukee, 1938
Real Photos

"Mass Production-Way down South in Fla."	15 - 18	18 - 22

CORAL-LEE (C)

4-1977 "Diana Ross"	3 - 4	4 - 5

9-1977 "Stevie Wonder"
20 "Diahann Carroll"

46-1979 "Muhammed Ali"	5 - 8	8 - 10
63 "Pres. Reagan and Willie Mays"	6 - 8	8 - 10
86 "Reagan and 'Sugar Ray' Leonard/Wife"	6 - 8	8 - 10
91 "Reagan w/Count Basie, others"	3 - 4	4 - 6
95 "N. Reagan visits St. Anne's Hospital"	1 - 2	2 - 3
114 "Queen Eliz./Philip and Dionne Warwick"	3 - 4	4 - 5

100/40 "J. Carter w/Dizzy Gillespie"

100/47 "J. Carter w/Harlem Globe Trotters"	4 - 5	5 - 8

SC17829 "Dave Winfield"
138 "Lt. Robert Goodman's Release"

CROAKER, C. L., 1906

"For Doodness Sate!" Black/White Babies	10 - 12	12 - 15
CROCKER, H. S. (C)	1 - 2	2 - 3

DETROIT PUBLISHING CO.

The Detroit Publishing Co. began producing postcards in the Private Mailing Card Era of 1898 to 1901, and continued until they were forced out of business during the Great Depression and were liquidated in 1932.   They produced outstanding U.S. views using their patented "Phostint" printing process. Basically, it was the photochrome process using stone plates, which was first developed in Switzerland.

Up to seven different etchings, one for each color, were made on the stone plates and resulted in beautiful and vivid lifelike color images. The plates, however, were prone to wear out after a few thousand cards were printed and more plates had to be etched to finish a large run. Many of the most popular earlier Detroit cards have several printings of the same image for this reason. For instance, the image for No. 5743 of "Bashful Billy and Sister" is first seen on a slim card; then a divided back card with a regular frame; one with an oval frame; and a divided back card with regular frame. All have the same number. The image is also seen later on a white border card and finally on a linen. The latter two, however, do not have the Detroit copyright since they were issued by other publishers after Detroit went out of business in 1932.

The Detroit company, although their printing process was one of the best, owed much of their success to pioneer photographer William Henry Jackson. Mr. Jackson brought 40,000 of his original photograph glass negatives with him when he became general manager of the firm. They were used continuously throughout the life of the company, greatly contributing to its success in the postcard industry.

Jackson's great wealth of photos had been taken from all over the United States, and helped record vital pages of history during the early years of the new century. Among these photos were hundreds taken in the South of blacks in their own surroundings showing meaningful real-life images...the way they lived, the hard and difficult way they had to work, and the fun they had when they were at play.

DETROIT PUBLISHING CO.

522 "Watermelon Jake"	20 - 25	25 - 28
5522 "Watermelon Jake" (PMC)		
5607 "Uncle Tom"		
5607 Also "My Old Cabin Home"		
5738 "Six Little Pickaninnies"		
5739 "Playing Hookey"		
5740 "Just As Easy"		
5741 "Mammy's Pet"		
5742 "A Treed Coon"	25 - 28	28 - 32
5743 "Bashful Billie and Sister"	20 - 25	25 - 28
One In Oval Frame and One with No Frame		
5744 "Waiting for the Circus"	18 - 22	22 - 25
5745 "Two Jacks and a Jill"		

5746 "Looking for a Job"		
5755 "A Native Sugar Mill"		
5809 "Little Eb Snow"	18 - 22	22 - 25
5971 "Seeing the Circus Go By"	15 - 18	18 - 22
6074 "Living Easy" (Copyright at Left)		
6074 Copyright on Bottom of Card		
6075 "Seben Come Leben"	22 - 25	25 - 28
6076 "Bliss"		
6330 "A Horseless Carriage"		
6397 "8 Little Pickaninnies Kneeling..."		
6470 "A Happy Family"		
6471 "Sunny Jim"		
6472 "Mammy Going to Market"	18 - 22	22 - 25
6819 "Cluster of Oranges"	12 - 15	15 - 18
6820 "First Hoeing of Cotton"		
6821 "Envy"	18 - 22	22 - 25
6822 "Anticipation"		
6823 "A Native Product"		
6824 "Coons in a Cotton Shed"	22 - 25	25 - 28
6825 "Brotherly Love"		
6826 "Discovered"		
6827 "A Study in Black and White"		
6831 "River Steamboat"	8 - 10	10 - 12
6832 "Train Load of Cotton for Export"		
6833 "Cotton Landing"		
6834 "I Wasn't Born to Labor"	18 - 22	22 - 25
6937 "Cotton Blossoms"	12 - 15	15 - 18
7018 "Happy Mitchell and His Boys"	18 - 22	22 - 25
7034 "Picking Cotton"	10 - 12	12 - 15
7035 "Cotton Compress"		
7036 "River Packet, Load of Cotton"		
7110 "Magnolia Blossoms"		
7438 "The Old Fisherman"	18 - 22	22 - 25
7439 "A Watermelon Feast"		
8210 "A Dark Corner of Watermelons"		
8211 "An Unbiased Opinion"		
8212 "Uncle Rastus"		
8282 "Loading Cotton into a Steamer"	8 - 10	10 - 12
8283 "Just Kids"	18 - 22	22 - 25
8394 "Polly in the Peanut Patch"		
8615 "Mammy"	18 - 22	22 - 25
9067 "Cattle for Export"	8 - 10	10 - 12
9068 "Cotton for Export"		
9139 "Unbleached Americans"	18 - 22	22 - 25
9161 "An Oyster Lugger"	8 - 10	10 - 12

Detroit Pub., 6755 (PMC)
"A Native Sugar Mill"

Detroit Pub., 10542 (DB)
"Out on Bale"

Detroit Pub., 5743
"Bashful Billy and Sister"

Detroit Pub., 5741 (DB)
"Mammy's Pet"

Detroit Pub., 5809 (UndB)
"Little Ed Snow"

Detroit Pub., 7438 (UndB)
"The Old Fisherman"

Detroit Pub., 10544 (UndB)
"Possum For Yo' Breakfast"

Detroit Pub., 8211 (DB)
"An Unbiased Opinion"

9162 "Weighing Cotton"		
9173 "Nigger in the Woodpile"	22 - 25	25 - 28
9195 "Buzzard Pete"	15 - 18	18 - 22
9220 "Golferino" (Golf)	30 - 35	35 - 40
9221 "Black Tee" (Golf)		
9234 "Free Lunch in the Jungle"	18 - 22	22 - 25
9540 "Bags of Rice Ready for Market"	8 - 10	10 - 12
9541 "The Water Carrier"	15 - 18	18 - 22
9542 "A Logging Train"	8 - 10	10 - 12
9543 "Tidings of Comfort and Joy"	15 - 18	18 - 22
9544 "Southern Lumber District"	8 - 10	10 - 12
9545 "A Southern Logging Camp"		
9547 "Picking Cotton"	12 - 15	15 - 18
10199 "Geo. Washington Lincoln Napoleon..."	22 - 25	25 - 28
10340 "A Typical Cotton Cart"	12 - 15	15 - 18
10342 "Unloading Bananas, Mobile"	10 - 12	12 - 14
10416 "A Mississippi River Packet"	8 - 10	10 - 12
10417 "River Landing"		
10418 "Coaling River Packet While Underway"		
10463 "Melon-Choly Days"	22 - 25	25 - 28
10542 "Out on Bale"		
10543 "Old Black Joe"		
10544 "Possum For Yo' Breakfast"		
10545 "Whoa Mule"		
10546 "Discovered"		
10547 "Picking in the Land of King Cotton"	10 - 12	12 - 15
10548 "A Basket Weaver in the Land..."	15 - 18	18 - 22
10549 "Products in the Land..."		
10551 "Saving Sinners"	22 - 25	25 - 28
10552 "A Southern Baptism"		
11276 "A Typical Cotton Picker"	12 - 15	15 - 18
11277 "Cotton Pickers in the Field"		
11278 "A Cotton Shed and Compress"	8 - 10	10 - 12
11279 "Drying Peaches at Isleta"		
11517 "A Bovinemobile"	18 - 22	22 - 25
12737 "Waiting for the Sunday Boat"		
13022 "Uncle Abe's Cabin"		
13023 "Stripping Tobacco"	8 - 10	10 - 12
13308 "Loading Cotton"	12 - 15	15 - 18
15661 "Uncle Tom's Cabin"	18 - 22	22 - 25
70738 "Products of Sun Kissed Southland"		
70739 "Pickaninnies"		
70910 "Aunt Charlotte"		

Detroit Pub., 5742 (PMC)
"A Treed Coon"

Detroit Pub., 9220 (DB)
"Golferino"

Detroit Pub., 8212 (UndB)
"Uncle Rastus"

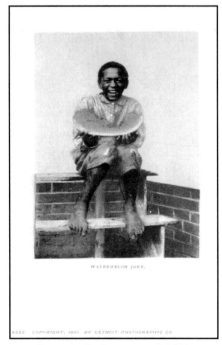

Detroit Pub., 5522 (PMC)
"Watermelon Jake"

DEXTER PRESS (L) (C)

120 Man and 3 Children in Cottonfield	3 - 4	4 - 5
65810 "Old Black Joe"	3 - 5	5 - 8
5S-29023B "Greetings From Dixieland"	1 - 2	2 - 3
5S-20925B "Cotton Pickin' Time in Dixie"		
S-5703B "Friends"		
DR-65865 "Every Yankee Tourist..."		
DR-66168 "Greetings From Down South..."		
DR-97258-B "Hot Dog!"		
DR-99087-B "Greetings from Middle Ga."		
32090B "Slave Market, Louisville, Ga."		
38552 "Lorraine Motel - Memphis, Tenn."		
Where M. L. King was killed.	3 - 4	4 - 6
Printed for many jobbers.		

Silvercraft

4415 "The Pilgrim Health and Life Ins. Co."	15 - 18	18 - 25

DIXIE NEWS CO. (B&W)

GP-3 Picking Cotton Near Blacksburg, S.C.	3 - 4	4 - 5

DOTHAN CIGAR & CANDY (C. Teich) (L)

2B409-N "Greetings from Ozark, Al." (L.L.)	2 - 3	3 - 4

DREW, H. & W.B. CO. (L)

"Florida Artistic Series"

A-21329 "His Last Prayer"	4 - 6	6 - 9
A-21445 "Scene in Grape Fruit Orchard..."		
A-21451 "Florida Products..."		
A-21458 "Study in Black and White..."		
A-21460 "A Coon Sextette"		
A-31120 "Florida Cantaloupes"		
A-31135 "Gathering Turtle Eggs..."		
A-31688 "Seven Up, Florida"		
R-38265 "A Lively Bunch of Alligators..."		
1517-12823 "A Still Hunt"	2 - 3	3 - 4

DUKANE PRESS (C)

D01281 "On Campus, Florida A & M..."	2 - 3	3 - 4
R26989 "Voodoo Priestess"	3 - 4	4 - 5

DUNBAR (B&W)

"Our Flag"	8 - 10	10 - 12

DUNN, O. G., New Bern

"Negro Baptism in Neuse River"	15 - 18	18 - 22
"A Cotton Pickin"	10 - 12	12 - 15
"Satisfied With Life"		

DUVALL NEWS (L)

S.A. 115 "Hold That Gator"	2 - 3	3 - 4

See Curt Teich Captions and Numbers.

Dexter "Silvercraft" -- Comptroller's Office
"The Pilgrim Health and Life Ins. Co., Augusta, Georgia"

EAS (E. A. Schwerdtfeger & Co.) Real Photos

576 Well Dressed Young Man Smoking	15 - 20	20 - 25
E.B. & E.	4 - 6	6 - 8

EASTERN PHOTO LITHO CO. (L)

4408 "Sponge Exchange, Tarpon Springs"	2 - 3	3 - 4
E-6680 "You All Come Down Honey..."	3 - 4	4 - 5

EDDY, E. C. (See Albertype and Real Photos)

EKSTONE, C. (1907)

"All to the Mustard" (Unidentified Male)	8 - 10	10 - 12

EHLER'S NEWS CO. (L)

5B-H1048 "Colored Masonic Temple, Birmingham, Alabama"	12 - 15	15 - 18

ELLCO (C)

5046 "The best of Friends Must Part"	2 - 3	3 - 4

ELMIRA TOBACCO CO. (C)

25533 "Mural" in Mark Twain Hotel, Elmira	2 - 3	3 - 4

ENVIRONMENTAL PHOTOART (C)

CP439 "G. Washington Carver Museum..."	2 - 3	3 - 4
CP440 "B. T. Washington Monument..."		

EPSTEIN, CHARLES, CO. (C)

74541 "A Cotton Field Near Houston"	1 - 2	2 - 3

EXPRESS PUB. CO. (C)

P77171 "Just a Closer Walk With Thee"	1 - 2	2 - 3
P319945 "New Orleans Jazz Band"		
X115685 "Armstrong Park, New Orleans"		

Florida Artistic, 917
"Enjoying Florida Watermelons"

A. P. Gerlach, Miami -- Series 14
"A busy day in Darky Town" -- Miami, Fla.

FARRIS COLOR VISIONS (C)
    Morris-Brown College
        2USGA45-B thru 51-B   1 - 2   2 - 3
FLORIDA ARTISTIC SERIES
        182 "Sugar Cane Grinders"   12 - 15   15 - 18
        883 "Sumatra Tobacco Plantation"
        905 "Tonsorial Artist"   15 - 18   18 - 22

EAS (E. A. Schwerdtfeger & Co.), Real Photo, 576
"In this hat the girls all love me, Think there's nobody above me."

George W. Harper, 26267
"Black Beauties" -- Bass Caught in Lake Parker, Lakeland, Fla.

915 "Aunt Venus, Hunting Florida Fleas"
917 "Enjoying Florida Melons"

1014 "Grape Fruit Groves"	10 - 12	12 - 15
1020 Fruit Pickers		
1024 "Grandma's Birthday Party"	15 - 18	18 - 22
A1338 "Up Against It"		
A1918 "At the Cabin Door"		
A13652 "Gator Bait"		
A31636 "Southern Negro Cabin"		
12829 "A Florida Boot Black"	18 - 22	22 - 26
13808 "Cutting Sugar Cane"	15 - 18	18 - 22
31620 "Music Hath Charm"		
66054 "Liza at the Tub"		

FLORIDA NATURAL COLOR (C)

FNC3067 "Famous Banana Market, Tampa..."	1 - 2	2 - 3
FNC5115 "The Southernmost Point..."		

FLORIDA NEWS CO. (C)

A-75667 "Honey Come on Down..."	1 - 2	2 - 3

FLORIDA P.C. CO. (L)

6A-H1418 "Waiting for a Bite in Florida"	4 - 6	6 - 8
6A-H2162 "Honey, Come on Down..."		

FLORIDA PREVUES - PC

15457 "Auction Time in Eastern Carolina"	2 - 3	3 - 4
S50846 "Tobacco Road..."		
S50861 "A Busy Day in a Cotton Field..."		
S50862 "Bales of Cotton Ready for..."		

FLORIDA SOUVENIR CO.

12824 "I Done Ketched 'Em, Florida"	15 - 18	18 - 22
12825 "Watermelon Time in Florida"		
12826 "Old Fashioned Southern Transit"		
12829 "A Florida Bootblack"	20 - 25	25 - 28
14610 "Dinner Time in Jungle of..."	15 - 18	18 - 22
14621 "Uncle Tom's Cabin"		
14824 "I Done Ketched 'Em, Florida"		
14825 "Watermelon Time in Florida"		
14826 "Old Fashioned Southern Transit..."		

Linens (Tichnor)

30186 "Oldest House in U.S."	2 - 3	3 - 4
60882 "The Old Market, St. Augustine"		
72471 "The Roundup at the World's..."		
72643 "Old City Gates, St. Augustine" (Kropp)		

Chromes (Tichnor)

K-15819 "The Old City Gate..."	1 - 2	2 - 3

FOSTER & REYNOLDS (L)

309 "Know Where to Go Fishin"	4 - 6	6 - 8

FROHMAN, L. H. (C)

No No. "Rev. W. Lawson and His Wife..."	2 - 3	3 - 4

GARDNER, H. F. (L)

C15062 "Paul Bascomb"	2 - 3	3 - 4

GARRISON COLOR CO. (C)

27782 "Old Market House, Fayetteville"	1 - 2	2 - 3
28261 "Greeting From Down South"		

GERLACH, A. P., Miami

Series 14 (B&W)

"A Busy Day in Darky Town, Miami, Fla."	12 - 15	15 - 18

GOODMAN (L) (Curt Teich)

A1343 "Weighing Cotton on Plantation"	3 - 4	4 - 5

GOWIN-COOK PRINTING CO. (L)

1173 "Rapid Transit in the South"	3 - 4	4 - 5

GRAY PHOTOGRAPHERS (C)

No No. ""Happy" at Harding Springs	2 - 3	3 - 4

GRAY & THOMPSON (C) (B&W)

GP1 "Picking Tobacco Near Halifax"	2 - 3	3 - 4
GP3 "Picking Cotton Near Edenton"		
GC-1C "Old Black Joe"		
GP-4C "Picking Cotton Near Perry, GA."		

GRAYCRAFT CARD CO. (L) (C)

Same as above

No No. "Cabin in a Cotton Field" (L)	3 - 5	5 - 6
GC-2C "Two Sunny Smiles" (C)		

Florida Artistic, 12829
"A Florida Bootblack"

Franz Huld (PMC)
Little Coons 3, "Shine Boss?"

GC-3C "Playing in the Cotton" (L)	3 - 5	5 - 6
GP-3 "Picking Cotton" (B&W)		
GROMBACH-FAISANS CO.		
Ser. 507 "Southern Coons, New Orleans"	10 - 12	12 - 15
Ser. 508 "Sleeping Darkey, New Orleans"		
GULF COAST CARD CO. (C. Teich) (L)		
8A-H1098 "Harvesting Florida's Orange..."	3 - 4	4 - 5
HAERTLEIN GRAPHICS (C)		
173340 "Milwaukee Boys Club"	1 - 2	2 - 3
HALLIS & CO.		
"Clipping Ostriches" (B&W)	6 - 8	8 - 10
HANNAU-ROBINSON (C)		
S-63366 "Viking Hotel & Motor Inn"	2 - 3	3 - 4
HARPER, GEORGE W.		
26267 "Black Beauties" Bass & Boys	15 - 18	18 - 22
HARRIS CO., W. J.		
Real Photos	10 - 12	12 - 15
Linens		
119839 "Slave Market and Old Cath..."	2 - 3	3 - 4
5A-HT22 "Old Slave Market, St. Augustine..."		
HARTMAN CARD CO. (L)		
E-6608 "You Can All Come Down..."	2 - 3	3 - 4

HEARST'S BOSTON SUN. AMER., 1908

No No. "Love Drop"   6 - 8   8 - 10

HERMITAGE ART CO. (Chester) (L)

No No. "Native Washer Woman"   2 - 3   3 - 4

HILBERT'S DRUG STORE (B&W)

B801 Home of *Emancipator*, the first
Abolitionist Newspaper, Jonesboro, TN   3 - 5   5 - 8

HORN'S PAVILION

Souvenir Post Card Co.

"A Flock of Blackbirds"   12 - 15   15 - 18

HOWARD SALES CO. (C) (Curteich)

3C-K27 "Rolling Chairs, Atlantic City"   2 - 3   3 - 4

HOWE, F. L. (UndB)

1283Y "Dis am Heben"   15 - 18   18 - 22

"A Regular Cut-up"

"Disturbing the Peace"

"Ole Mammy"

"Open and Above Board"

"Who's a Niggar?"   25 - 30   30 - 40

"You Should be Stocking Up..."   15 - 18   18 - 22

261 "Negro Hut in Georgia"

263 "Plowing in Georgia"

731-8 "I Want to Hear From You..."   3 - 4   4 - 7

HULD, FRANZ, N.Y.

"Darkey Series" (PMC)   25 - 30   30 - 40

1 Boy with Banjo

2 "Dere's No Lock on de Chicken..."

6 "Cake Walk"

"Little Coons" Series (PMC)   30 - 35   35 - 40

3 "Shine Boss?" Hand-Colored

4 "Watermelon Contest"

265 "Learning to Dance Early"

"Cake Walk (Negro Dance)" (PMC)

Elegantly Dressed Black Dancers (6)   30 - 35   35 - 40

"Cake Walk" Series 3, 1902 (8)

"Cake Walk (Negro Dance)" No. 1 through 8

"Correspondence Series 22"

"Welcome"   10 - 12   12 - 14

I. F. CO.

See Curt Teich

ILLUSTRATED POST CARD CO.

No No. "A Merry Christmas" (Emb.)   10 - 12   12 - 15

Series 78 (*) (**)

1 "A Dark Outlook" (UndB)   15 - 20   20 - 25

F. L. Howe, Atlanta
"Who's a Niggar?"

4 "Seven Little Pickaninnies" (UndB)	12 - 15	15 - 18
6 "One Jack and two black" (UndB)		
7 "Oh! dat ar watermellion" (UndB)	15 - 18	18 - 22
8 "A Horseless Carriage" (UndB)	12 - 15	15 - 18
9 "A Black Guard" (UndB)		
10 "A Quite Game" (UndB)		
15 "Who's a Nigger?" (UndB)	20 - 25	25 - 28
6-19 "An All-In-Gator Lunch in Fla."	15 - 18	18 - 22
5017 "Seven Little Pickaninnies" Same as 4	15 - 18	18 - 22
"A Dark Game" (B&W) (UndB)		
"Darkies" (B&W) (UndB)		
"The Schoolmaster" (UndB)	20 - 25	25 - 28
"Watermelon Jake"		
"Craps"		
8 "Florida Natives"	15 - 18	18 - 22
13 "Way Down South in Dixie"		

* For Silk Applique Clothing add $10.00.
** For Airbrushed Cards add $3.00.

Series 5

"You are Cordially Invited to Attend"	6 - 8	8 - 10

INTERNATIONAL P. C. CO.

1441 "Moving Cotton on the Levee..."	4 - 6	6 - 8

JORDAN, J. M.

26 "Cake Walk on the Pier"	12 - 14	14 - 18

KALTENBACH, JERRY L. (C)

5ED-433 "American Freedom Train, M.L.K."	3 - 5	5 - 8

Franz Huld (PMC)
"Cake Walk (Negro Dance)," No. 2

Franz Huld (PMC)
"Cake Walk (Negro Dance)," No. 6

KAUFMANN AND SONS (L)

A-75897 "Va. State School, Colored Deaf..."	15 - 18	18 - 22
R-30129 "Roasting Oysters, Cape Henry..."	2 - 3	3 - 4

KIRBY & CO. (L) (Curteich)

A-23582 "Colored Ind. School, Charleston"	15 - 18	18 - 22

KNAFFL & BROS., Knoxville
   1897-99 (B&W)

"A Bran New Coon in Town"	15 - 18	18 - 22
"Dead Game Sports"		
"Honey, Does yo' Lub yo' Man?"		
"Wake up and Join Us"		
"Chocolate Drops"		
"Us Fo' and No Mo"		
"Can I be yo' Mascot?"		
"Three Black Crows"		

   Copyright 1906

"A Job Lot"		
"Crying for You"		
"Wish you'd hush"		
The Wedding Series (B&W)	12 - 15	15 - 18
"Leave yo' Razor at de Door"		
"A Skin Game"		
Others		

KNOX, S. H. & CO.

Man in Donkey Cart	8 - 10	10 - 12
A-1772 "Fishing on the Wabash" (Curteich)	3 - 4	4 - 5

KOBER CO., PAUL (P.C.K.)

S-52 "Old Black Joe"	10 - 12	12 - 15
3813 "Waterproof Mose and His..."		
10922 "Their First Truck Garden"		

KOBERT COLOR PUBLISHERS

C24008 "J. Trammel, Cook for James Gang"	4 - 5	5 - 8

KOPPEL (C)

114849 "Martin Luther King Oil Painting"	4 - 6	6 - 8

KRESS, S. H.

"In the Good Old Summertime"	15 - 18	18 - 22
12102 "Boat Loaded With Cotton..."	2 - 3	3 - 5
12010 "A Typical Negro Home, Chattanooga"	3 - 5	5 - 7
A1350 "Southern Products..."		

KROPP, E. C., Milwaukee

"Black Ostrich Driver"	12 - 15	15 - 18
"Down in Sunny Dixie"		
"Negro Baptizing, Tennessee River"	15 - 18	18 - 22
"Delicious" (UndB)		
"Free Lunch in the Everglades"		
"Main Street, Kissimmee, Florida"	10 - 12	12 - 15
"Shack Near Bramwell, W.V." (UndB)		
"Street Scene, Albany, Ga." (UndB)		
4755 "Sunday Afternoon Down in Sunny..."	12 - 15	15 - 18

Illustrated P. C. Co., 78-5
"Two of a Kind"

E. C. Kropp, 4781 (L)
"Washington Lincoln ..."

Knaffl Brothers (Knoxville), 1898
"A Bran New Coon in Town."

Knaffl Brothers (Knoxville), 1906
"A Skin Game"

20309 "Anticipation"	10 - 12	12 - 15
452 "Three of a Kind"		
453 "Pickaninnies"	12 - 15	15 - 18
1170 "In the Cotton Fields"	8 - 10	10 - 12
1171 "Picking Cotton"		
1172 "Weighing Cotton"		
1174 "A Lot of Gay Cotton Pickers"		
1175 "Cotton Pickers Returning from..."		
1314 "Topsy, the Little Cotton Picker"		
1316 "Love in a Hut"		
1651 "In the Spring Run"		
1874 "Pulling Turpentine in the South" (UndB)		
1884 "Unloading Bananas" (UndB)		
2121 "Pulling Turpentine..." Same as 1874		
2978 " Southern Turpentine Still" (UndB)		
27487 Picking Cotton "Down in Sunny..."		
6743N "Drop In! A Hearty Welcome..."		

White Borders and Linens
"Natural Color" Numbers on Reverse

2675 "Strumming Away My Blues..."	3 - 5	5 - 7
2681 "Gathering Cotton"	2 - 3	3 - 5
2963 "Growing Pineapples, Florida"		
3763 "Cotton Pickers - Down South"		
4146N "Portrait of Uncle Alfred"		
4707 "Picking Cotton - Down South"	5 - 6	6 - 8

4707N Same		
4713 "Watermelon Jack"	6 - 8	8 - 10
4755 "Sunday Afternoon" Down...		
4755N "Happy Days - Down in Sunny..."		
4781 "Washington, Lincoln, Napoleon..."		
6023 "Man O' War, the Wonder Horse"	8 - 10	10 - 12
Also by **Kyle Co.**, Louisville	8 - 10	10 - 12
6116 "We's Waitin' Fo' You all Here..."	6 - 8	8 - 10
6116N Same		
6129 "Three Chocolate Drops..."		
6679 "Wide Open - A Hearty Welcome..."	5 - 6	6 - 8
6742 "Honey, Come on Down! We's..."		
6743 "Drop In! A Hearty Welcome..."		
7971 "Taking a Sunbath on a Lily Pad"		
7987N "I Heard a Good Story..."		
7996 "Two Jacks and a Jill" Down South		
8000 "Taking Life Easy"		
8000N "Taking Life Easy..."		
8014 "I'se Waitin' Fo' You Here..."		
8032 "Negro Baptism" Down South	8 - 10	10 - 12
8439 "A Coon in the Bananas in..."		
9456 "Transferring Bananas"	2 - 3	3 - 5
10401 "Happy Days" (Time Saver)		
12307 "Picking Cotton - Down in..."		
12307N "Cotton Fields, Near Raleigh"		
12398 "Two Staple Products - Down..."		
12430 "Gathering Rosin Gum"		
13637 "Roses are Red and Violets..."		
13788 "Music Hath Charm"		
13852N "Johnson's Colored Tourist Home..."	20 - 22	22 - 25
14519 "Honey, I's Waitin Fo You All..."	2 - 3	3 - 5
15130 "Honey, I's Waitin Fo You Down..."		
15564 "Having a Delightful Time..."		
17027 "A Joy Ride in Florida"		
17732 "Greetings From Mississippi"		
18677 "Realization"	6 - 8	8 - 10
18678 "Demoralization"		
18679 "Mastication"		
20309 "Anticipation"		
21216 "Honey We'se Waitin Fo'..."	5 - 6	6 - 8
22567 "Old Plantation Cabin - Down..."		
23795 "Pretty Soft Pickin's Down Here..."		
23795N Same		
23796 "Takin Life Easy Down South"		

24916 "A Row of Palms"	2 - 3	3 - 5
25084 "Br'er Johnsing Peaches..."		
25019 "Down in Sunny Dixie"		
25243 "Greetings from Down in Sunny Dixie"		
26047N "Br'er Johnsing Peaches..."		
26809 "Just a Small Family - Down in..."		
26809N "Just a Small Family - Down South"		
27487 Picking Cotton "Down in Sunny Dixie"		
28948 "Come to See Me - Down in Sunny..."		
30317 "Dixieland For Me - Down in Sunny..."		
32190 "On the Whole Army Life Agrees..."		

KYLE CO. (Kropp)

6023 Man O'War, "The Wonder Horse"	8 - 10	10 - 12

S. LANGSDORF & CO.

S. Langsdorf & Co.(or S.L. & Co.) published the embossed "Greetings From the Sunny South" Alligator Border cards, the most desired and most elusive series of all early African American related postcards. Many avid collectors have tried in vain to complete this beautiful 30-card series. Examples rarely come up for auction and dealers have few, if any, in their stocks...especially those in good condition.

Because of their quality and beauty, their popularity among collectors, their elusiveness, and the poor condition of those available on the market, values of the Alligator Border blacks have skyrocketed and will probably go even higher.

Langsdorf, S. & Co. (S. L. & Co.)

Alligator Borders
"Greetings From the Sunny South"

S631 "Tobacco Prizing, Florida"	80 - 90	90 - 100
S632 "Picking Cotton, Florida"		
S633 "Tobacco Ready for Cutting, Florida"		
S634 "Picking Tobacco, Florida"		
S635 "Tobacco Sale"		
S636 "Stemming Tobacco, Florida"		
S637 "Tobacco Seed Bed, Florida"		
S638 "The Smile That Wont...Florida"		
S639 "At Leisure, Florida"		
S640 "A Cotton Picker, Florida"		
S641 "A Typical Southern Negro, Florida"		
S642 "Old Uncle Joe, Florida"		
S643 "When Melon is Ripe, Florida"		

S644 "A Watermelon Feast, Florida"	80 - 90	90 - 100
S645 "Old Mammie, Florida"		
S646 "Musical Coons, Florida"		
S647 "Happy Coons"		
S648 "Negroes Carrying Freight, Florida"		
S649 "Come Seben Come Eleben, Florida		
S650 "Solid Comfort"		
S651 "Negroes Scrambling for Money"		
S652 "Horseless Carriage"		
S653 "Cotton Compress"		
S654 "In the Cotton Field"		
S655 "A Cotton Field at Picking Time"		
S656 "Transporting Cotton"		
S657 "Where the Cotton Blossoms Grow"		
S658 "Cotton Pickers"		
S659 "Weighing Cotton"		
S660 "The Latest Thing Out"		
Others		
S511 "Portion of Key West"	30 - 35	35 - 40
S549 "Hotel Ponce De Leon"		
S555 "Memorial Pres. Church, St. Aug..."		
S627 "Canary, Canary Date Palm, Fla."		
LAZARUS, J. (L)		
155631 "Harvesting Cranberries"	3 - 4	4 - 6
116602 "Harvesting Cranberries"		
LEE, JAMES, CO., 1907		
5629 "Charge of the Colored Troops"	18 - 22	22 - 25
LEIGHTON, HUGH C., Portland*		
A34 "Sunny South - A Coon Trees a..." *	20 - 25	25 - 30
L401 "A Coon Trees a Possum"	20 - 25	25 - 30
L410 "Aint Gwine to be None Left"	15 - 18	18 - 22
L426 "Dipping and Scraping Gum..."	12 - 15	15 - 18
590 "A Southern Ox Cart" *	18 - 22	22 - 25
723 "Home Sweet Home Down South"		
1815 "Seben Leben"		
1820 "Thanksgiving Morning in South" *		
1928 "Turpentine Still" *	12 - 15	15 - 18
1957 "A Brown Study" *	18 - 22	22 - 25
1958 "Anticipated"		
1959 "Deliberation" *		
1961 "A Native Product"		
1962 "A Bunch of Coons" *		
1963 "Three of a Kind" *		
1964 "Aint Going to be no Rine"		

S. Langsdorf & Company, S645
"Old Mammie"

S. Langsdorf & Company, S638
"The Smile that Won't Come ..."

S. Langsdorf & Company, S651
"Negroes Scrambling for Money"

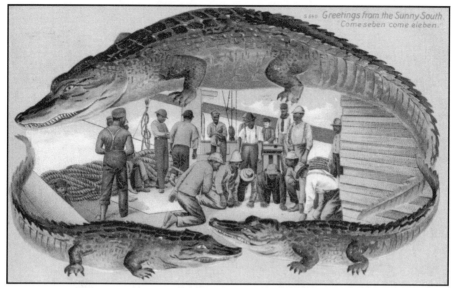

S. Langsdorf & Company, S649
"Come seben come eleben."

S. Langsdorf & Company, S646
"Musical Coons"

1976 "Race Suicide Down South" *	18 - 22	22 - 25
1979 "Typical Souther Negro Home" *		
2125 "Alligator Bait"		
2158 "A Florida Barber Shop"	18 - 22	22 - 25
2392 "On the Fence" *		
6748 Monday in "Coon Town"		

Dixie W. Leach
"Gaud Bless You, Honey"

6747 "Enough For One"	18 - 22	22 - 25
26359 "Female Vegetable Vendors"		
26360 "Male Vegetable Vendor..."		
26975 "White Man's Bar"		
29101 "P. Beach, Fla. Styx Negro Quarter"		
* Undivided Backs		

LEIGHTON & VALENTINE CO., N.Y.

208520 "Expecting a Bite"	10 - 12	12 - 15
2391 "Picking Cotton"	8 - 10	10 - 12
203559 "Seven Up"	12 - 15	15 - 18
203567 "A Southern Piccanniny"	15 - 18	18 - 22

LIEB PHOTO CO. (C) (Sepia)

107th Colored Infantry, Ft. Corcoran	2 - 3	3 - 5
Harriet Tubman		
Frederick Douglas		
M. L. King on Steps of Lincoln Memorial		
Mary McLead Bethune		
Civil War Sailor, USS New Hampshire		
Booker T. Washington		
M. L. King, 1963 March on Washington		

LIPSCHER SPECIALTY CO., New Orleans

13803 "Cutting Sugar Cane"	12 - 15	15 - 18
A1354 "Sugar Cane Plantation"		
A5867 "Hauling Cotton La. Sugar..."		
A1918 "At the Old Cabin Door"		
A1919 "Sunday Morning in Dixieland"		

Hugh C. Leighton, 1976 (UndB)
"Race suicide down South."

A1922 "In The Land of King Cotton"	12 - 15	15 - 18
A1927 "Down Where the Cotton Blossom..."		
LIVINGSTON, ARTHUR		
PMC Mule Race "Here Comes De Winner"	22 - 25	25 - 28
Series 26 (B&W)		
"Way Down South in Dixie"	15 - 18	18 - 22
"Blacks Dancing the Cake Walk"		
"Couples Cake Walk"		
"The Cake Walk on the Pier"		
219 "Oh! dem Watermillions"		
502 "A Shack," Southern Pines, N.C.		
686 "Old Aunt Liz, I Reckon..."	8 - 10	10 - 12
LOUISVILLE DRUG CO. (L)		
"Old Slave Market, Louisville"	2 - 3	3 - 4
358 "Old Slave Market" (B&W)	1 - 2	2 - 3
M.S.P., 1906		
X28 "I've Got a Feeling For You"	8 - 10	10 - 12
X29 "Life Aint Worth Living..."		
MᴀᴄFARLANE, W. G., Toronto		
911 "Picking Cotton, Louisiana"	12 - 15	15 - 18
912 "Roustabouts on the Levee"		
"Perfect Harmony"		
L114 "Food for Contention" (B&W)	10 - 12	12 - 14
I00323 "Hush Yo Fussin"		
I00326 "Warranted All Wool"		
100330 "A Drop in Cotton"		

Hugh C. Leighton, 6747 (DB)
"Enough for One."

Hugh C. Leighton, 34 (DB)
"... A Coon trees a Possum"

Hugh C. Leighton, 2158 (DB)
"A Florida Barber Shop"

Hugh C. Leighton, 26359 (DB)
"Female Vegetable Vendors ..."

Hugh C. Leighton, 26360 (DB)
"Male Vegetable Vendor ..."

Hugh C. Leighton, 1962 (UndB)
"A Bunch of Coons"

Hugh C. Leighton, 29101
"Palm Beach, Fla., Glimpse of Styx Negro Quarters ..."

MARK, M.
"Florida Artistic Series"

181 "Grandma's Birthday Party..."	12 - 15	15 - 18
203 "Native Coin Divers in Florida"	8 - 10	10 - 12
817 "Ostrich Race at Ostrich Farm"	12 - 15	15 - 18
872 "It's A Shame to Take the Money"		
914 "Chipping the Pine Tree"		

Linens

12822 "Waiting for the Circus"	4 - 6	6 - 8
1517-12823 "A Still Hunt..."		
12824 "I Done Ketched 'Em, Florida"		
12825 "Water Melon Time in Florida"		
14621 "Uncle Tom's Cabin, A Relic..."		

MASON, C. B. (L)

36 "Slave Block, Old Hotel R..., New Orleans"	2 - 3	3 - 4
101 "Louisiana Products, Sugar/Cotton"		

MATTOX, T. J. CO.

19 "Colored Baptizing in Flint River"	10 - 12	12 - 15

MAYROSE (L) (B&W)

"Scene Around Dillon, S.C."	3 - 4	4 - 5
"Scene Around Fitzgerald, Georgia"		

MERCHANTS ADVERTISING AGENCY

"Francis Marion Hotel, Charleston"	3 - 4	4 - 5

MERROW, E. L. (B/W or Hand-Tinted) (UndB)
"Greetings From Pinehurst, N.C."

"Cotton Pickers"	8 - 10	10 - 12
"Cotton Picking"		
"The Charcoal Burner, Pinehurst"		
METROCRAFT (W.B. and L)		
"A Turpentine Dipper at Work, Florida"	5 - 6	6 - 8
23470 "Listening to the Master's Word"	3 - 5	5 - 8
43052 "My Old Kentucky Home"		
43074 "A Darkey's Prayer"		
46735 "The Old Folks at Home"		
No No. "Papayas Growing ... St. Petersburg"		
MILLER, JOHN (UndB) (B&W)	6 - 8	8 - 10
"Nigger Heben" and "Cottonfield"	3 - 5	5 - 8
MILLER, WALTER H. (Koppell)		
2341 "Randolph Coach, Williamsburg"	1 - 2	2 - 3
118865 "Berkeley Plantation, Va."		
McCOY PRINTING CO., Moncton, B.C.		
242 "Roustabouts at Play" (B&W) (UndB)	8 - 10	10 - 12
McCRORY PRINTING (L)		
"Picking Cotton, Memphis"	2 - 3	3 - 4
McINTYRE DRY GOODS, INC., 1899		
"Camp Followers, Camp Marion, S.C."	8 - 10	10 - 12
MITCHELL, EDWARD H. (DB)		
1831 "Dixie Blossoms"	10 - 12	12 - 15
1832 "Happy go Lucky Coons"	12 - 15	15 - 18
MITLOCK & SONS (C) (Plastichrome)		
"Sammy Davis, Jr. performing on stage"	5 - 8	8 - 9
MOHAWK PRODUCTS CO. (L)		
"Dobbs House, Muni. Airport, Atlanta"	2 - 3	3 - 4
MONTGOMERY NEWS CO. (C)		
Tuskegee Institute Views	1 - 2	2 - 3
MOSS PHOTO SERVICE (B&W)		
"Lionel Hampton"	3 - 4	4 - 5
MULTIPLE PHOTO (C)		
"Hank Aaron's 715th Home Run"	8 - 10	10 - 12
MWM COLOR LITHO (L)	3 - 4	4 - 5
NATIONAL ART VIEWS (UndB) (B&W)*		
394 "A lonely Meal"	12 - 15	15 - 18
396 "Proof of Patience"		
747 "The Basket Maker"		
1078 "Singing For Grub"*	15 - 18	18 - 22
* Add $4 for Hand-Colored		
NATIONAL PC SERVICE (C)		
"America's Oldest House"	2 - 3	3 - 4
"Doing the Charleston Down South"		

Metrocraft, 46735 (L)
"The Old Folks at Home"

National Art Views (UndB) 1078,
"Singing for Grub"

"Harvest Time in the Southland"
"Peanut Harvest Time..."
"Peanut Pickers"
"Time Out for Watermelon"
"Turpentining in Dixie"

NEW ORLEANS NEWS
    6089/18 "Weighing Cotton - New Orleans"   3 - 4   4 - 6
    6094/24 "Old Plantation Cabin - Louisiana"

OHIO HISTORICAL SOCIETY
    38970 "Rev. John R. Kitchen, Abolitionist"   4 - 5   5 - 8

PCK (Paul C. Kober)
    2576 "The Three Graces"   15 - 18   18 - 22
    2582 "A Study in Black and White"
    2583 "Envy"
    2585 "Pals"
    3813 "Waterproof Mose and His..." (B&W)   10 - 12   12 - 15
    10922 "Their First Truck Garden"

PALMETTO NEWS CO. (L)
    2B-H1118 "Greetings from Laurens, S.C."   2 - 3   3 - 5

PFEIFFER, T. C., Daytona, FL.
    "Sinkie Sue and Lefty Lou"   10 - 12   12 - 15
    "George Washington Booker Brown, Florida"

PHOTO ARTS, Winnsboro, S.C. (C)

10860-B "Dancing the Charleston..."	2 - 3	3 - 4
31407-B "Cotton Picking Down South"		
38962-B "Marksmanship Coaching, P. Island"	3 - 5	5 - 8
85009 "Typical Carolina Scene"	2 - 3	3 - 4

PORTER, S.S.

170 "The Fortune Teller"	5 - 7	7 - 9

POSTCARD EXCHANGE (L)

8367 "At De Ole Cabin Door..." Alabama	3 - 4	4 - 6

RADIO CORP. OF AMERICA

"Duke Ellington"	20 - 30	30 - 40
"Lena Horne"		
"Fats Waller"		

REIDER, M.

175 "Dinner in Sight"	8 - 10	10 - 12
3229 "A Vineyard in California," Fresno	4 - 6	6 - 8
200 "A Vineyard in California" Red Grapes		

ROBERTS, MIKE (C)

SC1124 "Picking Cotton in Texas"	2 - 3	3 - 4
6454G "Feathery Cotton Can Be..."	1 - 2	2 - 3
C10668G Field of Cotton Pickers		
C15048 "State Senator Leroy Johnson"	3 - 4	4 - 5
C15054 "Johnny Mathis"	6 - 8	8 - 10
C15059 "Part of Nat King Cole's Family"	6 - 8	8 - 10
C15063 "Jesse Owens"	3 - 5	5 - 8
SC13361 "Twilight at Coco Palms"		
SC15265 "Pearl Bailey" Nugget	12 - 15	15 - 18
C15067 "Marching to Washington"	3 - 5	5 - 8
SC15803 "Juliet Prouse-Nipsey Russell" Nugget	6 - 8	8 - 10
C16222 "Eli Whitney" 1765-1825	1 - 2	2 - 3

ROBERTSON, GRANT L. (Crocker) (C)

GLR-445 "Preservation Hall-Kid Thomas Band"	3 - 4	4 - 5

ROBINSON, CHAS. D. (C)

34967 "The John A. Andrew Mem. Hosp."	2 - 3	3 - 4

ROCKY MOUNTAIN NEWS AGENCY

3B-H1096 "Greetings from Wilson, N.C." (L.L.)	3 - 4	4 - 5

ROGERS, H. TAYLOR (PMC)

"Greetings from Asheville, N.C." (B&W)		
"Thanksgiving in the South"	15 - 18	18 - 22

ROMBACK & GROENE, Cincinnati

711 "Who's a Democrat?" (B&W)	25 - 30	30 - 35

ROSIN & CO.

628 "My Old Cabin Home"	10 - 12	12 - 15
629 "Grandma's Birthday"		

630 "Coon Hunting in the South"	15 - 18	18 - 22
1273 "Rufus in De Cottonfield"		

ROST, H.A. 1900 (PMC) (B&W)

702 "Sunny South Shiner"	25 - 28	28 - 32
"Perfect Bliss"		

ROTARY PHOTO, E. C.

XS 246 Three Smiling Black Boys (R.P.)	15 - 18	18 - 22

ROTOGRAPH CO.

The Rotograph Company of New York was established in 1904 and began producing high-quality postcards at that time. They were a successor to National Art Views Co. Most earlier issues were printed on bromide photographic papers, and were probably printed by the Rotary Photographic Co.

Most of their images of blacks, however, were on regular card stock in black and white (mostly "A" numbers) in the beginning, and later the same issues were factory hand-colored. "C" numbers are the chromo, or color, cards. This group, both color, black and white, and hand-colored, was believed to have been printed by the famous Stengel and Co. of Dresden, Germany.

The majority of black cards have undivided backs, which means they were issued by Rotograph between 1904 and 1908, and could possibly be a carry-over from the National Art View Co. files. The Rotograph Co., for unknown reasons, left the postcard business in 1912.

ROTOGRAPH CO., N.Y. *
  Note: Rotograph has both Color and
  Black and White of the same cards.

B701 "Booker T. Washington" (R.P.) (UndB)	100 - 110	120 - 125
333Q "Pickaninnies, Florida" *	15 - 18	18 - 22
3341 "When You Make Dem Goo Goo..." *		
334H "Wheel Chairs at Palm B." (B&W) *		
3675 "Confed. Monument, Aiken, S.C." *	8 - 10	10 - 12
G15520 "Coons in a Rubber Tree" *	18 - 22	22 - 25
G15522 "Well I Should Smile" *	18 - 22	22 - 25
G15525 "A Quintette" *	18 - 22	22 - 25
G15526 "Sho, Done Got Him" *	18 - 22	22 - 25
G15527 "Oh! Dat Ar Watermelon"	18 - 22	22 - 25
A15521 "Pickaninnies, Florida" (B&W)		
G15533 "De Old Folks at Home"		

H. A. Rost, 1900 (PMC)
702, "Sunny South Shiner"

Rotograph Co., B701 (R.P.)
"Booker T. Washington"

G15555 "A Southern Express" *	10 - 12	12 - 15
A15555 "A Southern Express" (B&W) *	10 - 12	12 - 15
A15557 "Black Diamond Express" (B&W) *		
G15560 "On the Old Plantation...Florida" *		
G15561 "Uncle Tom's Cabin" *	18 - 22	22 - 25
G15564 "Southern Horseless Carriage" *		
G15565 "A Typical Coon" *		
A15653 "Gigging from a Steamer..." (B&W) *	10 - 12	12 - 15
64588 "Faithful Lewis of 70 years..."		

* Undivided Backs

ST. LOUIS GREETING CARDS (Kropp)

49830 "Homer G. Phillips Hospital"	15 - 18	18 - 22

ST. PETERSBURG NEWS
Metrocraft

43229 "Florida Natives, Pickaninnies..."	5 - 6	6 - 8

S.I.P.

Real Photo Series 144	15 - 18	18 - 22
Cake Walk		

SCENIC SOUTH
Mike Roberts (C)

C10668 Field Full of Cotton Pickers	2 - 3	3 - 4

XS 246

We mean to have no end of mirth,
Of frolic feast and folly,
We wish our friends, for all we're worth,
May Christmas-time be jolly !

ROTARY PHOTO. EC

Rotary Photo, XS 246
"We mean to have no end of mirth, Of frolic feast and folly ..."

C12377 "Greetings From Alabama"		
S15029-1 "Cooking a Pot of Burgoo Stew"		
C15044 "Dr. Martin Luther King"	3 - 5	5 - 8
C15056 "Joe Louis & Dr. M. L. King"	8 - 10	10 - 12
C15056 Same as above, but no Mike R. Logo		
C15639 "George Washington Carver"	3 - 4	4 - 6
C15640 "Booker T. Washington"		
C31567 "Carter & Carver"		
C15066 "Hank and Tommy Aaron"	5 - 7	7 - 9
S18509-8 "Watermelon Time Down South"	3 - 4	4 - 5
ICS-18509-9 Same as above		
S-18923-2 "Cotton Picking in the South"	2 - 3	3 - 4
S-19021-2 "Sorghum Syrup"		
S-26041-5 "A Scene in the Old South..."		
52/28261 "Greetings From Down South..."		
S-46156-1 "Uncle Remus"		

Koppell (C)

24323 "A Skin Game"	2 - 3	3 - 4
43238 "Wagonload Cotton & Pickaninnies"		
74310 "Beautiful Negro Homes"		
78498 "Alabama A&M College"		
78499 "Alabama A&M College"		
78512 "Alabama A&M College"		

Rotograph Co., G-15653 (UndB)
"Gigging from a Steamer"

Rotograph Co., G-15563 (UndB)
"In Nigger Heben"

Rotograph Co., A-15521 (UndB)
"Pickaninnies, Florida"

Rotograph Co., A-15557 (UndB)
"Black Diamond Express"

91117 "Booker T. Washington Monument"
91140 "Alabama A&M College"
93678 "Oakwood College, Huntsville"
93684 "Oakwood College, Huntsville"
96813 "Arlington Ante-Bellum Home..."
K-100893 "Atlanta-Resting Place M.L.K."
K-100894 "Rev. M.L.K. Born in House"
113237 "Morehouse College, Atlanta"
113349 "Ebenezer Baptist Church, Atlanta"
123797 "Memorial to Martin L. King"
113348 "National Office S.C.L.C., Atlanta"
91141 "Alabama A&M College, Normal"
93680 "Oakwood College, Huntsville"

SCHWABE PUBLISHING CO. (DB)

131B Scene Showing the Development of the "Industrial South" Sleeping Workers	12 - 15	15 - 18
149B "No such thing as Race Suicide" (C)		
123134 "An Old Horseless Carriage..."	1 - 2	2 - 3

SCORDILL, J. (L)

6264 "The Old Slave Block, St. Louis Hotel"	2 - 3	3 - 4

Schwabe Publishing Co. (DB)
"No Such Thing as Race Suicide in the Sunny South"

A-1922 "In the Land of King Cotton"
A-1927 "Down Where the Cotton Blossom..."
A-11129 "Old Creole Praline Candy Woman"
No No. "Typical Negro Homestead"

SELIGE, ADOLPH , St. Louis

5664 "Natural Sugar Cane Grinders"	15 - 18	18 - 22
No No. "A Good Time Coming"	15 - 18	18 - 22
5672 "Cotton Planting"		
2 "Southern Horseless Carriage"	12 - 15	15 - 18
3 "Negro Log Cabin"		
5 "Old Mammie"	18 - 22	22 - 25
6 "Uncle Tom"		
8 "Down in Dixie"		
9 "Happy Coons"		
10 "Musical Coons"		
12 "Negro Idlers"		
14 "Roustabouts at Play"		
15 "Negroes Carrying Freight"	12 - 15	15 - 18
16 "Negro Roustabouts" (UndB)	15 - 18	18 - 22
17 "Negro River Type"	12 - 15	15 - 18
18 "Negroes Scrambling for Money" (UndB)		
20 "Weighing Cotton"	8 - 10	10 - 12
26 "Cotton Compress"		
27 "Cotton Gin"	12 - 15	15 - 18
28 "A Good Days Work"	8 - 10	10 - 12
29 "A Day in the Cotton Field"		
30 "A Cotton Picker"		

Rudolph, Oxford, Pa. (UndB)
"Billy"

Adolph Selige, 5666 (UndB)
"Negro Home in a Freight Car"

243 "Roustabouts at Leisure" (B&W)	10 - 12	12 - 15
245 "The Old Mammie" (B&W)		
A1338 "Up Against It"		
"Rastus and Ned"	18 - 22	22 - 25
A1339 "Sho' do Love Melons"	18 - 22	22 - 25
A1356 "Down in Dixie"	18 - 22	22 - 25
"Ain't Gwine to be none left"	18 - 22	22 - 25
"Gathering Watermelons"	12 - 15	15 - 18
A1620 "I Have Hoed in Fields of Cotton"		
1886 "There is Money in Cotton" (B&W) *		
1889 "Down Where the Cotton..." (B&W) *		
2704 Blacks in Butterfly Wing Views		
"Souvenir of the South" (UndB) (B&W)	22 - 25	25 - 28
5662 "Turpentine Still, Georgia"	12 - 15	15 - 18
5663 "Gathering Fuel and Southern Prod."	12 - 15	15 - 18
5664 "Natural Sugar Cane Grinders..."	15 - 18	18 - 22
5666 "Negro Home in a Freight Car"	18 - 22	22 - 25
5668 "A Dark Outlook"	15 - 18	18 - 22
5672 Lady with Ox-drawn Plow		
5673 "Plowing"	10 - 12	12 - 15
5674 "I have hoyed the fields of cotton"		
6216 Weighing a Cotton Bale *		

Adolph Selige, 2704 (UndB)
"Souvenir of the South"

* Undivided Back

SIEBERT NEWS AGENCY (Colorama)		
C-13523 "Cotton Pickin' Time in Ark..."	1 - 2	2 - 3
SIMMONS DISTR. CO. (L)		
"Sitting Soft in Dixieland"	3 - 4	4 - 6
SOUTHCREST PRODUCTS (C) (Roberts)		
B6679 "Double View M. L. King"	3 - 5	5 - 7
B6680 "M. L. King Gravesite"		
SOUTHERN POST CARD CO. (C)		
4ED-38 "Charlie Pride"	5 - 7	7 - 9
P305593 "Old Slave Mart, Charleston"	1 - 2	2 - 3
SOUVENIR POSTCARD CO.		
No No. "Have You Seen the Klansman..."	22 - 25	25 - 28
No No. Close-up of Lady w/Feather in Hat	10 - 12	12 - 15
3029 "An Old Virginia Scene"	6 - 8	8 - 10
11118-1 "Down in Possum Country"	12 - 15	15 - 18
11118-5 "Roll Call"	12 - 15	15 - 18
13926 "An Old Basket Maker..."	10 - 12	12 - 15
13929 "Just in from the Field"	12 - 15	15 - 18
16800 "A Disagreement" (B&W)	8 - 10	10 - 12
16801 "Shrimp Vendor" (B&W)	10 - 12	12 - 15
16804 "Nut Cake Vendor" (B&W)		
16806 "Rag Pickers" (B&W)		
16809 "Labor Day" (B&W)		
16810 "Taking Their Sun Bath" (B&W)		
16812 "Whoa Mule" (B&W)		

16813 "Liza at the Tub" (B&W)
16815 "Roll Call" Eleven Kids (B&W)
SPELLMAN COLLEGE (L)

S25128 "Rockefeller Hall, Spellman College"	10 - 12	12 - 15

SUM HO BUN LEE (C) (B&W)

No No. Dr. M. L. King - "I Have a Dream"	4 - 5	5 - 7

T. C. CO.

Black Patriotics	35 - 40	40 - 45

T. P. & CO.

166 "Happy & Contented"	12 - 15	15 - 18
796 "You All Looks Good to Me"	10 - 12	12 - 15
Series 57 Two Boys Fishing	10 - 12	12 - 15

Series 226

"No Sir! You Don't Ketch Me..."	12 - 15	15 - 18

Series 836

1 "Old Swimming Hole"	8 - 10	10 - 12

7 "Southern Transportation"
8 "Cotton Pickers at Work"
14 "A Colored Church"
15 "Taking Cotton to the Gin"

Series 944

"Dates May Grow on Trees..."	6 - 8	8 - 10
202364 "Southern Transportation"		
202237 "Old Uncle Rastus"	10 - 12	12 - 15

TR CO.

"The Latest Thing in Hats"	12 - 15	15 - 18

TALBOT-ENO

C-7 "We Suah Am Winners at..."	6 - 8	8 - 10

TANNER SOUVENIR CO.

154 "Harvesting the Gubers, Southern Pines"	12 - 15	15 - 18

CURT TEICH CO.

The Curt Teich Co. of Chicago, founded in 1898, was one of the largest printers and publishers in the United States, and one of the most prolific publishers of African American postcards. Most other early postcard publishers sent their work to Germany. However, Curt Teich printed all their cards in their big Chicago plant. When the postcard era began, Teich perfected the color process by importing the skilled printing technicians from Germany, therefore becoming the leader in the U.S. field.

Their photographers roamed the rural areas of the southern states. They covered Alabama, Florida, Georgia, North Carolina, South

Carolina, Louisiana, Mississippi, Tennessee, and Virginia, gleaning terrific images of life as it was being lived by blacks around the turn of the century and up to the beginning of the depression years of the 1930's.

As can be noted on many black images, life was difficult and work methods of all types were primitive and without automation. In most instances, however, the people were depicted as contented and happy at work and play.

Curt Teich cards were issued by thousands of local distributors, drug stores and book stores, so it is important to know their numbering system for identification purposes. It would be impossible to list all these distributors and their numbers; therefore, we have tried to list, in most instances, the Curt Teich number which usually is shown on the reverse side of each card (some are even listed in stamp box). These numbers are normally shown in addition to the distributor's number on the front. Later linen issues also showed a small Curt Teich number on the front as well.

Undivided back cards of 1901-1907 usually have the C.T. Monogram on the back left bottom, and the image covers the entire card. Beginning with the "C.T. American Art" imprint on divided backs, there is either no number or the number is preceded by an "A." This is true on divided-backs, white borders and a number of the earliest linens. However, the C.T imprint was moved to a very small round circle in the "Post Card" imprint, also on the address side.

There were five different printing processes during this time, and all numbers have the "A" prefix. They include:

C.T. American Art - Full four-color process from black and white photo, some with linen finish.
C.T. Blue Sky - Black and white with colored blue sky.
C.T. Photo Cote - Black and white with glossy coating.
C.T. Bluestone - Black and white with blue tone over entire card.
C.T. Photo Finish - Same as Photo Cote but without gloss.

In 1929, they began a consecutive numbering system starting with 1-29. This system proved to be impractical because of the high numbers of cards produced and was discarded the following year. Beginning in 1930, letters listed before the manufacturing number indicate the decade in which the cards were issued. A - 1930's; B - 1940's; C - 1950's; D - 1960's and E - 1970's. Example: 6A at the beginning of a number means that the card was printed in 1936. Most early cards from 1900 though the 1920's (including many of the white borders) have no numbering system.

The second letter, or third digit in the number, denotes the type of process used:

H = C.T. Art Colortone - Started 1930, five-color process, linens. Made from black and white photos.

H = C.T. Colorit - Same as Art Colortone but cards have deckle edge.

P = C.T. Photochrom - Four-color process from black & white photos.

K = CURTEICHCOLOR - 1949, four-color process from color transparencies and plastic coated.

D = C.T. Photo Varicolor and C.T. Photo Platine. Varicolor uses black and white photo on cream color stock in blackish green with orange tint. Platine is the same except it does not have the orange tint.

Example: Card No. 4A-H1245 - The "A" = 1930 decade; the 4 = 1934; the H = C.T. Art Colortone; and 1245 = card number. Therefore, the card was printed in 1934 by Art Colortone process; the number of the card is 1245; when found in the listing the caption is "Working Hard for Family Dinner." The value in very good condition is $4 to $5, and $5 to $8 in excellent condition.

Curt Teich reproduced many of their best original divided-back early postcard images as "White Borders," from the 1915-1930 era; reprinted them as "early Linens," of 1930-1935; then again during the "Linen era" of 1935-1960; and continued with the Chrome Era which overlapped the years of 1939 and up to the 1970's.

TEICH, CURT, Chicago or **C.T.**

No No.		
"A Busy Day in the Cotton Field"	12 - 15	15 - 18
"A Happy Fiddler From Dixieland"	18 - 22	22 - 25
"A Horseless Carriage"		
"Music Hath Charm in Dixie Land"		
"A Southern Express"		
"A Southern Negro Cabin"		
"At the Old Cabin Door"		
"A Watermelon Feast"		

"Aunt Venus Hunting Florida Fleas"		
"The Blackville Serenade"		
"Cotton Ginning Day"	12 - 15	15 - 18
"Cotton Pickers at Work"		
"Dipping and Scraping Pine Trees..."		
"Down Where the Cotton Blossoms Grow"	15 - 18	18 - 22
"Drying Cotton"	12 - 15	15 - 18
"Enjoying Florida Melons"	18 - 22	22 - 25
"Free Lunch in the Everglades"		
"Fruit Pickers"	12 - 15	15 - 18
Girl stands in folds of U.S. Flag	30 - 35	35 - 38
"Grandma's Birthday Party"	15 - 18	18 - 22
"Grape Fruit Groves"	12 - 15	15 - 18
"Negro Baptism in Dixieland"	15 - 18	18 - 22
"Picking Cotton"		
"Plantation Life in Dixieland"	15 - 18	18 - 22
"Plowing With Ox on Old Plantation"		
"Rastus and Ned"	18 - 22	22 - 25
"Romeo and Juliet in Cotton Field"	15 - 18	18 - 22
"Sho' do Love Melons"		
"Solid Comfort"	15 - 18	18 - 22
"Southern Products"		
"Southern Products, Water Melons..."		
"Sugar Cane Grinders"		
"Thanksgiving Morning in the South"	18 - 22	22 - 25
"Tonsorial Artist"		
"Turkey Looks Good to Mammy"		
"Up Against it" Boy - Watermelon	15 - 18	18 - 22
"Waiting for the Parade"		
"Weighing Cotton"	12 - 15	15 - 18
"Uncle Tom"		

Note: Some listed below having same captions are reprints of above, usually White Borders.

28 "Uncle Tom"	15 - 18	18 - 22
50 "Getting Ready for a Feast"		
A-1338 "Up Against It"		
A-1342 "Dipping and Scraping Rosin..."	10 - 12	12 - 15
A-1343 "Weighing Cotton on the Plantation"		
A-1346 "The Overland Express"		
A-1347 "Plowing with Ox on Old Plantation"		
A-1354 "Sugar Cane Plantation, N. Orleans"		
A-1355 "Mischief Brewing"	15 - 18	18 - 22
A-1356 "Down in Dixie"		
A-1620 "I Have Hoed in Fields of Cotton"	10 - 12	12 - 15

Curt Teich, Chicago, 31600 (DB)
"Stripes but no Stars"
"Chain Gang at Dinner in Dixie Land."

Curt Teich, 5A-H732 (L)
"A Cranberry Scooper and ..."

Curt Teich, A-18104 (DB)
"Southern Products"

Curt Teich, A-31862 (DB)
"A Water Melon Feast."

A-1914 "Rastus and Ned"	15 - 18	18 - 22
A-1918 "At the Cabin Door"		
A-1921 "My Heart Turned Back to Dixie"	10 - 12	12 - 15
A-1923 "Cotton Pickers"		
A-1923 Same, "Cotton Pickers near Atlanta"	8 - 10	10 - 12
A-1923 "Cotton Pickers" without city	8 - 10	10 - 12
A-1924 "Picking Cotton"		
A-1946 "The Overland Oxpress"	12 - 15	15 - 18
A-11111 "Loading Cotton"	8 - 10	10 - 12
A-11726 "Fla. Prod., Pickaninnies & Aligat..."	15 - 18	18 - 22
A-13085 "Auto Race Course, Savannah, 1910"	10 - 12	12 - 15
A-13652 "Gator Bait"	18 - 22	22 - 25
A-13261 "Cotton Ginning Day"		
A-15386 "A Round Dozen"		
A-18104 "Southern Products"		
A-18105 "Cotton Harvest"		
A-21329 "His Last Prayer"		
A-21458 "A Study in Black & White"	15 - 18	18 - 22
A-24063 "Watching the Circus Go By"		
A-25647 "Sho Do Love Melons"		
A-30653 "Picking Cotton"		
A-31098 "Solid Comfort in Tropical Florida"	8 - 10	10 - 12
A-31434 "Drap Dat Chicken"	15 - 18	18 - 22
A-31435 "The Blackville Serenade"		
A-31587 "Uncle Tom's Cabin in Dixie Land"		
A-31588 "Bales of Cotton Ready for..."	8 - 10	10 - 12
A-31589 "A Southern Express"		
A-31591 "A Coontown Troubadour in..."	15 - 18	18 - 22
A-31592 "Aunt Venus Hunting in Dixieland"		
A-31596 "Next" in Dixie Land.		
A-31598 "Stripes But No Stars" Convicts	60 - 70	70 - 80
A-31600 "Stripes But No Stars" Dinner Time		
A-31601 "Weighing Cotton"	8 - 10	10 - 12
A-31603 "A Happy Fiddler from Dixieland"	15 - 18	18 - 22
A-31605 "Plantation Life in Dixieland"	12 - 15	15 - 18
A-31607 "Alligator Bait"	15 - 18	18 - 22
A-31611 "Dark Angels"		
A-31612 "Have a Drink Sir"		
A-31613 "Getting Ready for a Feast"		
A-31616 "A Southern Basket Maker"		
A-31617 "Dinner Time in Dixie Land"		
A-31620 "Music Hath Charm"		
A-31626 "Rural Transportation in the South"		
A-31627 "A Horseless Carriage"		

54. A Happy Fiddler from Dixie Land.

89. Drap dat Chicken.

Curt Teich, A-31603 (DB)
"A Happy Fiddler from Dixie..."

Curt Teich, A-31434 (DB)
"Drap dat Chicken"

Sho' do Love Melons.

Curt Teich, No No. (UndB)
"Sho' do Love Melons."

Curt Teich, A-31634 (DB)
"A Southern Delight, Chicken ..."

Curt Teich, 4A-H1243 (L)
"Yes Suh! Some Punkins ..."

Curt Teich, A-1946 (DB)
"The Overland Oxpress"

Curt Teich, A-31598 (DB) "Stripes But No Stars"
Convicts Marching to Work. "The Good Road Makers in Dixie Land."

Curt Teich, 17811-C (L)
"Nine Coons, Count 'em, in Dixie Land"

A-31630 "Cotton Blossoms"	15 - 18	18 - 22
A-31632 "Sunday Morning in Dixieland"		
A-31633 "Hauling Cotton to Market"	8 - 10	10 - 12
A-31634 "A Sou. Delight, Chicken/Possum"	18 - 22	22 - 25
A-31636 "Southern Negro Cabin"		

A-31637 "Weighing Cotton"	6 - 8	8 - 10
A-31639 "Mississippi River Packet-Cotton"	8 - 10	10 - 12
A-31648 "Wash Day in Dixieland"	12 - 15	15 - 18
A-31649 "Music Hath Charm in Dixieland"		
A-31651 "Sweet Contentment at Old Cabin..."	15 - 18	18 - 22
A-31652 "Seben Come Eleben"		
A-31654 "A Negro Home"	15 - 18	18 - 22
A-31655 "Going to Market in Dixieland"		
A-31659 "Turkey Looks Good to Mammy"		
A-31663 "At the Old Cabin Door"		
A-31664 "Sweet Contentment"		
A-31665 "My Old Log Cabin"		
A-31668 "A Southern Ox Team"	8 - 10	10 - 12
A-31669 "Cotton Ginning Day"		
A-31670 "Transportation of Cotton By Road"	8 - 10	10 - 12
A-31672 "Cotton Pickers Homeward Bound"		
A-31673 "Ox Team in Dixie"		
A-31675 "Three of a Kind"	15 - 18	18 - 22
A-31674 "Southern Products, Watermelons"		
A-31676 "Down in Dixie" Boys Wrestle		
"Razorbacks and Pickaninnies"	15 - 18	18 - 22
A-31679 "Solid Comfort"	15 - 18	18 - 22
A-31680 "Uncle Tom"		
A-31681 "Gathering Watermelons"	10 - 12	12 - 15
A-31682 "A Watermelon Feast"	15 - 18	18 - 22
A-31684 "My Heart Turned Back to Dixie"		
A-31685 "A Busy Day in Cotton Field"	8 - 10	10 - 12
A-31686 "Down Where to Cotton Blossoms..."		
A-31688 "Seven Up"	15 - 18	18 - 22
A-31689 "Thanksgiving Morning in..."		
A-31690 "Cotton Yards, Cotton Ready..."	8 - 10	10 - 12
A-31691 "On the Fence"	15 - 18	18 - 22
A-31692 "A Southern Barbecue"		
A-31694 "Cotton Harvest"	8 - 10	10 - 12
A-31696 "Scene at Cotton Gin"		
A-31697 "A Coon Sextette"	15 - 18	18 - 22
A-31698 "Cotton Pickers at Work..."	8 - 10	10 - 12
A-31699 "The Old Oaken Bucket in..."		
A-33328 "Picking Cotton"	8 - 10	10 - 12
A-63648 "Alligator Bait"	15 - 18	18 - 22
A-63649 "Southern Products"	18 - 22	22 - 25
A-63650 "Seven Up"	15 - 18	18 - 22
A-69213 "Alligator Bait"		
A-69377 "Uncle Tom's Cabin in Dixie Land"		

R-69210 "Alligator Bait"

41807-N "Greetings from Murfreesboro" — 6 - 8 — 8 - 10

"C. T. American Art" (DB and White Border)

29199 "Grand-Pap Embarrassed" — 5 - 7 — 7 - 10

60676 "A Coon Trees a Possum in Dixieland"

63649 "Southern Products"

63029 "Among the Orange Groves in Fla."

63650 "Seven Up in Dixieland"

93844 "Honey, I's Gwine to get you a..."

94218 "Fishing is great sport in Florida"

99706 "Three of a Kind"

104820 "Wash Day" in Dixie — 5 - 7 — 7 - 10

105350 "De Cabin Home" In Dixieland"

12851-C "The Darkey Preacher" — 5 - 7 — 7 - 10

21051 "Dipping and Scraping Pine..."

C-12822 "Waiting for the Circus in Dixieland"

OA3174 "Southern Products" "Time Saver" — 3 - 5 — 5 - 7

"C.T. Art-Colortone" (H = Linens)

OB-H35 "Sportsman in Dixieland" — 4 - 5 — 5 - 6

OB-H36 "Dixie Express" — 6 - 8 — 8 - 10

OB-H39 "Am Happy and Sitting Soft"

OB-H788 "A Darkey's Prayer" — 4 - 5 — 5 - 8

OC-H249 "Tobaccoland Smile"

OC-H250 "Tobacco is placed in Curing Barns..."

1B-H893 "Suga' Cane Sho' Am Good..." — 4 - 5 — 5 - 8

2B-H72 "Kitchen of Governor's Palace..."

2B-H643 "Honey Come on Down..."

3B-H1096 "Greetings From Wilson, N.C."

3C-H785 "Diorama of Stephen Foster..."

4A-H1244 "Picking Cotton in Sunny South"

4A-H1245 "Working Hard for Family Dinner"

4C-H75 "Old Slave Market, St. Augustine" — 2 - 3 — 3 - 4

5A-H545 "George Mason"

5A-H722 "Old Slave Market, St. Augustine" — 2 - 3 — 3 - 4

5A-H732 "A Cranberry Scooper..." — 4 - 6 — 6 - 8

5A-H1555 "Write Me, I'm on the Move" — 2 - 3 — 3 - 4

5A-H1305 "Yas Suh, Of Course, I'se..."

5B-H1048 "Colored Masonic Temple, Bg'ham" — 12 - 15 — 15 - 18

6A-H443 "Uncle Tom" — 6 - 8 — 8 - 10

6A-H444 "Solid Comfort"

6A-H445

6A-H446 "Aunt Venus Hunting..."

6A-H447

6A-H448 "Listening to the Master's Word"

Curt Teich, A-31697 (DB)
"A Coon Sextette"

Curt Teich, 104819 (DB)
"Hunting in Dixieland"

6A-H449 "Mammy Chloe"
Same Image and Caption as "Happy South
   Scenes" and Series No. S-314   5 - 6   6 - 9
6A-H450 "Give Us De Rine?..."
6A-H451 "Getting Ready for a Feast"
6A-H452 "Seben Come Eleben"

6A-H453 "Watermelon Feast"
6A-H454
6A-H455 "The Blackville Serenade"
6A-H456 "Dinnertime"
6A-H457
6A-H458 "A Lasses Party"
6A-H459 "Seven Up In Dixieland"
6A-H1418 "Waiting for a Bite in Florida"
6A-H1928 "My Heart Turned Back to Dixie"
6A-H1931 "Down Where the Cotton Blossoms..."
6A-H1932 "A Busy Day in the Cotton Field"
6A-H1932 Same, but with no borders.
6B-H1019 "All's Peaceful Along the Suwannee..."
6C-H30 "The Gallows, Old Jail, St. Augustine"   3 - 4   4 - 6
7A-H2601 "Which? ..."
7A-H2675 "Some Folks to Be Happy..."
7A-H2680 "Ah's About As Mad As..."
7A-H2681 "Ah Tries to be Puhlite an' Nice"
7A-H2993 "A Happy Pair in Dixieland"   3 - 5   5 - 8
7B-H264 Man Sleeping on Cotton
7B-H265 Four Blacks Picking Cotton
7B-H267 Wagon Loads of Cotton at Gin
7B-H268 Girl Sitting on Pile of Cotton
7B-H269 Girl Picking Cotton
7B-H272 Three Boys Bottle Feed Pigs   5 - 6   6 - 10
7B-H273 Boy/Girl Eating Watermelon
7B-H274 Four Boys Sit on Log
7B-H279 5 Women, 3 Boys in Front of Cabin
7B-H280 Boy Eating Strawberries"   5 - 6   6 - 8
7B-H1399 "Harvesting Sugar Cane in Florida"   3 - 5   5 - 8
7B-H1400 "Field Transportation in Florida"
* Many cards are overprinted with greetings
  from various cities.

CHROMES
"Curteichcolor" (Beginning 1949)
3CK-764 Three Men Load Barrels on Truck   2 - 3   3 - 4
3DK-851 "Uncle Remus Museum, Eatonton"
5C-K1354 "Way Down Upon the Suwanee.."
7CK-455 "Famous Dancing Waiter..."
8CK-3229 "Mechanical Cotton Picker"
8CK-3231 "Cotton Picking"
0DK2419 "According to Carver"   (3-D)   3 - 4   4 - 5

THOMAS, ROBERT (C)
  Plastichrome by Colourpicture
    P12106 "Rural Scene in Dixie"   2 - 3   3 - 5
    P12460 "Cotton Pickin' Time in South"
    P13002 "Collecting Pine Gum"
    P16338 "Way Down South in Dixie"

THOMPSON, C. H. 1909
    "Our Milk Man"   10 - 12   12 - 15

THOMPSON, W. R. & CO.
    640 "Street Scene - Colored Troops..."   8 - 10   10 - 12
    642 "Truck Maint., Colored Troops..."

THOMPSON COMMUNITY SERVICE (C)   1 - 2   2 - 3

THOMPSON & THOMPSON
    901 "Troubadours at Salisbury Beach"   5 - 6   6 - 8

TICHNOR BROS., Boston
    119728 "Weighing the Day's Picking..."   5 - 6   6 - 8
    129567 "Shipping Cotton...Galveston, Texas"
    (L) (C) "Lusterchrome"
    63027 "He'p Yo'se'f to Grapefruit"
    63029 "Among the Orange Groves in Florida"   4 - 5   5 - 7
    73897 "Cotton Blossoms in Dixieland"
    K-3155 "Harvesting Tobacco"   2 - 3   3 - 4
    K-4812 "Cotton Picking Time"
    K-7050 "Weighing Sacks of Cotton"
    K-9396 "Burley Tobacco Field"
    K-9435 "Nashua"   5 - 6   6 - 8

TOWN CRIER PUBLISHERS (C)
    137671 "Randolph Coach, Williamsburg"   1 - 2   2 - 3
    137695 "Gov. Palace Kitchen..."

TROUCHE, PAUL E. (C)
    "Cotton Field Near Eatonton, Georgia"   1 - 2   2 - 3

RAPHAEL TUCK & SONS

Raphael Tuck was an outstanding publisher and printer of post-cards. They were so good they were chosen to be "Art Publishers for the Kings and Queens of England." They took special pride in this title and their work was excellent during all of postcards' Golden Years. Much of their early printing was done in Germany by the Chromolithographic method of etching on stones. The beautiful colors and sharp features on these cards were greatly enhanced by their use of up to 10 to 12 stones per image.

The photographers from Tuck, as with Curt Teich and Detroit Publishing Co., invaded the Southern states for real-life pictures of blacks, some of which have become gems and highly collectible to hobbyists worldwide. A big plus for Tucks was their decision to publish cards in sets or series, usually six, but sometimes as many as 12 or more. This was a great marketing ploy as most collectors chose the whole set rather than just a single. Many of the series shown below have incomplete caption listings because they are very elusive, and many are believed to have been printed in small numbers.

Raphael Tuck's huge London factory was destroyed in World War II by German bombs. All their files, photos, cards, and records were turned to rubble. Their bad luck continued when their new factory in Northampton burned in 1954.

TUCK, RAPHAEL, London

"Old Uncle Elph, Salisbury"	18 - 22	22 - 25
Series 1092 "Dixieland"	15 - 18	18 - 22
Series 1098 "Dixieland" (12)	22 - 25	25 - 28
"Crap at Coonville"		
"De Lan' O'cotton"		
"De Ole Cabin Home"		
"Dis am de Wust Predicament ob Ma Life"		
"Give us de Rine"		
"Golly, Somebody's Comin"		
"The Mule Race at Coonville"		
"Old Mammy"		
"The Overland Express"		
"Picking Cotton"		
"We's in Heben"		
"Who's a Nigger?"		
Series 1298	12 - 15	15 - 18
"Friday will suit me very well"		
Series 2181 "The Sunny South" (6)	22 - 25	25 - 28
"Comrades"		
"Dinky & Titsy"		
"Melody"		
"Once Upon a Time"		
"Rapid Transit"		
"There's a New Coon in Town"		
Series 2362 "Plantation" (8)	18 - 22	22 - 25
"Dark Angels"		
"If Er Body Meets Er Body..."		
"Just in from the Field"		

R. Tuck, 2181, (The Sunny
South) "Melody"

R. Tuck, 2363 (Happy Darkies)
"A 'Spectable Cullud Pusson"

R. Tuck, 2421 (The Old Folks at
Home) "Four Score Years ..."

R. Tuck, 2181 (The Sunny South)
"Comrades"

"The Old Basket Maker"
"On the Old Plantation"
"So Near and Yet So Far"
"To De Wictor B'long de Spoils"
Series 2363 "Happy Darkies" (6)   22 - 25   25 - 28
  "A 'Spectable Cullud Pusson"
  "Dis Am Heben"
  "Golly, I'se Lucky"
  "Ise De Lucky Niggar"
  "Jes Nigger Luck"
  "The Man with the Spade"
Series 2368 "Happy Darkies" (6)   15 - 18   18 - 22
Series 2370 "In The Land of Cotton" (6)   12 - 15   15 - 18
  "Cotton Wharf"
  "On the Tombigbee River"
  "Rolling Cotton down the Bluff"
  "Unloading Cotton"
  "Way Down South in the Land..."
Series 2384 "Under Southern Skies" (6)   12 - 15   15 - 18
  "A Sugar Cane Mill"
  "Cutting Sugar Cane"
  "Down Upon the Mississippi"
  "Planting Sugar Cane"
  "Shipping Cotton"
  "Way Down Yonder in the Cornfield"
Series 2398 "Negro Melodies" (6)   15 - 18   18 - 22
  "Down in de Corn Field"
  "I'm Coming"
  "Old Black Joe"
  "Swanee River"
  "Swing Low Sweet Chariot"
Series 2421 "Old Folks at Home" (6)   18 - 22   22 - 25
  "At the Old Cabin Door"
  "At the Close of Day"
  "Aunt Ann and Uncle Nat"
  "By the Old Well"
  "Four Score Years and Ten"
  "In the Cotton Field"
Series 2524 "Scenes in Dixie" (6)   18 - 22   22 - 25
  "Colored Folks at Home"
  "Hunting Coons Skins"
  "Old Time Pine Log Hut"
  "Thanksgiving Morning in the South"
Series 2645 "Alligators"

R. Tuck, 6950 (In Dahomey)
"Full Dress"

R. Tuck, 2363 (Happy Darkies)
"The Man with the Spade"

"Look Pleasant"	12 - 15	15 - 18
Series 4400 "Way Down South" (6)	18 - 22	22 - 25
"Crap at Coonsville"		
"The Overland Express"		
"The Mule Race at Coonville"		
Series 4401 "Way Down South" (Darkies)	18 - 22	22 - 25
"Dis am de Wust Perdickermunt..."		
Series 5032	10 - 12	12 - 15
Black Groom and Ostrich		
Series 6909 "Negro Melodies"	10 - 12	12 - 15
"The Sun Shines..."		
"Way Down Upon De Swanee Ribber"		
Series 6950 "In Dahomey"		
"Full Dress"	12 - 15	15 - 18
Series 9050	10 - 12	12 - 15
"Down by the Riverside"		
Series 9227	12 - 15	15 - 18
"My Turn Next"		
"The Swimming Lesson"		
Series 9228	12 - 15	15 - 18
"In Polite Society"		
Series 9297 "Among the Darkies"	18 - 22	22 - 25

Series 9318	12 - 15	15 - 18
"After the Dip"		
Series 9457	15 - 18	18 - 22
Series 9899	12 - 15	15 - 18
"Worth a Paquin in Coonland"		

TUCKER, C. O., Boston
  692 "Boy - Shine em Up" (B&W)
  Shoe Shine Stand, Graigville, Ma."   15 - 20   20 - 25
  18388 Same as above   8 - 10   10 - 12

U. S. SOUVENIR P. C. CO.
  452 "A Pair of Suckers" 1905   12 - 15   15 - 18

UNION NEWS CO. (L)
  No No. "Natural Sugar Cane Grinding"   4 - 5   5 - 8
  OB-H36 "Dixie Express"
  6A-H1928 "My Heart Turned Back..."
  6A-H1929 "Drying Cotton"
Remaining are Curt Teich.
  106475 "At the Old Cabin Door"   4 - 5   5 - 8
  106478 "Seben Come Eleben"
  106479 "Negro Baptism in Dixie Land"   5 - 7   7 - 10
No. 1 Souvenir Album of the Sunny South"
  106473 "Seven Up"   4 - 5   5 - 8
  106474 "Aunt Venus Hunting in..."
  106475 "At the Old Cabin Door"

R. Tuck, 2362 (On the Old Plantation)
"To de Wictor B'long de Spoils"

R. Tuck, 2181 (The Sunny South)
"Rapid Transit"

106476 "Music Hath Charms in..."
106477 "A Water Melon Feast"
106478 "Seben Come Eleben" (above)
106479 "Negro Baptism in Dixieland" (above)
106481 "Sweet Contentment"
106482 "I'se Going Back to Dixie"
106477 "A Water Melon Feast"   4 - 5   5 - 8
V & O CHINESE GIFT SHOP (B&W)
"Diahann Carroll"   6 - 8   8 - 10
"Sidney Poitier"
VALENTINE'S (VALENTINE & SONS)
"Uncle Tom's Cabin" (UndB)
"Uncle Tom and Eva"   15 - 18   18 - 22
"The Death of Eva"
"Topsy and Miss Ophelia"
"Uncle Tom Bought by the Cruel Legree"
"The Death of Uncle Tom"
VALLEY VIEWS (Koppel)
151179 "John Henry, Negro Folk Hero"   4 - 5   5 - 6
VALENTINE & SONS
"Way Down South in Dixieland"   10 - 12   12 - 15
"Uncle Tom's Cabin"
"Topsy and Miss Ophelia"   12 - 15   15 - 18
W & G, Switzerland, 1986
Martin Luther King
"I Have A Dream"   5 - 6   6 - 8

WALERY, Paris

"The Florida Creoles Girls," Real Photo Types	30 - 35	35 - 40
Danse du Cakewalk		
"Miss Adams"		
"Miss Fitch"		
"Miss Hall"		
"Miss Hobson"		
"Miss Shippert"		

WESTERN NEWS CO.

169 "His First Offering"	5 - 6	6 - 8
171 "The Rivals"		

WESTERN PUB. & NOVELTY (L)

1B-H1015 "Home of Eddie 'Rochester'..."	4 - 5	5 - 6

WESTVILLE, Lumpkin, Georgia"

"Basket Making"	4 - 5	5 - 6
"Farmhouse Kitchen"		

WHEELOCK, C. E.

203 "Desolation"	4 - 5	5 - 6

WHITES (PCK)

11817 "A Southern Deserted Village..."	4 - 5	5 - 6
11527 "Columbus Ga. YMCA (Colored)"	12 - 15	15 - 18

WHITMAN'S PHOTOTYPE

"The Old Kitchen at Kenmore" (C)	3 - 4	4 - 5

WILES HOOD PHOTOGRAPHERS (Kropp)

4146N "Portrait of Uncle Alfred"	3 - 4	4 - 5

WOOLWORTH, F. W.

17806 "Possum and de Coon"	18 - 22	22 - 25
17811 "A Lucky Nigger"	15 - 18	18 - 22
"Picking Grape Fruit" (L)	3 - 4	4 - 6

WYCO COLOR PROD.

118420 "M.L.K., Am. War Museum..."	4 - 5	5 - 7

ZEMPE & DE PASS PUB.

"Cotton Fields, Camden, S.C."	2 - 3	3 - 4

ZIMMERMAN, H. G.

"Fishing is Great - Get Your Hook Out"	4 - 5	5 - 6

ANONYMOUS REAL LIFE

Pre-1920

2 "Sweet Contentment"	12 - 15	15 - 18
29 "A Day in the Cotton Field"	8 - 10	10 - 12
40 "Down Where Cotton Blossoms Grow"	12 - 15	15 - 18
52 "A Southern Delight-Chicken and Possum"		
53 "The Gamblers"		

C. O. Tucker, 692
"Ben (Shine-um-up)"

Valentine & Sons, No No.
"In the Cotton Field"

93 "Gathering Watermelons"
  "Gathering Kindling"
  "Reuben and Mary at the Seashore"
  "Seven Up, Florida" White Border
"Souvenir of New Orleans" (PMC) (B&W)   25 - 30   30 - 35
  "Southern Coons," New Orleans
  "No Place Like Home"
"Greetings from Charleston" (PMC)   25 - 30   30 - 35
  Old Man Carries Basket of Cotton
  "My Heart Turns Back to Dixie"
  Man with Beard
  "Gaud Bless You, Honey"
  Old Woman
"Greetings from Oklahoma"
  "Free Cotton and Free Wool" (B&W)   12 - 15   15 - 18
  Old Man, Woman and Child Pick Cotton
"Greetings From the Sunny South"
  "Aunt Nancy"   25 - 30   30 - 35
  Young Boy   25 - 30   30 - 35
  Old Man Carrying Cotton Basket   25 - 30   30 - 35
  "On The Plantation"   25 - 30   30 - 35
  "Your Dime Savings Bank"   25 - 30   30 - 35

Valentine & Sons (Uncle Tom's
Cabin) "Topsy and Miss Ophelia"

"Greetings from Charleston"
PMC, Anonymous

Photo by AZO
New Means of Transportation!

Anonymous

Photo by AZO
Sitting Pretty in the New Roadster

Real photo postcards are those taken with a camera and subsequently printed on photographic paper. Cards of this type have become extremely collectible, and tend to bring higher prices than colored or black and white images. The main reason for this is the limited supply and small numbers of an image that were actually printed. In some instances only one copy, or a few more to send to friends, was printed by the amateur photographer or studio ... and up to possibly 1000 or more of a train wreck or county fair by a commercial printer.

Early real photo cards have the distinction, at this time, of being both the most sought after and also those which have the highest values of any black-related cards. The primary reason for this, as mentioned above, is the very limited supply of cards printed of one image. Secondly, there are three major collecting fraternities who are in direct competition for them ... postcards, Black Memorabilia, and Photographica collectors. Added to these, of course, are collectors of various topicals such as sports, entertainment, and advertising.

With all these collectors vying for the best cards available, it is easy to understand why the values of these rarities have risen so dramatically. Results by the leading auction houses (listing located in Periodicals Section of the Appendix) over the past two years show a tremendous elevation in prices realized for better black-related real photo material. Among these are early issues of Jack Johnson in the $600-700 range; Josephine Baker - $125-175; hangings and lynchings - $600-800; convicts - $400-500; Ku Klux Klan - $200-500; and E. C. Eddy issues - $70-100. Since this material is so rare, and since there is so much demand for it, values should continue upward.

The values for secondary issues, which are usually pulled up by activity in rarer issues, have also been accelerating. Cards of entertainers, advertising issues, and various labor and school images are the leaders.

Real photo cards were in use as early as 1900 and were actually done using various papers and photographic processes, the names of which can be found in the stamp box area on the reverse. Among the most prominent were AZO (with 4 triangles pointing up, used from 1904-1918; 2 triangles up and 2 down, used from 1918-1930), CYKO, VELOX, KRUXO, ARGO, NOKO, PMO, ARTURA and VALTL which were used in the early years. Later users were AFGA, ANSCO, DOPS, EKC, EKO and KODAK (after 1950). Extreme care must be taken to assure that old photos have not been reproduced using newer processes. For instance, a card of boxer Jack Johnson who fought during the 1910 era would not have EKO or KODAK in the stamp box.

College Students at Storer College, 1911
Photo by AZO

Black Face Minstrel
Photo by VALTL

Golf Caddies, 1905
Photo by AZO

"Le Cake-Walk," French
S.I.P. 142 / 1

Lovely Little Lady
Photo by AZO

Cards listed in this section are used only as examples for values, and are assumed to be sharp, clear images. For instance, if a collector has an image of a golf caddy or caddies, similar to the photo and listed in the text at $60-70 and $70-80, he could assume that his card would have an equal value. Cards that are not clear and sharp and which are poorly printed would command a much lower price.

	VG	EX
AUTOMOBILES, WITH BLACKS		
1910 - 1925	25 - 30	30 - 40
Later Years	10 - 15	15 - 20
BABIES	15 - 18	18 - 22
Black Child with Santa Claus	80 - 90	90 - 100
BABY YEAR DATES	20 - 25	25 - 30
BAPTISING	60 - 70	70 - 80
BARBERS	50 - 60	60 - 70
BLACK-FACE PERFORMERS, ETC.	40 - 50	50 - 60
One-Man Band	50 - 60	60 - 70
Vaudeville Act		
Theater and Plays		
Al Jolson	90 - 100	100 - 120
BUSINESS, BLACK OWNERS	35 - 40	40 - 45

Tuskegee Students as Chefs and Waiters
O'Briens' Restaurant, Waverly, New York

Uncle Mark Thrash
Born near Richmond, Va. Dec. 25, 1820. Died Dec 17, 1943 at his residence in Chickamauga National Military Park only 8 days before his 123rd. birthday. He was married 5 times and the father of 29 children. Coat shown was presented to him by General Grant.

Uncle Mark Thrash
Lived 122 Years

A Sunday Pose
Anonymous

Watching the World Go By
Photo by AZO

A Handsome Couple
Anonymous

The Nanny
Anonymous

Out for a Lively Jaunt
Photo by AZO

Convicts, Lake City, Florida, 1911
Photo by AZO

Anglo-American Exposition
"Altogether."
The Famous Piccaninny Band

Writer States that She and Her
Husband are Honeymooning at
Niagara Falls. Photo by AZO.

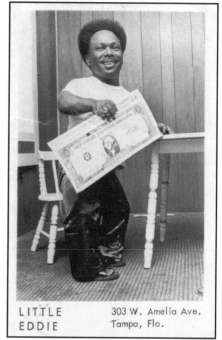

LITTLE
EDDIE   303 W. Amelia Ave.
                     Tampa, Fla.

Life Guards
at Kruse Pool

"Little Eddie"
Tampa, Florida

CHAIN GANG, CONVICTS

Many in Line, PM 1910 Lake City, Fla.	400 - 450	450 - 500
Black Prisoners in Stocks (Naval)	250 - 300	300 - 350
Black Women Prisoners in Stripes (N.C.)	450 - 500	500 - 550
"Women Convicts at No. Car. State Farm"	450 - 500	500 - 550
Others	350 - 400	400 - 450
CHILDREN	10 - 12	12 - 15
"Snowball" Young Boy With Basket (AZO)	20 - 25	25 - 30
CIRCUS		
Dwarfs	35 - 40	40 - 50
Other Performers		
COLLEGE STUDENTS		
Young Men with "Storer" College Banners	70 - 80	80 - 100
COUPLES	20 - 25	25 - 30
CRAP SHOOTERS	30 - 35	35 - 40
DANCERS	20 - 25	25 - 30
E. C. EDDY, Photographer		
Pinehurst & Southern Pines, N.C. Photos		
"By the Sand Road"	80 - 90	90 - 110
"Cotton Picking Time"		
"From Grand-daddy down"		
"Laundry-Special Delivery"		
"Life Saving Crew at 10th Hole..."	110 - 120	120 - 130

Staged Photo at Amusement Park
"Alabama Bound"

Beauty at Graduation Exercise
Photo by EKC

"Ned's Cabin"	80 - 90	90 - 110
"Ned's Family, Southern Pines"		
"No. 3 Course, Pinehurst"		
"Uncle Tom's Cabin"		
"Woman's Exchange, Pinehurst, N.C."		
EATING, Watermelon	25 - 30	30 - 40
FAMILIES AROUND CABIN HOMES	30 - 35	35 - 40
FANTASY POSING FOR PHOTOS	20 - 25	25 - 30
FAT LADIES	30 - 35	35 - 40
FIREMEN	40 - 50	50 - 60
FREAKS	30 - 35	35 - 40
GOLF CADDIE	60 - 70	70 - 80
HANGINGS, LYNCHINGS	500 - 600	600 - 750
LABORERS		
Chefs and Cooks	30 - 35	35 - 40
O'Briens, Waverly, N.Y.		
"Tuskegee Students as Chefs and Waiters"	50 - 60	60 - 70
Conductors, Train	40 - 50	50 - 60
Cotton Pickers	20 - 25	25 - 30
Hotel Servants	15 - 18	18 - 22
Milkman	40 - 50	50 - 60
Ministers, Preachers	30 - 40	40 - 50

School Children -- "F.C.C. Futures"
Photo by AZO

Named Chefs and Crew	20 - 25	25 - 30
Saw Mill Workers	25 - 30	30 - 35
Sugar Cane Grinders		
Stewards	15 - 20	20 - 25
Tobacco Pickers	20 - 25	25 - 30
Train Porters	30 - 35	35 - 40
Turpentine Scrapers	15 - 18	18 - 22
L. L. Cook, Milwaukee B-812		
"Gathering Raw Gum, Lewis Turp. Still"	30 - 35	35 - 40
"Pickaninnies at Lewis Turpentine Still"		
Wagon Drivers	20 - 25	25 - 30
Waiters, Waitresses		
KU KLUX KLAN	200 - 250	250 - 300
Black-Related	350 - 400	400 - 500
LADIES, Young and Old, Showing Fashions	15 - 20	20 - 30
MEN, Young and Old, Showing Fashions		
MIDGETS, DWARFS	30 - 35	35 - 40
"Little Eddie," Tampa, Florida	40 - 50	50 - 60
"Major White, Smallest Boy in World"	40 - 50	50 - 60

MINSTREL SHOWS

Minstrel Shows were, in most cases, a racist form of entertainment. The company normally consisted of white performers who appeared with black faces and stereotyped blacks in a humorous and usually degrading or demeaning manner.

Minstrel Group -- Afton, Iowa, 1909
Photo by AZO

French Real Photo
PC Paris, 3498

Mayomi
Danzatrice del Caffé Arobo

Father Divine and Mother Divine (White)
"Mountain of the House of the Lord -- Woodmont"

The names of some of the performers were usually "Rastus" and "Eliza," who were the leading man and lady of the show, while "Mr. Bones" and "Mr. Tambo" played the musical bones and the tambourine. Even though demeaning to the blacks, this was accepted as a part of the life and times of the era.

MINSTREL SHOWS		
Full Group or Company, Named	60 - 70	70 - 80
Unnamed Groups	30 - 35	35 - 40
Individual Black-Face Performers		
MUSICIANS		
Choirs	25 - 30	30 - 35
Gospel Singers, Named	20 - 25	25 - 30
Piano Players	25 - 30	30 - 35
Singers		
NANNIES	30 - 40	40 - 50
NUDES OR SEMI-NUDES	30 - 40	40 - 50
African Natives	15 - 18	18 - 22
NURSES	35 - 40	40 - 50
PARACHUTE JUMPER, "Dorothy Darby, 1935"	80 - 90	90 - 100
PEDDLERS	25 - 30	30 - 35
POLICEMEN	40 - 50	50 - 60
POOL, "Amateur Pool Sharks"	100 - 110	110 - 120
PORTRAITS	25 - 30	30 - 35
POSTMEN	40 - 50	50 - 60
RELIGION		

Soldiers of North America in 1916 Mexican Revolution
Photo by AZO, 20

Officer in WWI Campaign
Anonymous

Naval Officer, 1920's
Photo by AZO

Soldiers in Vienna after World War II, 1948
Photo by Rothstein

U.S. Army Gunner, 1909
Photo by AZO

Infantryman, WWI
Photo by AZO

Army Sergeant, WWII
Anonymous

*Dining Room and Kitchen Staff
Miami Terrace Hotel, Cook Photo*

*"Dorothy Darby, Parachute
Jumper, August 31, 1935"*

*Early Florida Ox Wagon
Photo by L. L. Cook (AZO)*

Teacher		
SCHOOLS, COLLEGES	25 - 30	30 - 35
SHOESHINE BOYS	50 - 60	60 - 70
SOLDIERS, WWI and Earlier	40 - 50	50 - 60
Soldiers of 92nd Div., Camp Funston, KS	90 - 100	100 - 110
Wounded Black of WWI (German Photos)	60 - 70	70 - 80
Officer	90 - 100	100 - 120
"Camping at Newport, N.Y." (10th Calvary)		
Soldiers with Revolvers and Rifles	40 - 50	50 - 60
Views of Camp with Blacks	30 - 40	40 - 50
Infantry Repl. Center Band (Colored)		
Camp Croft, S.C. EKC #46, 1940's	20 - 25	25 - 30
N. Amer. Soldiers in 1916 Mex. Revol. (AZO)	40 - 50	50 - 60
U.S. Army Gunner, P.M. 1909 (AZO)		
World War II	15 - 20	20 - 25
Integrated Blacks w/White Girls in Vienna	30 - 35	35 - 40
SAILORS, WWI and Earlier	60 - 70	70 - 80
Officer	90 - 100	100 - 120
STUDIO POSED PHOTOS	20 - 25	25 - 30
Man-Woman Tending Bar	40 - 50	50 - 60
TRANSPORTATION		
Goat Cart, with Children	50 - 60	60 - 70
Horse and Wagon	35 - 40	40 - 45

Infantry Replacement Center (Band, Colored), Camp Croft, S.C.
Real Photo, EKC, 46

U.S. Signal Corps Photo Reproduced by Photo Repro by Permission
Bureau War Photographs, "Our Men have Regular Inspection ..."

Father Divine & Mother Divine (White)		
"The Mountain of the House of the Lord"	70 - 80	80 - 100
SCHOOLS WITH CHILDREN	30 - 40	40 - 50
To 1940	30 - 35	35 - 40
Integrated, Showing Black and White	35 - 40	40 - 45
College Students	40 - 50	50 - 60

Pvt. Philip Warren

Pvt. Willie Hickman, Texas

Mascot Leslie Walker

Unknown

Soldiers from Camp Funston, KS, 3rd Co., 4th Battalion, who fought with the 92nd Division, the Official Black Division in WWI. This Division went into action in the front lines of France in August 1918.

"Women Convicts at the No. Car. State Farm" -- Anon. Real Photo

"Amateur Pool Sharks" -- Anonymous Real Photo

Ox Wagon and Driver "Early Florida" (AZO)	60 - 70	70 - 80
Others	40 - 50	50 - 60
WANTED NOTICES	60 - 70	70 - 80
WEDDING COUPLES	50 - 60	60 - 70
Black and White Couples	70 - 80	80 - 90

Blacks on early sports postcards up to the Twenties and early Thirties were limited mainly to boxing champions and contenders, amateur photos of baseball players and teams, and comical satires painted by artists of those eras. Heavyweight Champion Jack Johnson's cards, especially the real-photo types, have become the leader in this very sparse area. His cards seem to escalate in value each time one is placed in an auction or sale.

In the 1936 Berlin Olympics, Jesse Owens became the hero of the U.S. sports world with his outstanding performances. Several cards displaying Jesse and his triumphs were recorded on postcards, and are very much in demand. From 1898 until 1946, when the color line was broken by Jackie Robinson, black men were barred from baseball by a so-called "gentlemen's agreement" which kept some of the nation's greatest players in the relative obscurity of the Negro Leagues. Early postcards of players in the Negro Major Leagues surface occasionally, but are usually grabbed up by collectors before a price can be fixed on them.

Blacks on postcards became more abundant as many of the major league teams began issuing them as give-aways to promote their teams. These, plus amateur real photos, those done by enterprising small publishers, a small number by Exhibit Supply, and later Hall of Fame issues by The Albertype Co. and Perez-Steele (which we mostly used for autographing), began filling the void. Until this time, gum cards were the main fare for hobbyists.

	VG	EX
BASEBALL		
Black Baseball Teams, Identified		
Real Photos	40 - 50	50 - 60
Others	30 - 40	40 - 50
Black Baseball Teams, Unidentified		
Real Photos	20 - 30	30 - 40
Others	15 - 20	20 - 25
Prison Baseball Teams	50 - 60	60 - 75
Baseball Players, Identified		
Major League Issues		
1950's (Robinson, Mays, Paige, etc.)		
Real Photos,	30 - 35	35 - 40
Others (Chromes, B&W)	20 - 25	25 - 30
1960's (All Star Players)		
Real Photos	20 - 25	25 - 30
Others (Chromes, B&W)	10 - 15	15 - 20
Other Black Players	10 - 12	12 - 15

W. Munson (Uns.), Tichnor Bros.
69507, "Let's Play Around"

Hank Aaron, 715th Home Run
April 8, 1974

Leo Cardenas (Indians)
Cleveland Pro-Sports

Tony Taylor (Phillies)
Bob Bartosz

George Taliaferro
1956 Exhibit Supply Mutoscope

Earl "The Pearl" Monroe
Art Vue Postcard Co.

L. C. Phifer, E. L. Company Illustrated Song Series, 1820 "Goliath was struck out by David ..."

L. C. Phifer, E. L. Company Illustrated Song Series, 1820 "Rebecca went to the well with a pitcher ..."

L. C. Phifer, E. L. Company Illustrated Song Series, 1820 "The prodigal son made a home ..."

L. C. Phifer, E. L. Company Illustrated Song Series, 1820 "Eve stole first and Adam second ..."

Chandler's Zora Folley
"Top KO Contender" -- 1958

Orestes "Minnie" Minoso
Mutoscope Post Card, 1956

Hank Aaron
Multiple Photos, Los Angeles

6666 "Hank Aaron's 715th Home Run"	8 - 10	10 - 12
April 8, 1974 at Atlanta Stadium		

Baseball Players, Unidentified

Others (Color and B&W)	15 - 20	20 - 25
1940 - 1960	6 - 8	8 - 10

Other Issues
Bill and Bob Postcards, 1958

Hank Aaron	15 - 18	18 - 22
Billy Bruton	10 - 12	12 - 15
Wes Covington		

Louis Dormand Postcards

Roy Campanella	10 - 12	12 - 15
Elston Howard	6 - 8	8 - 10

Artvue Postcard Co., Hall of Fame (B&W)

Jackie Robinson	15 - 18	18 - 22

Spic and Span Dry Cleaners, 1956

Oversize Cards (B&W)		
Henry Aaron	18 - 22	22 - 25
Billy Bruton	10 - 12	12 - 15

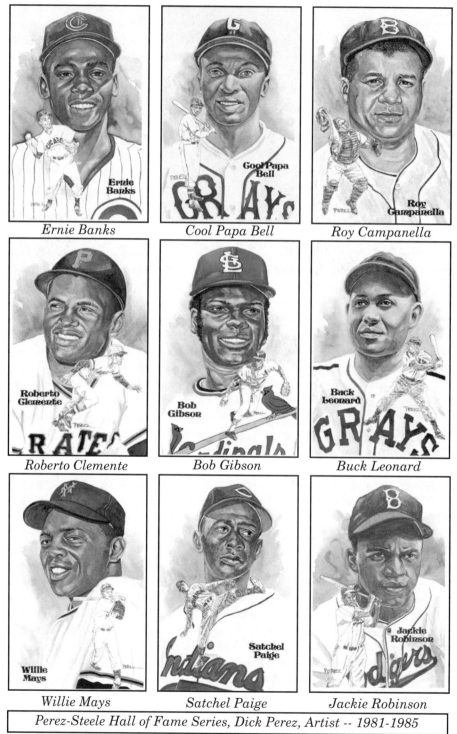

Ernie Banks   Cool Papa Bell   Roy Campanella

Roberto Clemente   Bob Gibson   Buck Leonard

Willie Mays   Satchel Paige   Jackie Robinson

Perez-Steele Hall of Fame Series, Dick Perez, Artist -- 1981-1985

Used with the Permission of Perez-Steele Galleries.

Van Patrick, 1949

Joe Black	15 - 18	18 - 22

Don Wingfield Postcards, 1955

Ernie Banks	8 - 10	10 - 12
Earl Battey	6 - 8	8 - 10
Elston Howard		
Willie Mays	15 - 18	18 - 22

George Brace, Chicago

All-Star Players	8 - 10	10 - 12
Others	4 - 5	5 - 6

H. F. Gardner Sports Stars

Hank and Tommy Aaron	8 - 10	10 - 12
Billy Bruton	4 - 5	5 - 6
Lee Maye		
Billy Williams	6 - 8	8 - 10

L. L. Cook Company, Milwaukee (B&W)

Tommy Aaron	4 - 5	5 - 6
Wes Covington		
Mel Bailey	1 - 2	2 - 3
Ed Broder	2 - 3	3 - 4
James Elder		
Doug Williams Photos .	1 - 2	2 - 3

1950's Baseball Stars, Team Issues

Henry Aaron	20 - 25	25 - 28
Ernie Banks	20 - 25	25 - 28
Roy Campanella	20 - 25	25 - 28
Roberto Clemento	25 - 30	30 - 35
Larry Doby	8 - 10	10 - 12
Elston Howard	8 - 10	10 - 12
Willie Mays	25 - 30	30 - 35
Willie McCovey	10 - 12	12 - 15
Minnie Minoso	8 - 10	10 - 12
Don Newcombe	8 - 10	10 - 12
Satchel Paige	25 - 30	30 - 35
Jackie Robinson	20 - 25	25 - 30

1960's Baseball Stars, Team Issues

Henry Aaron	15 - 18	18 - 22
Ernie Banks		
Lou Brock	12 - 15	15 - 18
Orlando Cepeda		
Roberto Clemente	15 - 18	18 - 22
Bob Gibson	12 - 15	15 - 18
Elston Howard		
Willie Mays	18 - 22	22 - 25

Joe Louis and Dr. King, "Two Champions"
Scenic South Card Co., C15056

Willie McCovey	12 - 15	15 - 18
Frank Robinson		
Perez-Steele *		
Dick Perez		
Ernie Banks	25 - 30	30 - 35

Jack Johnson Sits in His Corner with Handlers
Anonymous Real Photo

Jack Johnson, Jo3
Real Photo, Dana Studio

Sam Langford
Exhibit Supply, 1921

Roy Campanella	50 - 55	55 - 60
Roberto Clemente	15 - 20	20 - 25
Bob Gibson	25 - 30	30 - 35
Monte Irvin	15 - 20	20 - 25
Willie Mays	50 - 60	60 - 70
Satchel Paige	20 - 25	25 - 30
Jackie Robinson	20 - 25	25 - 30
Willie Stargell	25 - 30	30 - 35
Cool Papa Bell	10 - 15	15 - 18
Oscar Charleston	10 - 15	15 - 18
Martin Dihigo		
Rube Foster		
Josh Gibson		
Judy Johnson		
Buck Leonard		
John Lloyd		

* Cards of living players have high prices because
they are used for autograph purposes.

BASEBALL COMICS
Refer to Artist-Signed or Publisher's Sections.

Johnson and Cotton Sparring Match
This photo (by Cohn and Cann) shows his white wife at ringside.

FOOTBALL

Black Football Teams
Identified

Real Photos	30 - 35	35 - 40
Others	20 - 25	25 - 30
Knoxville College, 20's	20 - 25	25 - 30

Black Foot Teams
Unidentified

Real Photos	20 - 25	25 - 30
Others	15 - 20	20 - 25

Football Players, Identified
Claude Young
Tank Younger
Others

Real Photos	25 - 30	30 - 35
Color or B&W	20 - 25	25 - 28

1950's-1960's Football Stars

Jim Brown	15 - 18	18 - 22
Roosevelt Greer	12 - 15	15 - 18
Ollie Matson	15 - 20	20 - 25
Marion Motley		
Emlen Tunnell		
Paul Warfield		

1936 Olympics (Berlin)
Real Photo Showing Williams, USA, 400 Meter Gold Medalist

BASKETBALL

1950's-1960's Basketball Stars

Elgin Baylor	15 - 20	20 - 25
Wilt Chamberlain	20 - 25	25 - 30
Oscar Robertson		
Bill Russell		
Maurice Stokes	10 - 15	15 - 20

BOXING

Cassius Clay	10 - 15	15 - 25
Muhammed Ali	8 - 10	10 - 20
Zora Folley, Chandler, Arizona		
Real Photo of "Top K.O. Contender, 1958"	20 - 25	25 - 30
Jack Johnson		
Johnson-Jeffries Fight	40 - 50	50 - 60
Johnson-Willard Fight		
Jack Johnson, Heavyweight Champ, 1910	50 - 60	60 - 70
Real Photo-Champion Jack Johnson, "In front of his Training Quarters"	50 - 75	75 - 100
Real Photo W/U.S. Flag as Belt	75 - 100	100 - 125
Real Photo, Johnson/Cotton Sparring Match	75 - 100	100 - 125
Jack Johnson - Jo3		
Real Photo by **Dana Studio**	75 - 100	100 - 125

"Champion Jack Johnson In Front of His Training Quarters"
Real Photo

Sam Langford
   Boxing Series 613

"American Colored Heavyweight"	25 - 30	30 - 40

Joe Louis

Real Photos	25 - 30	30 - 40
Color or Black and White	15 - 20	20 - 25
In Army Uniform		
Scenic South Cards (C)		
C15056 With M. L. King, "Two Champions"	6 - 8	8 - 10

Jersey Joe Walcott

Real Photos	15 - 20	20 - 25
Color or Black and White	12 - 15	15 - 18

EXHIBIT SUPPLY CO.

Normally, the Exhibit Supply Co. printed their Mutoscope Arcade vending machine cards with blank backs. However, in some years they produced small groups of cards with Post Card backs. In 1956 they issued both baseball and football series which can be identified by the inscription, "Made In U.S.A." located on the front lower right. These are very elusive, especially on baseball, because collectors want them for autographing purposes.

BASEBALL

Gene Baker	10 - 15	15 - 20
Ernie Banks	35 - 40	40 - 45

Pvts. James Baggs--Florida and Fred Horrice--Georgia
Real Photo

Roy Campanella	30 - 40	40 - 50
Elston Howard	15 - 20	20 - 25
Willie Mays	80 - 90	90 - 100
Orestes "Minnie" Minoso	20 - 25	25 - 30
Don Newcombe	15 - 20	20 - 25
FOOTBALL		
Ollie Matson	20 - 25	25 - 30
Marion Motley	15 - 20	20 - 25
George Taliaferro		
Emlen Tunnell		
Claude Young		
Tank Younger		
Claude Young		
BOXING		
Sam Langford, 1921	18 - 22	22 - 25
Chick Suggs, 1927	15 - 18	18 - 20
Others		

OLYMPICS

1936 Olympics		
Jesse Owens	30 - 35	35 - 40
Others	20 - 25	25 - 30
Real Photo	40 - 50	50 - 60
Color or B/W	20 - 25	25 - 30
Williams, U.S.A., Winning 400 Meters	25 - 30	30 - 35

Black entertainers on postcards, especially those of the early era, are extremely hard to find in any volume because of the small numbers who succeeded in the profession. The most prominent was Josephine Baker, who became the darling of the French entertainment world for her performances in the Folies-Bergères in the early twenties. She was very beautiful and extremely talented, and the French displayed her charms to the utmost via the poster and postcard. The openness of the roaring 20's was very fruitful for her talents and she made the best of it. Her rising star provided an impetus for other blacks to follow.

Traveling minstrel shows, a great entertainment medium in most all cities in the U.S. in the late 1890's and early 1900's, were performed using white black-face actors and musicians. The most famous of all was the multi-talented singer and actor, Al Jolson. His renditions of black-related songs are legendary. Talented black performers began replacing white black-face actors in many of the revues after the turn of the century, and the rest is history. With his tremendous talents, the black performer carved an important niche in the entertainment field and made him acceptable to all.

Harlem, N.Y. became the cultural capital of the black community, and famous musicians, artists, and entertainers -- such as Louis Armstrong, Duke Ellington, Paul Robeson, and Claude McKay-- made it their home. Many entertainers also used it as a base for developing their talents and achieving success. Postcards of early black entertainers were very limited, but this is no longer the norm.

	VG	EX
AMOS & ANDY		
Exhibit Supply Mutoscope (1-16)	15 - 18	18 - 22
Real Photo	20 - 25	25 - 30
Others	12 - 15	15 - 20
PEARL BAILEY		
Mike Roberts (C)		
Pearl Bailey at the Nugget Hotel	10 - 12	12 - 15

JOSEPHINE BAKER

Josephine Baker, the famous black American dancer and comedienne was the rage of Paris in the early 1920's. She entertained on the stage of the famous Folies-Bergères and became the photographers' dream. Her famous semi-nude images have recently made her cards the most sought after of all entertainers of the era.

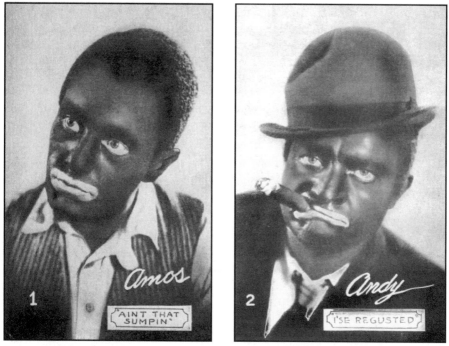

"Aint That Sumpin'"   "I'se Regusted"

The radio show "Amos and Andy," was created in 1928 by "white dialecticians" Freeman F. Gosden (Amos) and Charles J. Correll (Andy).

Josephine Baker
Real Photo, French

Josephine Baker, Jean Domerge
A.N., Paris, 6466, "The Parasol"

Josephine Baker (Dist. by "Iris")
Real Photo by Walery, 5293

Josephine Baker
Real Photo by Walery, 5176

Gabriel Domerge, a French Art Deco artist of the time, painted a most beautiful and classical nude series of Josephine. These renditions, with Domerge's Deco touch, were an immediate success as prints. They were then released as real-photo postcard types and are in great demand today. The Walery Salon, Paris, also produced many fine semi-nude and dressed real photo postcard images of her that have survived through the years.

BAKER, JOSEPHINE

S/Jean Gabriel Domerge, Paris
Artist-drawn Nude, Real Photo types   100 - 120   120 - 140
S/Walery, Paris
Semi-Nudes Real Photos by "Iris" (5176)   130 - 140   140 - 150
Real Photo by "Iris" (5293)
Tinted Photo, "Folies Bergéres"
Tinted Photo, Semi-Nude (see back cover)   140 - 150   150 - 160
Topless, with Boa Snake   120 - 130   130 - 150
S/Za, A-74, Published by E. Zacchelli
Continental size, color   110 - 120   120 - 130
NADAR, 124 Real Photo   90 - 100   100 - 110
Other Semi-Nude Real Photos   100 - 110   110 - 120
Others, Non-Nude   70 - 80   80 - 90

"Our Gang" -- Hal Roach's Rascals
Eagle Postcard View Co. (Farina, Jean Darling and Joe Cobb)

Buckwheat
Eagle Postcard View Co.

Lionel Hampton
Moss Photo Service, 1958

Ray Charles
H. F. Gardner, C15068

Dizzy Gillespie and Jimmy Carter
Coral-Lee, 1981

Paul Robeson
Real Photo

Sarah Vaughn
Real Photo

Advertising Card, 1948
"George Gershwin's 'Porgy and Bess' at the Majestic Theatre"

Duke Ellington
RCA Victor

"Fats" Waller
RCA Victor

Tiger Lily
1928 Real Photo by WM

Charley Pride
Curt Teich, Chrome

CALLOWAY, CAB Big Band of 40's (R.P.)	15 - 20	20 - 25
CARROLL, DIAHANN		
V&O Chinese Gift Shop (B&W)	8 - 10	10 - 12
DAVIS, SAMMY, JR.		
Plastichrome	5 - 8	8 - 10
FISK JUBILEE TRIO, Mocara, McAdoo & Carr	30 - 40	40 - 50
LAYTON & JOHNSTONE, Columbia Records	35 - 40	40 - 50
LILI DAMITA & BLACK GROUP	30 - 35	35 - 40
MUSICAL JOE, "The Ideal Entertainer"	30 - 40	40 - 50
ORIGINAL JUBILEE SINGERS, Nashville	25 - 30	30 - 35
OUR GANG BLACKS		
Eagle Postcard View Co.		
"Buckwheat" (B&W)	20 - 22	22 - 25
Real Photos	20 - 25	25 - 30
Exhibit Supply Mutoscopes	18 - 22	22 - 25
Others	20 - 22	22 - 25
POITIER, SIDNEY		
V&O Chinese Gift Shop (B&W)	8 - 10	10 - 12
ROBESON, PAUL		
Real Photo	15 - 18	18 - 22
TIGER LILY		
Real Photo	25 - 30	30 - 35

"*Fisk Jubilee Trio*"
(Macara, McAdoo & Carr)

"*Musical Joe*"
The Ideal Entertainer

"*Layton and Johnstone on
Columbia Records*" *(R.P.)*

"*Lili Damita*"
Anonymous (R.P.)

E. C. Kropp Company, 6000, "Original Jubilee Singers"
Nashville, Tennessee

Others	15 - 18	18 - 22
VAUGHN, SARAH		
Real Photo, Foreign Publisher	10 - 12	12 - 15
WEBB, CHICK Singing star of 30's (R.P.)	15 - 20	20 - 25
MUSICIANS, SINGERS - 1940's-1950's *		
Count Basie	8 - 10	10 - 12
Ray Charles		
Cozy Cole		
Nat "King" Cole		
Fats Domino		
Duke Ellington		
RCA Victor	20 - 30	30 - 40
Ella Fitzgerald	8 - 10	10 - 12
Erskine Hawkins (Band Leader)		
Lena Horne		
RCA Victor	20 - 30	30 - 40
Eddie Oliver	8 - 10	10 - 12
Ben Pollack		
Charley Pride		
Sarah Vaughn		
Fats Waller		
RCA Victor	20 - 30	30 - 40
* Real Photos - Add $5.00 each		
THEATER		
"Porgy & Bess" Advertising Card (1948)	15 - 18	18 - 22

"The Bride"
Real Photo by AZO

Real Photo by AZO

Black Face Minstrel Group
Dover, Illinois, 1912

Etats-Unis.
Blanc et Noir.

Theodore Roosevelt assumed the Presidency in 1901 and voiced his favor of "equality of all men," and even invited Booker T. Washington to dine at the White House. Racists picked up on this sudden about-face, and many cartoons emanated from it. One of the better ones was recorded on a postcard by a French publisher -- "Black and White."

Topical postcards play a major role in the collections of hobbyists. This is especially true in collecting African American cards, as some of the very important historical and social types are included. Of these, most are real life types that were issued to tell about an upcoming event or to recount it just after it happened. They are important events recorded and dated by the image, by the caption, by the postmark, or by the name of the publisher, and preserved for all generations. There are also photos taken of the happy owners of the new car, an artist's rendition of the up-coming county fair, or the picture of a store front with the proud owner in the door. The topics in this section are only those that relate to African Americans.

Topical collectors are usually those who specialize in only one or many different motifs. If their special topic happens to be women with big hats they will search diligently through all dealers' stocks of beautiful ladies to find those of interest. However, after looking through the beautiful lady cards the collector will realize that he also likes those of women participating in various sports. So... another topic to collect. The number and kinds of topics are limitless, and there is always one or more to fit anyone's budget, whether he is rich or poor. This unlimited number of different topics makes the collecting of postcards interesting as well as rewarding.

Unless cards or sets are named, listed values are for a generalized selection in each particular topic. Outstanding cards may be valued at much higher values while lower standard cards may be much lower.

	VG	EX
BAPTIZING	12 - 15	15 - 20
Linens	6 - 8	8 - 12
Chromes	2 - 3	3 - 4
BLACK-FACE (Whites)	15 - 18	18 - 22
"Rufus and Roberta" Radio Show Ad (B&W)	20 - 25	25 - 28
BUSINESS, BLACK-OWNED		
"Atlanta Life Insurance Co." (L)	20 - 22	22 - 25
Albertype (B&W) 1930's		
"Douglas Life Ins. Co., New Orleans"	20 - 22	22 - 25
E. C. Kropp		
13802N "Johnson Colored Tourist Home"	20 - 22	22 - 25
Silvercraft (Dexter)		
"Pilgrim Health & Life Ins., Augusta, Ga."	20 - 22	22 - 25
B. M. Styron Co.		
"The Biltmore Hotel," Durham, NC	18 - 20	20 - 22
Anonymous		
"Southern Aid Society of Virginia"	15 - 18	18 - 22

Black-Face and White Lady
Anonymous

Colored Masonic Temple
Birmingham, CT, Teich 5B-81048

THE BLACK BUSINESSMAN AND PROFESSIONAL

Frequent denial of employment by some whites caused blacks to begin developing businesses of their own. Starting a business, however, was always a task for them because of inadequate capital and the reluctance of white-owned banks to lend them money. This, in some ways, was alleviated by 1900 as four black-owned banks were founded to serve black clientele. Because they made it easy for blacks to secure a loan, these institutions became very successful and enabled new businesses to spring up in many areas. Pictures taken of various shop fronts and buildings, along with their proud owners, are preserved and dated on postcards of the era. Real photo types of these scenes are of particular interest to all collectors. The white professionals, including doctors, dentists, beauticians, lawyers, undertakers and barbers, became reluctant to serve blacks because of fear of alienating their white patrons. Although at that time these actions made life unpleasant and created many hardships, it proved to be a Godsend for the black race in America. The black community was practically forced to develop their own professionals to serve their own people. They began investing millions of dollars in the training of professionals and teachers at all levels. This not only was the answer to the service problem, but it helped create thousands of good jobs. Black schools and colleges began to spring up all over the South, and training grounds were established for the middle class and future community leaders.

CADDIES	15 - 20	20 - 30
CAMPS FOR CHILDREN	8 - 10	10 - 15
CHAIN GANG, CONVICTS		
A. L. Vidal & Co. (UndB) (B&W)		
"Convicts in mine - digging rock"	40 - 50	50 - 60
Albertype (DB) (B&W)		
"Atlanta, Chain Gang & Ga. Ferry"	50 - 60	60 - 70
S. H. Kress		
"Stripes but no Stars," Asheville, N.C."	50 - 60	60 - 70
Curt Teich		
A-31597 "Stripes but no Stars"		
"Chain Gang at work..."	50 - 60	60 - 70
A-31598 "Stripes but no Stars"		
"Convicts marching to work"	50 - 60	60 - 70
Others in Series	50 - 60	60 - 70
CHURCHES		
American News Co.		
"Colored Baptist Church, Darien, GA" (UndB)	20 - 22	22 - 25

Detroit Publishing Company, 10551 (DB)
"Saving Sinners" (Scene Along the Mississippi)

Anonymous
"Zion Mem. Church, Federalsburg, MD (R.P.)   20 - 25   25 - 30
CIRCUS   15 - 20   20 - 25
COLLEGES
Curt Teich
R21277 "Georgia State Industrial College"   15 - 18   18 - 22

"Johnson Colored Tourist Home and Dinette"
Orangeburg, S.C., E. C. Kropp, 13802N

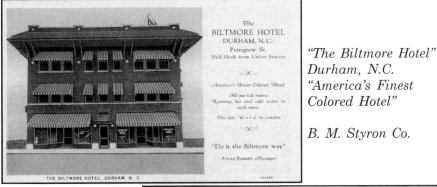

*"The Biltmore Hotel"
Durham, N.C.
"America's Finest
Colored Hotel"*

B. M. Styron Co.

*"Douglas Life
Insurance Company,
New Orleans"
Dr. E. N. Ezidore,
President*

Albertype Co.

Ad on Reverse.

Ad on Reverse.

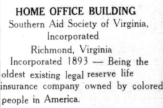

Colored Baptist Church, Darien, Georgia (UndB)
American News, 190282

A-23582 "Colored Ind. School, Charleston"	18 - 22	22 - 25
Anonymous		
"Upton Home, Spellman College"	15 - 18	18 - 22
COLLEGE STUDENTS	15 - 18	18 - 22
COUPLES	12 - 15	15 - 18
DANCERS	15 - 20	20 - 25
EXPOSITIONS		

"Zion Memorial Church, Federalsburg, Md.
And its Pastor Rev. W. H. Johns." Photo by AZO

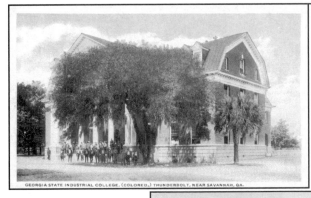

"Georgia State Industrial College (Colored), Thunderbolt, Savannah, Ga."

Curt Teich, R21277 (L)

"Colored Industrial School, Charleston, S.C."

Curt Teich, A-23582

"Upton Home, Spellman College, Atlanta"

Anonymous

"Hampton Institute Choir, Hampton, Virginia"

Albertype Company

"Convicts in Mine, digging Rock"

A. L. Vidal & Co.

Convicts in Mine, digging Rock

THE WHIPPING POST, DOVER, DEL.

"The Whipping Post, Dover, Delaware"

Kaufmann & Sons

"Stripes But No Stars, Asheville, N.C."

Curt Teich, A-31597

Stripes But No Stars, Asheville, N.C.

"Stripes but no Stars," Chain Gang at work in Dixie Land.

"Stripes but no Stars."

Chain Gang at Work in Dixieland.

S. H. Kress

Negro Building,
Chilhowee Park,
National Conservation
Exposition Grounds,
Knoxville, Tenn.

"Negro Building, Chilhowee Park, National Conservation Exposition Grounds, Knoxville, Tenn.," Curt Teich, A-14037

Cotton States and Int. Expo., Atlanta, 1895
  Baum Officials by H.A.K. Co.
    "The Negro Building"   350 - 375   375 - 400
  Leipzig Ausstellung, 1897
    "Gruss Aus Ost Afrika" **(S/Arth Thiele)**   50 - 60   60 - 70
Anglo-American Expo, 1914
  Gale & Polden (R.P. Type)
    The Famous Piccaninny Band   35 - 40   40 - 50
    "The Band"
    "The Conductor"
    "Full Play"
    "Master and Man"
Appalachian Expo, Knoxville
    "The Negro Building"   20 - 25   25 - 30
Jamestown Expo, 1907
  Jamestown A. & V. Co.
    "The Negro Building"   20 - 22   22 - 25
National Conservation Expo, Knoxville
  Curt Teich A-14037 "Negro Building"   15 - 18   18 - 25
EXAGGERATIONS
  Martin
    Blacks and Big Watermelons   12 - 15   15 - 18
    Blacks "Carving our Watermelon"

HOMER PHILLIPS HOSPITAL FOR COLORED, ST. LOUIS, MISSOURI

"Homer Phillips Hospital for Colored, St. Louis, Missouri"
Colourpicture, 15390 (L)

HOSPITALS
Colourpicture (L)
    15390 "Homer Phillips Hospital for Colored"   15 - 18   18 - 22
Curt Teich
    D7662 "Domestic Science Bldg., Piney Woods"   18 - 22   22 - 25

Good Samaritan Hospital, Charlotte, N. C.   3

"Good Samaritan Hospital, Charlotte, N.C."
Oldest Private Negro Hospital in U.S., Tichnor, 79458 (L)

Tichnor (L)
    79458 "Good Samaritan Hospital, Charlotte"   15 - 18   18 - 22
HANGINGS, LYNCHINGS
  Hugh C. Leighton (UndB)
    28295, "Lynched"   200 - 250   250 - 300
    "Lynching at Russellville, Ky., July 31, 1908"   200 - 250   250 - 300
    "Scene in Sabine Co., Texas, June 22, 1908"   200 - 250   250 - 300
  Springfield Riot, 1908 (Anonymous)
    "Tree where Negro was Lynched"   40 - 50   50 - 60
INTER-MARRIAGE   25 - 30   30 - 35
KU KLUX KLAN   (White Border)
  J. N. Chamberlain, Miami
    19431 "Ku Klux Klan, Pageant Day,
        Flagler St., Miami, Fla."   150 - 175   175 - 200
  Black-Related   200 - 220   220 - 250
LABORERS
  Basketmakers   12 - 15   15 - 18
  Chefs, Cooks   10 - 15   15 - 20
  Cobblers   15 - 18   18 - 22
  Conductors   15 - 20   20 - 25
  Cotton Pickers   10 - 12   12 - 15
  Firemen   20 - 25   25 - 28
  Hotel Servants   12 - 15   15 - 18
  Mailmen   20 - 25   25 - 30
  Named Chefs and Crew   15 - 20   20 - 25
  Nannies/Nurses
  Peddlers   15 - 18   18 - 22
  Policemen   20 - 25   25 - 28
  Porters   15 - 18   18 - 22
  Sawmill Workers
  Stewards/Sugar Cane Grinders
  Tobacco Pickers   12 - 15   15 - 18

NOVELTIES

AIR-BRUSHED (Heavily Embossed)
  Illustrated P.C. Co.
    Two Kids and Mule   15 - 18   18 - 22
    Playing Marbles
    Eating Watermelon
BASKET APPLIQUE
  Livermore & Knight Co., 1900 (Oversize)
    Lady with Big Basket with Adv. Pull-out   50 - 60   60 - 70
BAS-RELIEF   15 - 18   18 - 22
BUTTON FAMILY   30 - 35   35 - 45

I love you fair maiden, nay prithee don't start,
When I open my mouth, 'tis to show you my heart.

Mechanical Valentine
"I love you fair maiden, may ..."

Mechanical Moving Faces;
Blacks and Whites Appear

Jervis		
"Buttons Pickaninny"	25 - 30	30 - 35
DOUBLE-FOLD		
"Alexander's Rag Time Band"		
Black Uniformed Band	25 - 30	30 - 35
HOLD-TO-LIGHT		
Transparency	50 - 60	60 - 70
S/Ellam		
Minstrel Man	40 - 50	50 - 60
INSTALLMENTS		
Syndicate Publishing Co.		
S.I. Weatherbee		
"I"	15 - 20	20 - 25
"Want"		
"You"		
"Mah Honey"		
KISS-O-GRAM		
Valentine & Sons		
"A Kiss from your own dear boy"	50 - 60	60 - 70
"A Kiss from your own sweet girl"		
LEATHER		
Blacks with Cotton	12 - 15	15 - 18

Livermore & Knight, No. 262
Real Feathers -- When Pulled, An Ad or Ads Appear.
"No Ma'am, I Aint Seen No Stray Rooster Over Heah."

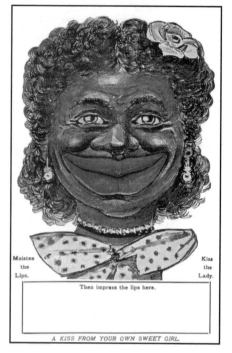

Valentine & Sons, "A Kiss
From Your Own Dear Boy"

Valentine & Sons, "A Kiss
From Your Own Sweet Girl"

---

*Installment cards were a complete series usually mailed to the same
recipient for arrival on succeeding days or weeks to eventually complete
the set. A series was usually composed of four or more cards.*

F. I. Weatherbee, Syndicate Publishing Company
"I -- Want -- You -- Mah Honey"

Blacks with Chickens & Watermelon	15 - 18	18 - 22
Others	10 - 12	12 - 15

MECHANICALS
Signed **Ellen Clapsaddle**
Series 1286 Halloween

"A Jolly Halloween" (S/**A. Hutaf**)	350 - 400	400 - 450

Rotograph Co.

Double-fold Mechanical	60 - 65	65 - 75

Anonymous

Valentine "I love you fair maiden ..."	40 - 45	45 - 50

Raphael Tuck Series 3394

Black Girl W/Golliwog Doll, "I's Topsy"	125 - 150	150 - 175

Face-Change

Face Changes from White Child to Black	90 - 100	100 - 110

Others

"Squeeze Me" Early German, DRGM	40 - 50	50 - 60
"Glass Eyes" or "Movable Eyes"	20 - 25	25 - 30
Black Man Plays Banjo -- Eyes, Hands and Mouth Move.	50 - 60	60 - 70
"Dinah Black Enamel" Advertising	40 - 45	45 - 50

Die-Cut Folder Mechanicals
Livermore & Knight

Man with Applique Crate	25 - 30	30 - 35
Woman with Applique Basket		

PUZZLES
Ullman Mfg. Co.

	70 - 80	80- 90

"Pick the Pickaninnies"
REAL FEATHERS
Livermore & Knight

#262 "No Ma'am, I ain't seen no stray..."	30 - 35	35 - 40

Hugh C. Leighton, 28295
"Lynched"

W&G, 5145C, M. L. King, Jr.
"I have a dream" (1986)

Dr. King, Scenic South Card Co.,
Bessemer, Alabama, C15044

Ku Klux Klan, Pageant Day, Flagler St., Miami, Fla.

"Ku Klux Klan, Pageant Day, Flagler St., Miami, Fla."
J. N. Chamberlain, 19431 (White Border)

The Ku Klux Klan, which thrived in the South immediately after the Civil War, started their revival around 1915. Migrations of blacks from the south to the north and west, plus heavy immigration of many dark-skinned Southern and Eastern Europeans, gave them a new purpose. Their well-known cross burnings, public marches and scare tactics were used to try to keep their opponents in line or, if warranted, to make them move to other areas ... or to completely disappear altogether.

The Klan was well organized and, because of their invisibility, they could almost do as they pleased -- not only with blacks but also with Jews and other foreign-born Americans. They often called themselves the "Protectors" of White American Civilization and were truly a "thorn in the side" of blacks for many years. The movie *Birth of a Nation,* which contained extreme racial prejudice, was associated with the revival of the Klan because it was based on material taken from the novels by Thomas Dixon, *The Leopard's Spots* and *The Klansman.*

"Taken from Death." Lynching at Russellville, Kentucky, July 31, 1908
Photo by Jack Morton, Nashville, Tennessee

History has recorded that 214 blacks were lynched in 1901 and 1902 alone, and the number was up to 1100 by 1914. These atrocities were committed mostly in the South. However, blacks started wholesale migration from the south to northern and mid-western states to some areas where they were not welcome. This caused very hostile feelings among residents and the strong anti-black factions, such as the Ku Klux Klan and various vigilante groups, and helped create further racial disorder. In many instances, blacks were lynched in an effort to scare other blacks away.

Some of these macabre lynching scenes were photographed and preserved on picture postcards, and are seldom recorded elsewhere. Although most of the known images are of inferior grade and the published works are usually of poor quality, they are still among the most collectible of all black-related material in any condition. As in white-related lynchings, government intervention and prosecution of violators finally brought an end to these proceedings.

Ullman Mfg. Co., Mechanical Puzzle
"Pick the Pickaninnies"

"The Protecting Angel" (DB)
Anonymous

"Jesus Died for Both" (DB)
Anonymous

REAL PHONOGRAPH RECORDS
Blacks Singing and Dancing
"Under the Yum-Yum Tree"   30 - 35   35 - 40
SILKS
  Silk Applique
  Illustrated P.C. Co.
  "One Jack and Two Blacks"   22 - 25   25 - 28
  Others
  Woven Silks
  Grant & Co., England
  "Golly Don't I Like Chicken"   100 - 110 110 - 125
X-RAY CARDS
"Gaze on Dem Bones"   15 - 20   20 - 25
MIDGETS   15 - 20   20 - 25
MINSTREL SHOWS
Named   20 - 25   25 - 35
Unnamed   15 - 18   18 - 22
Performers   20 - 22   22 - 25
PIONEER CARDS, ANONYMOUS
"Praline Woman," New Orleans (B&W)   35 - 40   40 - 45
"Greetings from Galveston" 3 Children (B&W)   40 - 45   45 - 50
POLITICAL
Theodore Roosevelt and Black Man
  Anon. French, "Etats-Unis, Blanc et Noir"   200 - 225 225 - 250
Theodore Roosevelt
  S/B. Moloch
  Roosevelt Painting Negro White   100 - 125 125 - 150
Black Man Kicks T. Roosevelt's Hat
  "You Aught'a Quit Kickin that Hat..."   50 - 60   60 - 70
RACIAL HISTORY
  Working Black Lady says:
  "Who' Dat Said De Nigger Am Free"   150 - 175 175 - 200
  Young Child Sits on U.S. Flag
  "Tell 'em We're Risin"   40 - 45   45 - 50
  Black & White Children
  Franz Huld "North and South United"   30 - 35   35 - 40
  Whipping
  Kaufmann & Sons, Baltimore
  "The Whipping Post, Dover, Delaware"   30 - 35   35 - 40
RELIGION
Anonymous
  "Jesus Died for Both" (Sepia)   10 - 12   12 - 15
  "The Protecting Angel" (Sepia) (DB)   12 - 15   15 - 18
  "Please Come Back!" (Sunday School)   10 - 12   12 - 15

Romback & Groene, Cincinnati
711, "Who's a Democrat?"

B. Moloch, French, "États-Unis"
Roosevelt Painting Negro White.

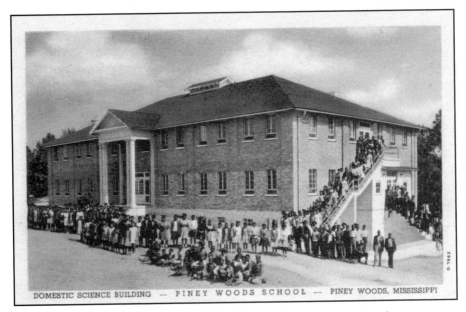

"Domestic Science Building -- Piney Woods School
Piney Woods, Mississippi" -- Curt Teich, D-7662 (L)

THE VICTIMISATION OF NEGROES IN AMERICA,

8 million out of the 12 million Negroes in America are destitute workers in the South where race hatred on the part of the white masters and middle classes is as never before. Conditions are far worse than slavery.

These boys, the eldest 22, the youngest 14 were arrested on a fake charge of assaulting 2 white girls, [the stock accusation] who themselves denied it, but were bullied by the police into telling the lie that would have caused the legal lynching

At the first "trial" a crazy mob of 10,000 clamoured for a real lynching on the spot.

Only the world-protests have saved them so far!

THE 9 SCOTTSBORO BOYS.

The 9 Scottsboro Boys' Fund-raising Card.
"The Victimisation of Negroes in America."

THEY MUST NOT DIE!

Against Race Discrimination!

Against Lynching!

Scottsboro Boys, "They Must Not Die!"
"Against Race Discrimination! Against Lynching!"
Thousands of Cards Mailed to Alabama Governor B. M. Millard.

Churches	10 - 15	15 - 20
Pastors, Preachers	15 - 20	20 - 25
SANTAS (Others, See Publishers)		
FP, Algiers		
Yellow Robe, French Caption	175 - 200	200 - 225
HWB, Sweden		
Blue Robe, "God-Jul!"	25 - 30	30 - 35
Illustrated P. C. & Novelty Co.		
Santa in Overcoat with Turkey		
"A Merry Christmas"	30 - 40	40 - 50
Ch. Hzoney -- White Robe	100 - 110	110 - 120
Anonymous, French		
Orange Robe, "Joyeux Noël"	110 - 120	120 - 130
SCHOOLS	10 - 15	15 - 20
With Children	15 - 20	20 - 25
Integrated	22 - 25	25 - 28
Named Schools for "Colored"	15 - 20	20 - 25
Albertype (B&W)		
"Hampton Institute Choir, Hampton, Va."	15 - 18	18 - 22
Yates & Milton (L)		
3911 "Atlanta U. School of Social Work"	20 - 22	22 - 25
Connor Drugs, New Albany, In.		
"School for Colored People"	12 - 15	15 - 18
S. H. Kress		
19361 "Magnolia Colored H.S., Valdosta" (L)	8 - 10	10 - 15
E. C. Kropp		
19058 "Attucks Colored High School,		
Hopkinsville, Kentucky"	12 - 15	15 - 18
Linens	8 - 10	10 - 15
Chromes	2 - 3	3 - 5

SCOTTSBORO BOYS

In the early 1930's nine young black men, the youngest of whom was thirteen, were arrested and jailed in Scottsboro, Alabama. They were charged with raping two white women on a freight train, found guilty by the court, and sentenced to death. The "Scottsboro Boys" case gained nationwide publicity. Appeals by the NAACP and other factions (including results of distribution of the three postcards listed in this chapter) produced a new trial after it was proven that the defendants did not have adequate counsel in the original trial. The new trial was beneficial in that the death penalty was revoked and the Scottsboro boys were sentenced to terms of up to 90 years. By 1950 all had been released.

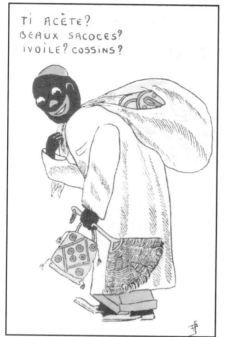

FP, Yellow Robe
Anonymous Publisher

Ch. Hzoney, French, White Robe
Anonymous Publisher

HWB, Sweden, Blue Robe
"God-Jul!"

Anonymous, French, Orange Robe
"Joyeux Noël"

Ill. P. C. & Novelty Co.
"A Merry Christmas"

*"Colored Community Hall, Aluminum Co. of America,
Maryville, Tenn."*

"USO Rainbow Club -- Hawaii"
Photo by EKC

SCOTTSBORO BOYS
1. Card addressed to Supreme Court
   "Don't Let Them Burn"   300 - 350 350 - 400
2. Card addressed to Gov. of Alabama
   "They Must Not Die"   200 - 250 250 - 300

3. Appeals for Funds
"The Victimisation of Negroes..."   300 - 350   350 - 400

SEGREGATION

Black Grandstand Signs   15 - 20   20 - 25
Others

SEGREGATION, INDUSTRIAL

Aluminum Co. of America
"Colored Community Hall," Maryville, Tenn."   18 - 22   22 - 25
National Malleable Castings, Indianapolis
"No. 2 Colored Women's Dressing Room"

SPANISH-AMERICAN WAR

James Lee Co., Chicago
"Charge of Colored Troops, San Juan"   15 - 18   18 - 22

WORLD WAR I

Camp Humphreys, Va.
"In Line for Mess, Colored Section"   18 - 22   22 - 25
Camp Lee, Va. (B&W)
640 Street Scene -- Colored Troops
Black Soldiers   15 - 18   18 - 22

WORLD WAR II

Black Servicemen   8 - 10   10 - 12
Black Soldiers-White Women   15 - 20   20 - 25

THE BLACK SOLDIER

African Americans, although small in number, served in segregated units in the Spanish-American War. Of the thirty serving on the Battleship "Maine," twenty-two were killed when it exploded. When war was declared, several states permitted African Americans to organize outfits and enter the service. These were in addition to two calvary and two infantry units already there.

When Congress authorized the four new outfits the War Department insisted on white officers, or those above the rank of second lieutenant, to lead them. This was a problem for military leaders from the very beginning as only one unit, the Third North Carolina Infantry, had all black officers. Even though they were in uniform and fighting for the United States, they were still subjected to Jim Crow segregation laws and garrisoned away from the whites and public accommodations.

The four units saw considerable action, and it was reported that the Ninth and Tenth Calvaries saved the Rough Riders in one of their most crucial battles. They were praised by many white officers, including Teddy Roosevelt, for their gallantry and bravery.

"A Message from a Race."
Anonymous, 1725

Sunday School Visitor's Card
"Please Come Back"

At the beginning of World War I there were approximately 10,000 African Americans in units of the regular Army, which consisted of the Ninth and Tenth Calvaries and Twenty-fourth and Twenty-fifth Infantries. Over 700,000 blacks registered to enter the service on registration day, and over two million were finally registered by the Selective Service. Of this total, 367,000 were called into the service. Questions concerning black officers and segregation of troops were again debated as the black community pushed for equality in these areas.

From a special camp in Des Moines, Iowa, 639 blacks were commissioned as officers and later, at nonsegregated camps, others were also commissioned to be leaders in the Army. These were two important victories; however, admittance of blacks to the Navy was limited and they were barred altogether from entering the Marines. Although many served as stevedore regiments at the start of the war, a great number of battalions and units were in the thick of fighting and gained much acclaim for their bravery and fighting prowess. White officers and enlisted men, as well as French officers, praised them for their heroics in helping to liberate France and win the war.

Anonymous
"A Mother's Joy"
(Blessed are the little Children)

"Scene in Sabine Co. Texas,
June 22, 1908"
(The Dogwood Tree)

In 1940 there were fewer than 5000 African Americans in the four black units named above. As the U.S. neared involvement in World War II the Selective Service Act, passed in 1940, forbid discrimination in drafting and training men. It seemed, however, that the U.S. was still committed to having a white Army and a black Army. Just over 2000 blacks were drafted during the first year; 100,000 joined or were drafted in 1941, and 370,000 in 1942. By 1944 there were over 700,000 in the Army alone, and by the end of the war over 4000 Black American women had enlisted. The issues concerning black officers and segregation were still apparent, but blacks were slowly gaining the equality they had been seeking. Almost a half million served the U.S. in foreign theaters.

VEHICLE DRIVERS
    Slaton-Green Drugs (UndB) (B&W)
        "Driver, Rapid Transit Car, Wash., Ga."   15 - 20   20 - 25
Y.M.C.A.
    Whites, Columbus
        11527 "Columbus, Ga. Y.M.C.A. (Colored)"   12 - 15   15 - 18

POSTCARD PUBLISHERS & DISTRIBUTORS

Following are some of the major publishers of postcards worldwide. Minor publishers can be found under each particular listing throughout this book.

AMAG, Germany — Artist-Signed and Better Comics
A.M.B. — Meissner & Buch, Quality Greetings, Artist-Signed
A.S.B. — Greetings
Ackerman — Pioneer Views of New York City
Albertype Co. — Pioneer & Expo Views; Local Views
Alphasia Pub. Co. — Artist-Signed and Comics
Am. Colortype Co. — Expositions
Am. News Co. — Local Views
Am. Post Card Co. — Comics
Am. Souvenir Co. — Pioneers
Anglo-Am. P.C. Co. (AA) — Greetings, Comics
Art Lithograph Co. — Local Views
Asheville P.C. Co. — Local Views, Comics
Auburn P.C. Mfg. Co. — Greetings, Comics
Austin, J. — Comics
Ballerini & Fratini, Italy — Chiostri, Art Deco
BKWI, Germany — Artist-Signed, Comics
Bamforth Co. — Comics, Song Cards
Barton and Spooner — Comics, Greetings
Bergman Co. — Comics, Artist-Signed Ladies, etc.
Julius Bien — Comics, Greetings, etc.
B.B. (Birn Brothers) — Greetings, Comics
B.M., Paris — Comics
Bosselman, A.C. — Local Views, Others
Britton & Rey — Expositions, Battleships, etc.
Brooklyn P.C. Co. — Views

Campbell Art Co. — Comics Rose O'Neill, etc.
Chapman Co. — Greetings, College Girls, etc.
Charlton, E.P. — Expositions, Local Views
Chisholm Bros. — Expositions, Local Views
Colonial Art Pub. Co. — Scenics, Comics, Sepia Lovers
Conwell, L.R. — Greetings
Crocker, H.S. — Local Views
Davidson Bros. — Greetings, Artist-Signed
Davis, London — Artist-Signed and Better Comics
Dell Anna & Gasparini, Italy — Art Deco
Delta, Paris — French Fashion
Detroit Pub. Co. — Prolific Publisher, All Types
Eagle Postcard Views — Views and Comics
Fairman Co., Cincinnati — Comics
Faulkner, C.W., British — Artist-Signed, Greetings
Finkenrath, Paul, Berlin (PFB) — Greetings
Gabriel, Sam — Greetings
Gartner & Bender (G&B) — Artist-Signed and Comics
German-American Novelty Art — Greetings, Comics
Gibson Art Co. — Comics, Greetings
Gottschalk, Dreyfus & Davis — Greetings
Gross, Edward — Artist-Signed
Hammon, V.O. — Local Views
Henderson & Sons — Artist-Signed, Comics
Henderson Litho — Greetings, Comics, Local Views
Hey, E. J., London — Comics
Huld, Franz — Installment Sets, Expositions, etc.
Ill. Postal Card Co. — Greetings, Artist-Signed and Many Others
Inter-Art, London — Artist-Signed and Comics
Int. Art Publishing Co. — Greetings by Clapsaddle, etc.
Knapp Co. — Artist-Signed
Koeber, Paul C. (P.C.K.) — Comics, Artist-Signed
Koehler, Joseph — H-T-L, Expositions, Local Views
Kropp, E.C. — Local Views, Battleships, etc.
Langsdorf, S. — Alligator and Shell Border Views, Local Views, Greetings
Lapina, Paris — Color Nudes and French Fashion
Leighton, Hugh — Local Views
Leubrie & Elkus (L.&E.) — Artist-Signed
Livingston, Arthur — Pioneers, Local Views
Lounsbury, Fred — Greetings, Local Views, etc.
Manhattan P.C. Co. — Local Views, Comics
Marque L-E, Paris — French Fashion
Meissner & Buch, German — Artist-Signed, Greetings
Metropolitan News Co. — Local Views
Mitchell, Edward H. — Expositions, Battleships, Local Views
Moore & Gibson — Comics
Munk, M., Vienna — Artist-Signed, Comics, etc.
Nash, E. — Greetings
National Art Co. — Artist-Signed, Greetings, etc.
Nister, E., British — Artist-Signed, Greetings
Novitas, Germany — Artist-Signed
Noyer, A., Paris — Nudes and French Fashion
O.P.F. — Quality German Artist-Signed
Owen, F.A. — Greetings, Artist-Signed

Phillipp & Kramer, Vienna — Artist-Signed, Art Nouveau
Platinachrome — Artist-Signed, Earl Christy, etc.
Reichner Bros. — Local Views
Reinthal & Newman — Artist-Signed, Greetings
Rieder, M. — Local Views
Rose, Charles — Greetings, Song Cards, Artist-Signed, Comics
Rost, H.A. — Pioneer Views, Battleships
Roth & Langley — Greetings, Comics
Rotograph Co. — Local Views, Expositions, Battleships, Artist-Signed, etc.
Sander, P. — Greetings, Comics, Artist-Signed
Santway — Greetings
Sborgi, E., Italy — Famous Art Reproductions
Schlesinger Bros. — Artist-Signed, Ladies and Comics
Selige, A. — Expositions, Western Views, People, etc.
Sheehan, M.T. — Local Views, Historical, Artist-Signed
Souvenir Post Card Co. — Local Views, Greetings, etc.
Stecher Litho Co. — Greetings, Artist-Signed
Stengel & Co., Germany — Famous Art Reproductions
Stewart & Woolf, British — Comics, Artist-Signed
Stokes, F.A. — Artist-Signed, Comics
Strauss, Arthur — Local Views, Historical, Expositions
Stroefer, Theo. (T.S.N.), Nürnburg — Artist-Signed, Animals, etc.
Taggart Co. — Greetings
Tammen, H.H. — Expositions, Historical, Local Views
Teich, Curt — Local Views, Artist-Signed, Comics
Tichnor Bros. — Later Local Views, Comics
Tuck, Raphael & Sons, British — Artist-Signed, Views, Comics, Greetings, etc.
Ullman Mfg. Co. — Greetings, Artist-Signed, Comics
Valentine & Sons, British — Artist-Signed, Comics, Views, etc.
Volland Co. — Artist-Signed, Greetings
White City Art Co. — Comics
Whitney & Co. — Greetings, Artist-Signed
Winsch, John — Greetings, Artist-Signed
Wirths, Walter — Pioneer Views

BIBLIOGRAPHY

American Advertising Postcards, Sets and Series, 1890-1920, Frederic and Mary Megson, Martinsville, NJ, 1987
The American Postcard Guide to Tuck, Sally Carver, Brookline, MA, 1979
The Artist-Signed Postcard Price Guide, J.L. Mashburn, Colonial House, 1993
The Black Experience in America, Norman Coombs, Twayne Pub., NY, 1972
The Black Vanguard, Origins of the Negro Social Revolution, Robert H. Brisbane, Judson Press, 1970
The Collectors Guide to Postcards, Jane Wood, Gas City, IN
Encyclopedia of Antique Postcards, Susan Nicholson, Wallace-Homestead, 1994
Guide to Artists' Signature and Monograms on Postcards, Nouhad A. Saleh, Minerva Press, Boca Raton, FL, 1994
From Slavery to Freedom, A History of Negro Americans, 3rd Edition, John Hope Franklin, Published by A. A. Knopf, 201 E. 50th St., New York, NY 10022
Official Postcard Price Guide, Dianne Allman, House of Collectibles, NY, 1990
Prairie Fires and Paper Moons, The American Photographic Postcard: 1900-1920, Hal Morgan and Andreas Brown. Pub. by D. R. Godine, Boston, MA, 1981
What Cheer News, Mrs. E. K. Austin, Rhode Island Postcard Club

PERIODICALS

The Antique Trader Weekly, P.O. Box 1050, Dubuque, IA 52004-1050
Antiques and Auction News, P.O. Box 500, Mount Joy, PA 17552 Monthly Tabloid
Barr's Post Card News, (The Mail Auction Specialist), 70 S. Sixth St., Lansing, IA 52151, Weekly Tabloid
Collector News & Antique Reporter, P.O. Box 156, Grundy Center, IA 50638
Paper Collector's Marketplace, P.O. Box 128, Scandinavia, WI 54977, Monthly Magazine
Paper Pile Quarterly, P.O. Box 337, San Anselmo, CA 94979
Picture Post Card Monthly, 15 Debdale Lane, Keyworth, Nottingham NG12 5HT, England
The Postcard Album, H. Luers, Anton-Gunther-Str. 12, W-2902 Rastede, Germany
Postcard Collector, P.O. Box 1050, Dubuque, IA 52004-1050, Monthly Magazine

MAJOR AUCTION HOUSES

Antique Paper Guild, P.O. Box 5742, Bellevue, WA 98006 Real Photo Specialists
Bennett's, Pickering Road, Dover, NH 03820
Butterfield & Butterfield, 220 San Bruno Ave., San Francisco, CA 90046
The First National Postcard Auctions, P.O. Box 5398, Hamden, CT 06518
Swann Galleries, Inc., 104 East 25th St., New York, NY 10010

Index